Deregulation and Labour Law

Deregulation and Labour Law

In Search of a Labour Concept for the 21st Century

Bulletin of Comparative Labour Relations 38 – 2000

Editor: R. Blanpain

Guest Editors: R. Yamakawa
T. Araki

Contributors: R. Eklund
C. Engels
D. H. Foote
D. Joost
M.-A. Moreau
H. Morito
M. Tiraboschi
G.H. van Voss

2000
Kluwer Law International
The Hague/London/Boston

Published by Kluwer Law International
P.O. Box 85889
2508 CN The Hague, The Netherlands

Sold and distributed in North, Central and South America by
Kluwer Law International
675 Massachusetts Avenue
Cambridge, MA 02139, USA

In all other countries, sold and distributed by
Kluwer Law International
Distribution Centre
P.O. Box 322
3300 AD Dordrecht, The Netherlands

Library of Congress Cataloging-in-Publication Data is available from the Library of Congress

Printed on acid-free paper

Cover design: Peter Gerretzen

ISBN 90-411-1370-3

Printed and bound in Great Britain by Antony Rowe Limited.

Table of Contents

Introduction

1. JIL COMPARATIVE LABOUR LAW SEMINAR (JIL TOKYO SEMINAR)

The Japan Institute of Labour (JIL) held the fifth JIL Comparative Labour Law Seminar (JIL Tokyo Seminar) on November 11 and 12, 1998, in Tokyo, Japan. The JIL Tokyo Seminar was originally organised by Professor Kazuo Sugeno (Faculty of Law, The University of Tokyo) and Professor Yasuo Suwa (Faculty of Sociology, Hosei University) who were at that time senior research fellows at JIL. This seminar has two purposes: first, to discuss contemporary issues regarding labour law with distinguished guests from foreign countries; second, to provide young Japanese scholars with opportunities to participate in international academic activities. The topic of the first seminar held in 1991 was 'Management Flexibility in an Era of Change: the Method of Accommodating Working Conditions and Work Organisations.' In 1993 the second seminar focused on the issue of 'The Influence of Foreign Law on Union Rights Policies in Asian Countries.' The third seminar was held in 1994 under the title 'Working Life and Family Life: Policies for Their Harmonisation.' The topic of the fourth seminar in 1996 was 'The Process of Industrialisation and the Role of Labour Law.'

2. THE FIFTH JIL TOKYO SEMINAR

The theme of the fifth seminar was 'Deregulation and Labour Law: In Search of a Labour Law Concept for the 21st Century.' Eight national reporters from European countries, the United States, and Japan participated in the four-session seminar. The reporters were:

Professor Ronnie Eklund, Stockholm University (Sweden)
Professor Chris Engels, Katholieke Universiteit Leuven (Belgium)
Professor Daniel H. Foote, University of Washington (United States)
Professor Gustaaf Heerma van Voss, Rijksuniversiteit Leiden (Netherlands)
Professor Detlev Joost, Universität Hamburg (Germany)
Professor Marie-Ange Moreau, Universite Aix Marseille III (France)
Professor Hideyuki Morito, Seikei University (Japan)
Professor Michele Tiraboschi, University of Modena (Italy)

The objective of the fifth JIL Tokyo Seminar was to review the deregulation in labour law in each country and examine what the general trend means. The term 'deregulation' in this seminar was defined broadly, including matters usually discussed under the notion of 'flexibility.' After examining the factors causing deregulation in Labour law and evaluating its ramifications, this seminar purported to ask a fundamental question: Do we need a new concept of labour law for the 21st century? If so, what should it be? In this light, the co-ordinators sent the following outline to each national reporter.

3. OUTLINE OF NATIONAL REPORTS

Introduction

Deregulation of Labour Law in Respective Countries

1. Labour market regulations
   For example:
   - the abolishment of the state's monopoly of employment placement services and the legalisation of private fee-charging employment placement businesses
   - the legalisation of temporary work services and worker dispatch services
   - the deregulation of fixed-term contracts
   - the deregulation of dismissal regulations
2. Individual labour relations
   For example:
   - the flexibilisation of working-hour regulations
   - lifting the ban on women's night work
   - expansion of derogation from the legal norms set by protective Labour legislation through collective bargaining agreements, other agreements at plant or establishment level, or (where it exists) individual consent
3. Collective Labour relations
   For example:
   - the decentralisation of collective bargaining, i.e., moving from centralised bargaining to company- or plant-level bargaining and from trade unions to works councils
   - re-examination of the relation between trade unions (collective bargaining) and individuals (individual bargaining)

Driving Forces of Deregulation

A national paper should describe what factors cause deregulation mentioned above, such as

- counter measures against unemployment
- pressure of global competition
- international pressure to harmonise regulations (harmonising competition rules in the EC, judgement by the European Court of Justice, ILO convention, etc.)
- structural changes in industries
- structural change in the Labour force (demographic change, ageing work force, diversified work force, individualisation of workers, etc.)

Evaluation of Current Deregulation and Reforms of Labour Law

- Is deregulation a universal phenomenon in labour law in your country, or are there any areas where regulations are increased or strengthened (e.g., employment discrimination, privacy of workers)?
- What are the general reactions (pros and cons) to deregulation in your country? Is it a temporary phenomenon or a perpetual one? Does deregulation simply

mean abolishing regulations, or can it be regarded as a modernisation of regulations through abolishing outdated regulations and introducing new ones?

The Role of Labour Law in the 21st Century: Do We Need a New Concept of Labour Law?

Considering various changes surrounding labour and employment relations and the current deregulation phenomena, what do you think the role of labour law in the coming century should be? Should we promote a market-oriented approach to labour law? How should we react to the individualisation of the labour force? Do we need a new concept of Labour law? What might it be?

4. OVERVIEW OF DISCUSSION

The whole seminar was divided into four sessions. The following is a brief summary of the discussions in each session.

A. First Session: Introductory Remarks on 'Deregulation' and Labour Law in Respective Countries and the Deregulation of Labour Market Regulations

The first session began with introductory remarks by each national reporter regarding the general situation of deregulation in labour law. In most countries, the movement toward deregulation in labour law is more or less in progress. An exception is the United States, where the regulation of employment relations has rather been strengthened in the 1990s through such legislation as the Americans with Disabilities Act of 1990 and the Family and Medical Leave Act. However, the basic legal principle underlying employment relations in the United States is the employment-at-will doctrine. In this sense, American labour law from the beginning had less regulation than its European counterparts. Even so, there has been so-called 'effective' deregulation in the United States, such as layoffs of white-collar workers and the increase in contingent workers. On the other hand, in Europe and Japan regulation has been strengthened in certain areas. This is especially true in the area of employment discrimination and workers' privacy.

In this session, participants also discussed the deregulation in labour market law. Many European countries have experienced deregulation in this area. In recent years, for example, Sweden, Germany, and Italy have abolished the state monopoly regarding employment placement services and legalised private fee-charging employment placement businesses. Japan has taken a similar course: the scope of such private employment placement businesses has been broadened, and further expansion is around the corner. In Belgium, where regulation remains relatively strong, such business has become legalised with respect to persons with higher functions.

The regulation of temporary work services and worker dispatch services has also been relaxed. For example, the Netherlands recently abolished licensing systems for such businesses. This is also the case with the restriction on the use of fixed term employment contracts. Although the restriction has basically remained in many

European countries, some countries, such as Germany and Sweden, have allowed a wider range of exceptions for the use of such contracts.

B. Second Session: Deregulation of Individual Labour Relations Law

The second session covered deregulation in the area of individual labour relations – e.g., working time. The flexibilisation of working time regulations has been carried out in many countries. The average working time scheme has been introduced or expanded in a number of European countries, as well as in Japan. The main purpose of such flexibilisation is to enable parties to labour relations to adjust working time arrangements according to business necessity without increasing overtime wages, while maintaining employment in slack seasons.

It must be noted that more often than not such flexibilisation is conditioned upon the conclusion of collective agreements. Furthermore, collective bargaining agreements or other types of agreements at the establishment level can function as a means of derogation from legal norms set by protective labour legislation. This is the case in such countries as France, Germany, Belgium, and Japan. Meanwhile, although the ban on night work by women has been lifted in European countries, this has been carried out in accordance with the EC Directive regarding equal treatment of men and women rather than the deregulation drive.

In Japan a discretionary working time scheme was introduced as another means of deregulation in terms of working time. Under this scheme, working time is determined according to the labour-management agreement at the establishment level or the resolution of the labour-management committee, without regard to actual time worked ('conclusive presumption'). This scheme is applied to certain non-exempt professionals and white-collar employees working at core management sections. In the same vein, the scope of exemption has been expanded in the United States. Outside the context of the working time regulation, such flexibilisation took place in the Netherlands when case law declared that employers might reserve the right to change working conditions unilaterally.

C. Third Session: Deregulation and Reforms of Collective Labour Relations Law

In the third session, the issue of 'deregulation' included the decentralisation of collective bargaining, i.e., from centralised bargaining at the industrial or national level to company- or plant-level bargaining. Since collective bargaining has been carried out at the company or plant level in the United States and Japan, such decentralisation is discussed or carried out mainly in European countries. However, with respect to deregulation, it has been debated in the United States whether the National Labour Relations Act should be amended in order to legalise employee participation programs established by employers in non-union workplaces.

In addition to the change in the practice of collective bargaining, there have been changes in the legal framework regarding collective bargaining. In France, for example, a member of a works council or a worker chosen by a trade union is allowed to negotiate collective bargaining agreements when there is no trade union representative in the enterprise, although there are certain conditions, such as recognition by an industry-level collective agreement.

D. Fourth Session: Evaluation of Current Deregulation and Future Prospects of the Labour Law Concept

The previous three sessions clarified that deregulation is a common tendency in most countries of the participants. Even in the United States, where regulatory statutes have been increasing, so-called 'effective' deregulation is in progress. Although there are differences from country to country with respect to the subject and measures of deregulation, flexibilisation in the regulation of the labour market and working time appears to be a major trend.

There are a number of factors that may have influenced this deregulation trend. In many countries, employers are facing global competition as well as structural changes in the economy. As a result, some regulations have become obstacles to the competitive edge; others have become outmoded in the face of new systems of business operations or new styles of working. Also, especially in European countries, deregulation has been regarded as one of the measures to combat unemployment, since flexibilisation of the labour market is expected to produce more employment opportunities.

With regard to the evaluation of 'deregulation', all the national reporters basically agreed that 'deregulation' in some areas must be accompanied by stricter regulation in other areas, such as employment discrimination. It should also be noted that deregulation is more often than not conditioned on certain safety valves, such as the involvement of trade unions. Thus, some reporters stated that as a whole labour law is in the process of 're-regulation' rather than simple deregulation. As a means of such 're-regulation', the flexibilisation of regulation generally received favourable comments. On the other hand, some concerns were expressed about the likelihood of a decrease in the role of trade unions, and others mentioned the necessity to re-examine the representational function of unions in light of the diversified workforce.

Since the basic framework of labour law remains intact in many respects, the discussion in the fourth session did not reach a firm conclusion of what the new concept of labour law should be in the 21st century. However, there was agreement that, while adapting to socio-economic changes, labour law would maintain its role as one of the most important instruments of social ordering.

5. ACKNOWLEDGEMENTS

Throughout the four-session seminar, all the reporters and other participants enjoyed stimulating and fruitful discussions. We firmly believe that the goal of this seminar was achieved and that all of us were able to gain insights into the future of labour law.

We would like to thank all the participants who actively took part in the discussions. Our sincere gratitude goes to the distinguished guests from abroad who submitted excellent national papers and made splendid contributions to the two-day seminar. We are also grateful to Professor Sugeno and Professor Suwa, who provided invaluable suggestions for the seminar both in the preparatory stage and during the sessions.

Finally, special thanks go to Prof. Roger Blanpain who gave us excellent international exposure for the JIL Tokyo Seminar. Our deep gratitude also goes to Ms Lisa Engels Salas for her kind assistance in making this publication possible.

July, 1999

Ryuichi Yamakawa, Associate Professor of Law,
Tsukuba University (Senior Research Fellow,
The Japan Institute of Labour)
Takashi Araki, Associate Professor of Law,
The University of Tokyo (Senior Research Fellow,
The Japan Institute of Labour)

Notes on Contributors

Ronnie Eklund, Professor, School of Law, Stockholm University
Chris Engels, Professor, Institute for Labour Relations, Katholieke Universiteit Leuven
Daniel H. Foote, Professor, School of Law, University of Washington
Detlev Joost, Professor, Seminar für Arbeitsrecht, Universität Hamburg
Marie-Ange Moreau, Professor, Institut de Droit des Affaires, Université Aix-Marseille III
Hideyuki Morito, Associate Professor, Faculty of Law, Seikei University
Michele Tiraboschi, Researcher of Labour Law, Dipartemento di Economica Asiendale Ufficio, University of Modena
Gustaaf Heerma van Voss, Professor, Faculteit der Rechtsgeleerdheid, afdeling Sociaal Recht, Rijksuniversiteit Leiden

1. Deregulation and Labour Law: The Belgian Case

Chris Engels

1. INTRODUCTION

The deregulation of Belgian labour law has been discussed in many seminars since the 1980s. It is still of interest to look at the Belgian experience, in as much as this much discussed phenomenon did not lead to an abolition of Belgian labour law all together. Quite often deregulation and re-regulation have gone hand in hand. This shows that deregulation is not considered an ideal in itself, but is a means to arrive at a more flexible system of labour law that allows employers to remain competitive in an increasingly competitive market.

The Belgian experience is also interesting because the deregulation and the flexibility that were introduced remained at all times 'controlled.' The new rules did not merely replace the old ones, they gave a decisive voice to those in closer contact with the industry and business than Parliament itself, namely the social partners.

While the Belgian experience in deregulation and flexibility goes back to the 1980s, there is still a lot to be done to reach a level of flexibility that will be indispensable in the global competitive market.

2. LABOUR MARKET REGULATIONS

2.1 Placement of Workers – Private Fee-Charging Agencies

a. European background

The European Court of Justice has addressed the issue of Placement of Employees and the state monopolies that often exist on two occasions.[1]

In the *Macroton* decision the Court challenged the monopoly of public employment offices in the activity of finding work for persons seeking employment.[2] The case concerned the exclusive right in Germany of the *Bundesanstalt für Arbeit* (Federal Employment Office – 'the BA'), on the basis of the *Arbeitsförderungsgezetz* (Law on the Promotion of Employment – 'the AGF'), to put people seeking work in contact with employers. Notwithstanding that exclusive right, a specialized

1. R. Blanpain and C. Engels, *European Labor Law*, 5th ed., 1998, Kluwer Law International, The Hague, London, Boston, 240 e. s.
2. COJ, 23 April 1991, *K. Höfner and F. Elser v. Macroton GmbH*, no. C-41/9 *ECR*, 1991, 1979.

R. Blanpain (ed.), Deregulation and Labour Law, 1–42

recruitment and placement business has developed for business executives. It is carried on by recruitment consultants to some extent tolerated by the BA. The fact remained that measures that contravened a legal prohibition were void under Article 134 of the German Civil Code and that, according to decisions of the German courts, that prohibition applied to recruitment activities carried on in breach of the AGF. In the case under review the recruitment consultants had presented a candidate to a client whom the client decided not to recruit, refusing as well to pay the consultants' fees since the contract with them was void. In the case which was ultimately submitted to the Court in Luxembourg, the Court was asked whether the provisions of the Treaty on the freedom to provide services precluded a legal provision prohibiting private recruitment consultants from finding placements for business executives, and whether the monopoly on the placement of executives tested in a public employment office constituted an abuse of a dominant position. The Court ruled as follows:

> '*A public employment office engaged in the activity of finding work for persons seeking employment is subject to the prohibition in Article 86 of the Treaty, provided the application of that provision does not defeat the specific task entrusted to it. A Member State which has conferred an exclusive right to carry on that activity upon that public employment office is in breach of Article 90(1) of the Treaty where it creates a situation in which that office is obliged to infringe the terms of Article 86 of the Treaty. That is the case, in particular, where the following conditions are met:*
>
> – *the exclusive right extends to finding employment for business executives;*
> – *the public employment office is manifestly incapable of satisfying demand on the market for such activity;*
> – *the actual pursuit of that activity by private personnel consultants is rendered impossible by the maintenance in force of a statutory provision prohibiting it, with the annulment of the corresponding contracts as a penalty for contravention;*
> – *the activity in question may extend to nationals or to the territory of other Member States.*'

A second case[3] concerns the Italian Law of 23 October 1960, which prohibits acting as an intermediary in employment relationships, whether as an employment agency, or as an employment business. Failure to comply with the statute gives rise to penal sanctions.

The question that was asked is essentially whether the provisions of the Treaty preclude national legislation under which any activity as an intermediary between supply and demand in employment relationships is prohibited unless carried on by public employment agencies.

The Court decided in a landmark decision that:

1. Placement of employees is an economic activity, even if entrusted to public offices;
2. a body such as a public placement office may therefore be considered a business for the purposes of the Community competition rules;

3. COJ, *Non-contentious proceedings brought by Job Center Coop. arb.*, Case no. 55/96, *ECR*, 1997, 7119.

3. public placement offices remain subject to competition rules unless, and to the extent to which it is shown that their application is incompatible with the discharge of their duties;
4. before the application of Article 86 of the Treaty can obstruct the performance of a particular task assigned to placement offices, it must be determined that they are manifestly unable to satisfy demand in that area of the market;
5. pursuant to Article 86(b) of the Treaty, such abuse may in particular consist in limiting the provision of a service, to the prejudice of those seeking to avail themselves of it;
6. as the Commission has rightly pointed out, the provision of services relating to the placement of employees is both a very extensive and extremely diverse market. Supply and demand within that market cover all sectors of production and relate to a range of jobs requiring anything from unskilled labour to the scarcest and most specialised professional qualifications;
7. in such an extensive and varied market, subject moreover to enormous changes as a result of economic and social developments, public placement offices may well be unable to satisfy a significant portion of requests for services;
8. by prohibiting, on pain of penal and administrative sanctions, any activity as an intermediary between supply and demand on the employment market unless carried on by public placement offices, a Member State creates a situation in which the provision of a service is limited, contrary to Article 86(b) of the Treaty, if those offices are manifestly unable to satisfy demand on the employment market for all types of activity;
9. a potential effect of abusive conduct on trade between Member States is sufficient and arises in particular where the placement of employees by private companies may extend to the nationals or to the territory of other Member States.[4]

In many countries placement of workers was still by and large a monopoly of the Public Employment Offices who, as practice showed, were manifestly unable to satisfy demand. It is clear that this situation is both illegal and obsolete.

First of all, the monopoly of the Public Employment Office is contrary to the letter and the spirit of Convention No. 181 of the ILO (1997) and to European competition law. It is evident that the Official Employment Offices can no longer *de facto* satisfy the demand in the market for all types of activity. The national Public Employment Offices cannot cope with the diversity of the modern labour markets at European level.

In conclusion one can say that:

1. the monopoly of the Public Employment Offices has to be abolished;
2. enterprises must be able to propose a total package of services on the labour market, vocational training included;
3. the scope of possibilities to put workers at the disposal of users/enterprises must be widened.[5]

---

4. For a discussion on the impact of the last European Court case: E. Traversa, The Role played by the Court of Justice of the European Community in opening up the market for private employment agencies, in *Private Employment Agencies: The impact of ILO convention 181 (1997) and the judgment of the European Court of Justice of 11 December 1997, Bulletin of Comparative Labor Relations,* Kluwer Law International, forthcoming.
5. R. Blanpain and C. Engels, *European Labor Law*, 5th ed., 1998, Kluwer Law International, The Hague, London, Boston, 242 e.s.

b. The Belgian situation

1. The Royal Decree of 28 October 1975[6]
The activity of paid private placement of employees is prohibited.[7] The placement of employees is defined as the activity of any physical or legal person acting as an intermediary in order to provide an individual with a job.[8]

An exception to the prohibition of fee-charging placement is made for the placement of artists.[9] This nationally established principle is further refined for the Flemish *region.*[10]

2. Flemish Decree of 19 April 1995[11]
The constitutional reforms of 1980 transferred the competence to deal with matters such as employment placement from the federal government to the regions. A Flemish Decree of 19 April 1995, presently regulates the matter. The 1975 Royal Decree ceased to be applicable to Flanders as of 1 December 1997.[12]

The placement activity is defined as 'the activity where a go-between tries to match between supply and demand on the labour market and provide an employee with a job against the payment of a fee or a retribution or with the aim of obtaining a material advantage.'

While the 1995 Decree still contains a blanket prohibition on fee-charging placement, it nevertheless allows the government to permit such private placement in case the Public Employment Office is clearly unable to adequately match supply and demand on the labour market in a satisfactory way.[13]

A special license will need to be obtained from the government. Stringent conditions need to be satisfied before such a license will be granted. Sanctions, including criminal sanctions such as imprisonment, are established for those violating the applicable regulations.

3. Flemish Decree of 21 October 1997
A decree of 21 October 1997 makes private placement for a fee possible for 'persons with a higher function.' The decree itself defines what it understands to be a higher function, referring to the person's prospective annual income. At the time

6. Royal Decree, 28 November 1975, concerning the running of Fee-charging Offices of Placement, *Official Gazette*, 22 January 1976.
7. Art. 2, Royal Decree, 28 November 1975, concerning the running of Fee-charging Offices of Placement, *Official Gazette*, 22 January 1976.
8. Art. 1, Royal Decree, 28 November 1975, concerning the running of Fee-charging Offices of Placement, *Official Gazette*, 22 January 1976.
9. Art. 3, Royal Decree, 28 November 1975, concerning the running of Fee-charging Offices of Placement, *Official Gazette*, 22 January 1976.
10. Decision of the Flemish government in furtherance of the Decree of 19 April 1995 regarding the Fee-charging Placement within the Flemish region in relation to artists, *Official Gazette*, 26 November 1997.
11. Flemish Decree, regarding the Fee-charging Placement within the Flemish region, 19 April 1995, *Official Gazette*, 26 July 1995.
12. Decision of the Flemish government in furtherance of Article 31 of the Decree of 19 April 1995 regarding the Fee-charging Placement within the Flemish region, *Official Gazette*, 26 November 1997.
13. Art. 4, Flemish Decree, regarding the Fee-charging Placement within the Flemish region, 19 April 1995, *Official Gazette*, 26 July 1995.

the decree was passed the income level that was referred to was 1.2 million BEF. This amount will be adjusted to inflation on an annual basis starting from 1 January 1999.[14]

The definition of the term 'higher function' refers to notions that are used in the legislation dealing with the election of the members of works councils. The definition refers to the concepts of *cadre* and of *leading personnel* that are both developed within the context of works councils. Leading personnel are those white-collar workers who are charged with the daily management of the operation or the persons immediately below them in rank but still involved in the daily management of the operation. Cadre or white-collar workers are employees who perform functions in the enterprise that are normally reserved to a holder of a degree of a given level or to someone with equivalent job experience.[15]

These definitions have been the subject of heated discussion in many companies where elections for employee representative bodies had to be organised. Ample case law also exists on the subject.[16] The actual definition of higher personnel in the Flemish Decree refers to:

> 'persons who perform a higher function in the enterprise which is usually reserved to the holder of a certificate of a given level or to someone with equivalent job experience or persons who are charged with the daily management of the undertaking and who are empowered to represent the employer and to engage him legally, as well as the employees who are immediately subordinate to them when they equally perform tasks of daily management.'[17]

Blue-collar workers who perform mainly manual work are excluded from the scope of the decree. For them employment placement for a fee remains illegal.

The prospective minimum income of 1.2 million BEF referred to is not very high. Most higher level white-collar workers will earn this kind of money on an annual basis. Taking into account that monthly salaries in most sectors of industry are paid 13.89 times a year, the employee has to earn around 86,000 BEF per month (all benefits included). This corresponds to 6 $\pm$ 2400 US dollars (rate of 36 BEF/$).

Offices that want to engage in fee-charging employment placement have to be recognised by the Flemish region.[18] The Flemish Decree even *regulates the fees* that the placement agency can charge. The level of the fees has to be the subject of a written agreement between the employer that wants to make use of the placement

---

14. Decision of the Flemish government in furtherance of the Decree of 19 April 1995 Regarding the Fee-charging Placement within the Flemish region in relation to persons with a higher function, *Official Gazette*, 26 November 1997.
15. See: R. Blanpain and C. Engels, in 'Belgium', in: *International Encyclopaedia for Labor Law and Industrial Relations*, R. Blanpain (ed.) Kluwer Law International, s.d., no. 25, p. 33.
16. See: C. Engels, 'Het begrip werknemer' (The Notion of Worker) in *Sociale Verkiezingen 1995* (Social Elections 1995), C. Engels, R. Parijs and M. Stroobant (eds.) Leuven, Peeters, 54 e.s.
17. Art. 1, 7, Decision of the Flemish government in furtherance of Article 31 of the Decree of 19 April 1995 Regarding the Fee-charging Placement within the Flemish region in relation to persons with a higher function, *Official Gazette*, 26 November 1995.
18. Art. 3 e.s., Decision of the Flemish government in furtherance of Article 31 of the Decree of 19 April 1995 Regarding the Fee-charging Placement within the Flemish region in relation to persons with a higher function, *Official Gazette*, 26 November 1995.

services and the office providing such services. The decree provides for three possibilities:

a. a percentage of the annual income of the candidate;
b. a lump sum amount; or
c. an hourly rate.

The commission, however defined, needs to be within the following range: not less than 18% and not more than 55% of the gross annual income of the candidate.[19] The reimbursement of costs incurred by the placement agency is not included in this amount.

Records have to be kept about every job placement that the agency performs and an annual report needs to be filed with the Ministry of Employment. An exchange of information with the official employment office needs to be established.

An office that engages in placement activities for fees is neither allowed to engage in the activity of *search and selection*,[20] nor in the activity of *outplacement*.[21]

2.2 Temporary Worker Services

Temporary work in Belgium is regulated by the Act of 24 July 1987,[22] adopted by almost unanimous vote in Parliament, indicating that a wide consensus has been reached on a topic which for a long time was a subject of heated debate. Temporary work has thus been consolidated and has acquired a limited but definite place in our labour law system. On the average temporary work firms employed 52,000 workers in 1997 and 44,000 in 1996.[23]

The 1987 Act confirmed options that were already part of the provisional 1976 Act on temporary work and the consecutive collective agreement No. 36 of 1981 concluded in the National Labour Council. One of the compromises that led to the unanimous agreement allowed not only that temporary workers could be employed by private enterprises but that the State Employment Agency could act as an employer of temporary workers as well.

Lines of force are:

1. *The social protection of the temporary worker*
   The temporary worker is regarded as an employee, enjoying the full protection of labour law and social security law. He/she is categorised as a white-collar or blue-collar worker in accordance with the manual or intellectual nature of his work. His/her employer is the temporary work firm.

---

19. Art. 8, Decision of the Flemish government in furtherance of Article 31 of the Decree of 19 April 1995 Regarding the Fee-charging Placement within the Flemish region in relation to persons with a higher function, *Official Gazette*, 26 November 1995.
20. Collective Bargaining Agreement no. 38 concerning Search and Selection of Employees, rendered generally binding by Royal Decree of 11 July 1984, *Official Gazette*, in July 1984, thereafter amended by Collective Bargaining Agreement no. 38 bis of 29 October 1991 and Collective Bargaining no. 38 ter of 17 July 1998.
21. Collective Bargaining Agreement no. 51, concerning Outplacement, 10 February 1992, rendered generally binding by Royal Decree of 10 April 1992, *Official Gazette*, 1 May 1992.
22. Act of 24 July 1987 on Temporary Labour, Interim Labour and the Putting at Disposal of Workers to Users, *Official Gazette*, 20 August 1997, hereafter often amended, [hereafter referred to as Act on Temporary Employment].
23. X, Universele Formule, Europa in Deban, *VBO Bulletin*, 1998, 92.

2. *The safeguarding of the interests of the permanent worker*
   - through the strict limitations on the kind of work temporary workers can perform, so as not to threaten the jobs of permanent workers;
   - by providing that the wages of the temporary worker are not less than the salary that would be earned if he/she had been engaged by the user as a permanent worker in order that temporary workers will not be considered as cheap labour, pushing permanent workers out of the market.
3. *The protection of the user*
   - through a system of licenses (called 'recognition') by which the Regional Government permits only '*bona fide*' firms to operate. This system also guarantees respect for the social rights of the employees.
4. Finally, the Act gives the *Government the necessary powers to eliminate abuses* through surveillance, penal and other sanctions.[24]

An employer (that is the user) who needs a temporary worker has recourse to different measures to meet its needs. It can hire temporary workers directly, or can call upon the employees of another employer within the framework of the legal placement of employees at the disposal of an employer-user. However, the Act drastically restricts the possibility of putting workers at the disposal of another employer.[25]

Temporary work firms can only handle 'temporary work' as defined by the Act. If they operate outside the scope of the Act, they will be punished by sanctions and their license may be suspended or withdrawn.

Temporary work is strictly defined in the Act. It is an activity which involves:

(a) the replacement of a permanent worker (for example in case of sickness, vacation, maternity leave, etc.);
(b) help in case of a temporary increase in workload (due, for example, to an increase in orders);
(c) enabling exceptional work to be carried out (caused by an accident, or the creation of a new department for which the employer has not yet been able to engage permanent employees, or a similar situation).

The labour contract for temporary work can be concluded in one of three forms:

(a) a contract for a definite period of time;
(b) a contract for a precisely indicated job;
(c) a contract for replacement.

Employment contracts for an indefinite period of time between the temporary work agency and the temporary worker are prohibited.

2.3 Dispatching of Employees

a. Principle

The Parliamentary Act of 24 July 1987 on temporary work, work through temporary work agencies and putting workers at the disposal of users, regulates this matter in a

24. R. Blanpain and C. Engels, 'Belgium', in *International Encyclopaedia For Labor Law And Industrial Relations*, R. Blanpain (ed.), Kluwer Law International, The Hague, Boston, London, 5th ed. nos. 120–123, 86–87.
25. See *infra*.

very stringent way.[26] Article 31ff of the Act deals with the issue of putting workers at the disposal of users outside the context of temporary work and work through temporary work agencies. The Act severely limits the activity of a physical person or legal entity that puts employees at the disposal of third parties that exercise any of the employer's normal authority.[27]

Previously the Act contained an exemption for non-profit organisations (VZW/ASLB) that were recognised for this purpose through a Ministerial Decree.[28] This exception was repealed by an Act of Parliament of 13 February 1998 in order to maintain the general prohibition of putting workers at the disposal of a user accompanied by a uniform exception to the general rule.[29]

The prohibition is restricted in its scope to subordinate workers. This means that a company can contract with an *independent* consultant/specialist in order for the latter to perform certain jobs at the premises of a third party (=the client). Since a company does not exercise any authority on a consultant rendering services to it, it obviously cannot delegate authority to the user. Should the user exercise authority over the consultant, it does so on its own account.

The 1987 Act only *prohibits putting subordinate workers at the disposal of users* when accompanied by the delegation of some part of the employer's authority. The Act applies to any transfer, however minimal, of the employer's authority.

b. Exceptions to the prohibition

1. Putting a worker at the disposal of a user without any delegation of authority – implicit exception

The 1987 Act only prohibits workers being put at the disposal of a user with a transfer of authority from the original employer to a user. A *contrario* one could state that putting a worker at the disposal of a user is allowed when it is not accompanied by any delegation of authority.[30]

In order to fall within the scope of the prohibition the original employer need not have transferred its entire authority. It suffices that part of the authority is transferred to the user. The user may therefore not exercise any authority over the workers for the restrictions not to come into play. In order to determine whether the user is exercising any form of authority over the consultants, the same indicia are taken into account as those used to determine whether an employment relationship exists.

It is important to stress in this context that *Belgian labour courts* are *quite liberal* when deciding whether an employment contract exists. This means that courts are willing to accept the existence of an employment relationship in circumstances where the alleged employer's actual or potential exercise of authority over the alleged employee is not apparent. Quite often the employer's authority is derived from secondary instead of primary indicia of subordination. Primary indications would be the fact that the (alleged) employer gives the worker mandatory

26. Act, on Temporary Employment.
27. Act 31, § 1 Act on Temporary Employment.
28. Act 71, Act containing Measures to stimulate Employment, 13 February 1998, *Official Gazette*, 19 February 1998.
29. Chamber of Representatives, 1997–1998, December 16, 1997, Amendment no. 14, Document number 1269/3 – 97/98, 5.
30. See: Brussels, 7 September 1994, *J.T.T.*, 1996, 81; Labor Tribunal Brussels, AR. no. 33.539/93, re: *Eltzroth c. Morgan Lewis & Bockius*.

instructions with respect to what, where, and when to perform. The same is true when the employer effectively controls the worker's performance of services.[31]

While a sub-contractor (performing as part of a relationship that is not a contract of employment) may also receive instructions and guidelines, these are of a different nature. The Belgian Supreme Court accepted as compatible with the independent status of the sub-contractor the fact that the sub-contractor's counterpart was giving instructions, provided these were general.[32] Furthermore, as the same Court held, the independent contractor can agree to deliver certain services at a predetermined place and time.[33]

Given the fact that highly skilled workers are often granted an extremely large freedom in the performance of their work (e.g. as far as time, place and manner of performance is concerned), labour courts had to look for other indicators that would allow them to make a distinction between the subordinate and the self-employed worker. Courts therefore started to look more and more at the external circumstances of a job for an indication of the existence of an employment relationship.

The external and material organisation of the work being performed is more and more relied on to establish the existence of an employment relationship. This tendency is especially apparent with regard to medical doctors performing in hospitals. The question arose as to whether these medical doctors could be considered employees of the hospital or not, taking into account that they have complete technical independence. Courts started to look at factors such as where the medical acts were performed, the equipment used, the team the doctor could/had to rely on, etc. In other words, courts were trying to establish whether the medical doctor was in fact being submitted to an organisation controlled not by the doctor him/herself but by somebody else or some other body.[34]

Courts are thus willing to find that one party exercises authority over the other within the work relationship on the basis of criteria that relate to the external circumstances of the job rather than to the way the job is performed.

It is obvious from the above that only under the clearest circumstances of sub-contracting, one is *not* dealing with workers being put at the disposal of an employer without transferring even part of the employer's normal authority.

2. *Putting workers at the disposal of a user with delegation of authority*

In exceptional cases an employer can put some of its workers at the disposal of another employer and thereby delegate some of its normal authority over the worker concerned. However, as a general rule, *a government authorisation* is required. In order to obtain this authorisation, the consent of the trade union delegation within the user's company is required as well.

---

31. See: C. Engels, De Juridische duiding van de overeenkomst tussen ziekenhuis en ziekenhuisgeneesheer, Arbeidsovereenkomst of overeenkomst tot zelfstandige samenwerking (The legal identity of the agreement between a hospital and the hospital medical doctor. Contract of services or for services), in *Arbeidsrecht, een confrontatie tussen theorie en praktijk* (Labor Law, Confrontation between theory and practice), O. Vanachter (ed.), *Antwerpen – Apeldoorn*, Maklu Uitgevers, 1993, 31, 56–63.
32. Supreme Court, 13 October 1957, *Arr.Cass.*, 1958, 48.
33. Supreme Court, 11 September 1978, *Arr.Cass.*, 1978–79, 32.
34. C. Engels, Belgium, in *Employed or Self-employed*, B. Brooks and C. Engels (eds). *Bulletin of Comparative Labor Relations*, no. 24, 1992, 29 e.s., especially 31–32.

However, *neither* the trade union delegation's *consent, nor* the government *authorisation is required* if a worker – whose original contract of employment is preserved – is exceptionally put at the disposal of a user:

1. within the framework of a collaboration between employers of the same economic and financial entity;
2. for the *performance during a limited time period of specialised tasks* that require special professional qualifications.

No authorisation or consent is needed under these circumstances. However, the government needs to be *notified* 24 h in advance of putting the worker at the disposal of the user.

A written document needs to be drafted and signed by the three parties involved: the original employer, the user and the worker concerned.

The contract of employment between the original employer and the worker remains in force. However, the original employer and the user become jointly liable for the payment of all wages, indemnities, benefits and social security contributions.

The 1987 Act furthermore states that the worker who is put at the disposal of a user should not be treated less favourably than the normal workers of the user who perform the same kind of jobs. This means that the conditions of employment (including wages and all kinds of benefits) of the worker put at the disposal of the user should in no way be inferior to the wages of the user's employees with the same job description.[35]

The February 1998 amendment of the 1987 Act makes a few provisions that deal with temporary work agencies, also applicable to the situation of workers put at the disposal of a user. For the period during which a worker is at the disposal of a user, the latter shall be answerable for the observance of those provisions of labour regulation and protection that are applicable in the workplace.[36] The Act itself specifies what kind of provisions are meant. It deals with provisions relating to:

- working hours
- public holidays
- Sunday rest
- female labour
- work by young people
- night work
- internal company work rules
- health and safety of workers and salubrity of work and the workplace.

The permission to put a worker at the disposal of a user with a delegation of authority 'in light of the short term performance of specialised tasks that require special professional qualifications' is meant to cover situations such as sending *computer specialists* to other companies.

Another example from case law is the leasing of a crane along with the qualified crane operators to run the crane for a specific job.[37]

35. Art. 32, §4, Act on Temporary Employment.
36. Art. 19, §1, Act on Temporary Employment.
37. Court of Appeals Liège, 12 March 1983, *J.L.M.B.*, 1994, 126.

According to the Act prior to its modification on 13 February 1998, putting a worker at the disposal of another employer *has to remain exceptional*. While it was not exactly clear what the term 'exceptional' really meant in this context, it appeared to exclude the possibility of permanently putting workers of one company at the disposal of another.

A very broad interpretation of the Act and the particular concept at hand was proffered and implied that there would be no real time restriction. This lenient interpretation, however, made a distinction between the activity the employer is ordinarily engaged in, and the exceptional activity of putting workers at the disposal of another employer. Some authors then defended the position that the Parliamentary Act allows – with the two exceptions mentioned above – putting workers at the disposal of another employer as long as this does not become the normal or regular activity of the employer.[38]

The latest modification of the Act of 24 July 1987 on 13 February 1998, makes it clear that there are not only *time restrictions* on the circumstances in which normal workers can be put at the disposal of users. The amended version of the 1987 Act now states that 'the employer, contrary to the general prohibition (stated in Article 31 of the same Act), is allowed to put its permanent employees at the disposal of a user if a number of conditions are *cumulatively* satisfied:

- the workers can be put at the disposal only for a limited period of time; and
- putting workers at the disposal of a user can be done by the employer only in addition to the employer's ordinary activities.'

The Parliamentary discussion highlighted that putting workers at the disposal of a user should not belong to the employer's normal activities. The fact that the employer engages in such an activity should remain occasional. It was stressed that should such activity become the employer's normal activity, it should be exercised through a temporary employment agency.

Both the occasional nature and the limited duration of putting workers at the disposal of users are stressed in the current version of the legal text.[39]

The authorities should be able to determine whether or not putting workers at the disposal of users belongs to a company's normal activities, although even in this respect difficult questions are weighed as to the importance of the activities an employer is engaged in.

How to determine an employer's ordinary activities? Does one look at the main activities of the employer? Must an employer be primarily engaged in putting workers at the disposal of users in order to establish that this is part of the employer's ordinary activities? Or, should one only consider an activity the employer has engaged in over a long period of time as (part of) an employer's ordinary activity, regardless of the fact that this activity represents only a minor part of the employer's

38. See in general: F. Tilleman, *Tijdelijk Arbeid uitzendarbeid en ter beschikkingstelling van werknemers* (Temporary Work and putting Employees at the Disposal of Users), Kluwer Rechtswetenschappen, 1982, 151–152; V. Petry, Detacheringen ter beschikkingstelling: een gespleten identiteit (Secondment and putting Workers at the Disposal: a split Personality), *Orientatie*, 1993, 195, 198–199; J.F. Gérard, La mise de travailleurs à la disposition d'utilisateurs (Putting Workers at the Disposal of Users) *Orientations*, 1992, 14, 21–22.
39. Chamber of Representatives, 1997–1998, 16 December 1997, Amendment no. 15, Document number 1269/397/98, 6.

business (figure)? Taking into account that the modified text of the 24 July 1987 Act explicitly refers to the employer's ordinary activit*ies*, in plural, the latter interpretation seems to be the correct one.

Furthermore, the Act expressly states that it is possible to put permanent workers at the disposal of a user for a limited period of time only (beperkte duur/durée limitée). Neither the discussion leading to the adoption of the Act, nor the Parliamentary Act itself offers any indication as to what the concept implies. The authorities who will have to grant/refuse the requests for approval are left without any (official) guidance as to the limits on the duration of the leasing of personnel that the law obviously intends. It is striking here that the Parliamentary Act uses the term *limited* and not *fixed* duration. In either case, the authorities will have to judge whether the duration of putting the worker at the disposal of a user is justified under the circumstances.

While it may be difficult to come up with hard and fast rules in this area, some general guidance from the legislator would have been helpful, for example an indication of which criteria should be taken into account to verify the legitimate nature of putting a worker at the disposal of a user.

c. Sanctions in case of violation of the Act

1. Triggering of the sanctions

Both criminal and civil sanctions can be imposed in case the provisions of the Act of 24 July 1987 are violated.

However, the principle prohibition of putting workers at the disposal of users, contained in article 31 of the Act of 24 July 1987, does not come into play:

1. If the subordinate workers are put at the disposal of the users without any delegation of authority;
2. when the subordinate workers are put at the disposal of users
   - for a limited period of time,
   - putting workers at the disposal of users does not belong to the employer's normal activities, and
   - when a government approval or government notification has taken place;
3. when dealing with self-employed workers.

The Courts' liberal construction of the concept of authority under Belgian Law, and the emphasis that is put on the integration of the worker in an organisation run by the other party (alleged employer) in deciding whether an employment relationship exists, may make it quite difficult to lease personnel to a user without the delegation to the user of any part of the authority normally exercised by the employer.

When the leasing takes place over an extended period of time, it is not unlikely that the personnel that is put at the disposal of a user will become at least partly integrated into the organisation of the user. Such integration could be seen as an exercise of authority of the user over the leased personnel. If so, the leasing of the personnel may well be contrary to the provisions of the Act of 24 July 1987, if and when:

- not all government notifications have been made, nor approvals obtained, or
- when the leasing is not for a limited period of time, or

- when leasing of its personnel belongs to the regular normal activities of the employer.

It should furthermore be stressed that it does not suffice for an employer that is leasing out its personnel to a user to formally state in the agreement between the employer and the user that the former retains the entirety of the authority over the workers who are leased out. A user that is exercising part of the authority normally exercised by the employer, even in violation of the explicit provisions of the agreement between the employer and the user, may trigger the sanctions under the law.[40]

2. *Civil sanctions*

a. Presumption of a contract of employment for an indefinite period of time with the user. The Act explicitly states that if any form of prohibited employment of this kind takes place, a contract of employment for an indefinite period of time is presumed to exist between the worker and the user. This presumption cannot be appealed.[41]

b. Termination of the contract of employment of an indefinite period of time, by the employee, and without term of notice.

   A worker put at the disposal of a user in violation of the 1987 Act can terminate his/her contract of employment with the user on the spot, without respecting any term of notice, and this for the period that was contracted for putting him/her at the disposal of the new employer.[42] If the worker was specifically hired to be put at the disposal of a user and the activity was carried out in violation of the 1987 Act, the employment contract is null and void.[43]

c. Joint liability between the (original) employer and the user. Both the original employer and the user will be liable (jointly) for the payments of:
   - all indemnities, wages, benefits and
   - all social security contributions.

This joint liability includes liability for the termination indemnities.[44]

The sanctions could be particularly severe if the original contract of employment (now considered void, since the conditions for acceptable leasing of personnel have not been satisfied) was a contract for a specific period of time.

Since the contract is to be considered null and void and replaced by virtue of the law by a contract of employment for an indefinite period of time, the contract will not automatically come to an end at the date that was set in the original agreement. In case the work for which the leasing took place has come to an end, the contract will have to be terminated in accordance with the rules dealing with terminations of contracts of employment for an indefinite period of time (see *infra*).

---

40. See: Criminal Court Charleroi, 5 June 1985, *Soc. Kron.*, 1986, 23.
41. Art 31, §3, al. 1, Act on Temporary Employment.
42. Art 31, §3, al. 2, Act on Temporary Employment.
43. Art 31, §2, Act on Temporary Employment.
44. F. Tilleman, Het sluipend gewoon van de terbeschikkingstelling (The creeping Danger of putting Workers at the Disposal of Others), *Orientatie*, 1997, 121, 123.

Both employers (original employer + the user) will then be jointly liable for the termination indemnity.

3. Criminal sanctions

The 1987 Act provides for criminal sanctions at the following level:

* 8 days to 1 month imprisonment for the employer or its agents who violate the relevant provisions of the Act and/or
* a fine of between 26 and 500 BEF, to be multiplied by 200 (for adjustment to inflation). This sanction can be applied as many times as there are workers who are employed in violation of the Act, with a maximum of 50,000 BEF (also multiplied by 200). The maximum fine is therefore 10,000,000 BEF.
* The judge can take mitigating circumstances into account when determining the level of the criminal sanctions. However, the criminal fine cannot be set below 40% of the minimum amount mentioned above.[45]
* In case of repetition within the year, the sanction can be doubled.
* If the authorities decide not to press criminal charges, administrative fines can be imposed by the Ministry of Labour. The fines could run from 2,000 BEF up to 50,000 BEF and are multiplied by the number of employees that is illegally employed in violation of the 1987 Act. The absolute maximum of the administrative fine is 800,000 BEF. Mitigating circumstances can be taken into account. However, the fine can never be below 40% of the minimum mentioned in the law.[46]

d. Interim management

Interim management companies deliver managers (of all kinds) to companies that have (temporary) vacancies. If the interim management company wants to organise its services with *subordinate employees*, it will fall squarely within the scope of the basic prohibition of putting workers at the disposal of users. Questions would not only be raised about the temporary nature of the management assignments, more importantly, putting its workers at the disposal of users will be seen as the normal activity of the interim management company. This is clearly contrary to the mandatory provisions prohibiting an employer to lease out personnel as part of its normal activities. This holds only when there is at least a partial delegation of the employer's normal authority. In the absence of such delegation of authority the arrangement whereby the interim management firm leases out its subordinate manager (employee) seems to be valid, even when this is done over an extended period of time.

In this case one is dealing with true sub-contracting where the sub-contractor (interim management firm) is performing the requested services with its own personnel.

Should the employer's authority be delegated to the user, the services can only be delivered within the framework of interim labour, through an interim labour agency, otherwise, for a restricted period of time, or as part of the company's normal activities.

45. Art. 43, §2, Act on Temporary Employment, as amended by the Parliamentary Act of 13 February 1998, *Official Gazette*, 19 February 1998.

46. Art. 1ter Act on Administrative Fines, 30 June 1971, as amended by the Parliamentary Act of 13 February 1998, *Official Gazette*, 19 February 1998.

The above applies to interim managers who perform as subordinate employees and belong to the work force of the interim management firm or company. It is therefore of the utmost importance to determine the true nature of the relationship between the interim manager and the interim management firm or company.

The way the parties themselves label the relationship that exists between them is not the determining factor. Most interim management firms claim not to work with subordinate employees but with *independent contractors*. The basic activities the interim management firm performs are very similar to the activities performed by interim agencies or temporary work agencies as the concept is defined by the Act of 24 July 1987.

Arguments have been advanced that the interim management firms are actually interim labour agencies and that the contracts they conclude with the managers can irrefutably be considered contracts of employment.[47]

This interpretation of the Act is not entirely sound. It would prevent long standing relationships between contractors and sub-contractors whereby they enter into a so-called framework agreement that contains the basic principles for collaboration when/if sub-contracting jobs come up. Whenever a job comes up, contractor and sub-contractor enter into a specific agreement outlining the details of the work to be performed. If the framework agreement is devoid of any references to an exercise or potential exercise of authority and is not contradicted by actual practice, the relationship between the contractor and the sub-contractor cannot be considered an employment relationship.

The presumption found in article 8 of the Act of 24 July 1987 should not come into play at all. It aims at confirming the fact that the temporary employment agency is the employer of the subordinate worker. The agency retains the general authority over the worker concerned while the worker is performing at the user's premises and receives direct instruction from him.[48]

When dealing with a framework agreement between an interim management firm and an (interim) manager through which the agency cannot/does not retain even the general authority over the worker, the provision on temporary work agencies (including the irrefutable presumption of the existence of a contract of employment) should not come into play at all.

Given the fact that there is no relationship of authority between the interim agency firm and the interim worker, what the interim management firm does is nothing more than matching supply and demand for independently delivered services. One could compare this service more to placement of self-employed (against a fee) than to interim labour agencies.

Since the existing Belgian laws dealing with placement of workers only relate to the placement of subordinate employees, they are not at all applicable to the placement of independent workers.

It is reported that four interim management offices operate in Belgium:

- Price Waterhouse Coopers;
- Robert Half Belgium;

---

47. See: F. Tilleman, Het sluipend gevaar van de terbeschikkingstelling (The creeping Danger of putting Workers at the Disposal of Others), *Orientatie*, 1997, 121, 128.

48. See: R. Blanpain, *Uitzendarbeid* (Interim Labor), in Arbeidsrecht, R. Blanpain (ed), Brugge, Die Keune, s.d., 37, no. 60 referring to the Parliamentary preparatory work of the Act that preceded the 1987 Act.

- Executive Temporary Management (ETM, belonging to Ernst & Young); and
- KPMG Interim Management.

These four offices are grouped in BIMA (Belgian Association of Interim Management).

Interim managers often work through their own management corporation. They perform as independent workers for the interim management firm. On the average they charge between 20,000 and 40,000 BEF per day (±550 and 1100 US $). The interim management office will likely add a 20% surcharge in its bill to the client.[49]

e. *Conclusion*

True independent contractors, acting as sub-contractors, perform a pre-determined service at a given time and place, as agreed upon beforehand. They are not (should not) be subject to any authority from any third party. They may receive some general instructions with regard to the work to be performed.

When subordinate workers are leased out to other companies, outside the context of the strictly regulated interim work agencies, a general prohibition of this kind of activity comes into play. Leasing of ordinary personnel cannot validly be part of the employer's normal activities, nor can the leasing last for a long period of time. This is the case when the normal employer of the worker delegates some of its normal authority over the workers to a user.

Leasing out subordinate workers to an employer without any delegation whatsoever of the authority normally belonging to the employer will, in practice, prove quite difficult, at least when dealing with activities that have to be integrated into the larger framework that makes up the user company.

Furthermore, Belgian Labour Courts have interpreted very broadly the relationship of subordination/authority that needs to be present for a contract of employment to validly exist. This implies that courts are willing to find an employment relationship quite easily, and quite often on the basis of factors that relate to the external circumstances under which the work is performed.

Against this background, the leasing of personnel is likely to go hand in hand with at least some delegation of the employer's normal authority.

For companies ordinarily engaging in services performed at a client's location for an extended period of time, the above implies that they are likely involved in activities that are subject to criminal sanctions under Belgian Law.

This situation is hardly compatible with modern business developments of the network society in which 'companies' consist of separate independent entities performing services for each other and at each other's premises. Companies outsource activities which do not belong to the core of their business.

Canteen and cleaning services are transferred/outsourced to independently operating businesses. These services have to be delivered on the premises of the 'user' company. It may be hard for the user to avoid *any* indication of the exercise of authority over the workers. However, that is what Belgian Law requires. And why?

If an employer is putting part of its normal employees (under a contract of employment for an indefinite period of time) at the disposal of users and thereby

49. B. De Keyser, Interim Management, *VBO Bulletin*, 1998, 95, 82.

transfers part of its normal authority in order to make sure services are delivered properly, there seems to be no reason to generally prohibit this kind of activity.

The same is true when agencies try to match supply and demand on the market of independent service providers. Interim employment agencies for self-employed, better referred to as placement agencies, should be able to operate on our labour market. Overregulation of this kind of activity for which there is apparently room in our economy, ought to be avoided at all cost.

2.4 Dismissal Regulations

a. *Introduction*

Dismissal regulations have not been deregulated to a large extent in the recent past. The basic provisions dealing with dismissal law are part of the Act on contracts of employment of 3 July 1978. This act makes a major distinction between white-collar and blue-collar workers. It would not be unfair to state that white-collar workers, certainly those that earn the highest salaries, are *very well*, if not *over* protected.

The difference in treatment for blue and white-collar workers is considered inflexible. Theoretical arguments have been advanced and thereafter cases were introduced before the Cour d'Arbitrage (Constitutional Court) claiming the unconstitutionality of the difference in treatment, particularly with regard to the length of the term of notice.[50]

The Cour d'Arbitrage, however, did not consider the difference in treatment to be unconstitutional. The court stated that the difference and the criterion on which the difference is based would be hardly constitutional if such a distinction were introduced into law at this point in time. It considered the distinctive criterion to be neither reasonable, nor objective. However, the court held that additional forms of protection have been granted to blue-collar workers either by sector level collective bargaining agreement (see *infra*) or by law (e.g. protection against abusive dismissal granted to blue-collar workers only) that soften the impact of the difference in treatment.[51]

b. *White-collar workers*

Terms of notice for white-collar workers are set at three months for each five year period of employment begun with the same employer.[52] This holds for white-collar workers earning less than 947,000 BEF annually (valid through 1999, and adjusted

50. See: C. Engels, De statuten van werkman en bediende: een juridische benadering (The Status of blue and while-collar Workers: a legal Approach) in *Statuut Werkman-Bediende, Arbeidsrechtelijke en sociologische kanttekeningen* (The Status of blue and white-Collar Workers, Labor Law and sociological Observations), Belgische Vereniging voor Arbeidsverhoudingen, Brugge, Die Keure, 1990, 7, 42–47; C. Engels, Het onderscheid werkman/bediende, een ongrondwettige discriminatie in strijd met de artikelen 6 en 6bis van de Belgische grondwet, *R.W.*, 1991–92, 729–742; C. Engels, De toenadering tussen de statuten van werkman en bediende en de ongrondwettelijkheid van het nog bestaande onderscheid (The difference between blue and white-collar workers: an unconstitutional discrimination violating the articles 6 and 6bis of the Belgian Constitution), *Or.*, 1992, 13–24.
51. Cour d'Arbitrage, 8 July 1993, case no. 56/93, *Official Gazette*, 27 August 1993, 18926.
52. Art. 83, Act concerning Contracts of Employment, 3 July 1978.

on an annual basis). For those earning more than this amount the three months notice per five year period of employment begun is an absolute minimum. The law states that the parties should have come to an agreement on the length of a term of notice at the time notice is given. In the absence of an agreement, the labour courts should *post factum* (after the termination has occurred) determine the appropriate indemnity in lieu of notice.

Terms of notice for white-collar workers being paid over 947,000 BEF gross yearly are normally significantly higher than the three month minimum period. In order to be able to make reasonable predictions of what courts would grant as compensation in lieu of notice, several theoretical formulae were developed. The *Claeys* formula is most commonly applied. It does not bind any court of law, but is routinely used. The result of an application of the Claeys formula is most often the employer's ultimate liability.[53]

The Claeys formula applies as follows:

Term of notice expressed in months = 0.89 (Seniority) + (0.08 (Age) + 0.0013 × (Remuneration) − 2)

Seniority is calculated as follows:

1 month	= 0.08
2 months	= 0.16
3 months	= 0.25
4 months	= 0.33
5 months	= 0.42
6 months	= 0.50
7 months	= 0.58
8 months	= 0.67
9 months	= 0.75
10 months	= 0.83
11 months	= 0.91
12 months	= 1

The **Age** factor is calculated in the same way as seniority.

Salary/annual salary expressed in units of 1000; e.g. 1,000,000 BEF are written in the formula as 1000.

The annual salary that is taken into account includes the worker's full salary, including the financial value of all benefits in kind the worker receives from his/her employer.

The annual salary is adjusted to changes in the cost of living.

It should be mentioned that an application of the Claeys formula quite often determines the maximum compensation an employer may have to pay to an employee in case of termination of the employment contract. Courts often grant less than the result of the Claeys formula. This is especially the case when the employee's annual salary is extremely high.

53. See: C. Engels, *De Opzegging van de arbeidsovereenkomst voor onbepaalde tijd* (The Termination of a Contract of Employment for an indefinite Period of Time, by giving Notice), Brugge, Die Keure, 1995, 97 e.s.

Since 1994 the legislator tried to make the rules with regard to the termination of high level white-collar workers more flexible (read: less costly). A Parliamentary Act of 30 March 1994, allows the parties to the employment contract under certain conditions to contractually determine the term of notice the employer has to respect in case of termination.

Contract stipulations with regard to the term of notice to be respected by the employer hold only upon the satisfaction of the following conditions:

1. one is dealing with a white-collar worker who earns more than 1,893,000 BEF per year. This amount is adjusted to inflation on a yearly basis. The amount mentioned is valid through 1999;
2. only terms of notice that apply to the employer can be contractually determined;
3. the minimum term of notice to be provided is three months per five year period of employment started;
4. the contract stipulation regarding the term of notice has to be agreed upon by the parties prior to the actual employment taking effect.[54] It has been argued in this respect that contract stipulations would also be valid in case the employee was already in the employment, but was promoted to a completely new job. If he/she concludes a new agreement prior to actually starting the new job, the clause should be considered valid.[55] In a recent case, the labour court of Brussels approved this theory.[56]

If all the above conditions are *cumulatively* satisfied, it is possible to contractually stipulate the term of notice at a level that is considerably lower than what is to be expected if such contract stipulation did not exist.

Although it is impossible to have a clear picture of how widespread the use of such clauses has become in Belgium since their introduction in 1994, practice points out that they are clearly still the exception to the rule. Most high-level white-collar employees are aware of the level of their legal protection in the absence of contract stipulations and are not prone to give that up.

c. *Blue-collar workers*

As far as blue-collar workers are concerned, the Act on contracts of employment provides for only minimal terms of notice that differ only – and even then only marginally – in function of the seniority of the employee:

Seniority	*Term of notice in calendar days*
Less than 20 years	28
20 years or more	56

54. Art. 82, para 5, Act of 3 July 1978 concerning Contracts of Employment.
55. C. Engels, *Opzegging van de arbeidsovereenkomst voor onbepaalde tijd* (The Termination of a Contract of Employment for an indefinite Period of Time, by giving Notice), Brugge, Die Keure, 1994, 110–113.
56. See: Labour Court Brussel, 15 January 1998, *J.T.T.*, 1998, 378.

The Act on contracts of employment allows that deviations from these terms of notice can be introduced by Royal Decree on the basis of a sector level collective bargaining agreement.[57] The Act specifies that such a Royal Decree can be passed if it is in the interest of specific categories of employees or for social and economic reasons. Courts are reluctant to verify whether these conditions were actually present when the Royal Decrees were passed.

Terms of notice have been agreed upon between the employee and employer representatives in about 30 sectors of industry. While there are some sectors of industry that have reduced the terms of notice for blue-collar workers, the large majority of the other sectors of industry have substantially increased the length of the terms of notice for blue-collar workers, without, however, reaching the level of protection that is granted to white-collar employees.[58] Collective bargaining agreements often offer a protection similar to the agreements in the metal working sector. The protection that is granted increases with the employees' seniority:

Seniority	*Term of notice in calendar days*
Less 5 years	28
5–10 years	35
10–20 years	70
20–25 years	154
25 and over	196[59]

The laws that establish the framework for the social partners to negotiate an agreement at sector level (sector of industry) in the first place and then have the collective bargaining agreement rendered generally binding, came into being, together with the Act on contracts of employment itself, in 1978. It allows the social partners to determine what they see fit as terms of notice for the blue-collar workers in their industry or sector. Since the Collective Bargaining Agreements are presumed to be the result of free collective bargaining, the terms of notice that are established should be adapted to the requirements of the particular industry for which the collective bargaining agreement is concluded.

2.5 Fixed Term Contracts of Employment

a. General regime

The Act on contracts of employment (3 July 1978) allows for the conclusion of fixed term contracts of employment without obligation of government approval, without

57. Art. 61, Act concerning Contracts of Employment, 3 July 1978.
58. See: C. Engels, Contractuele afspraken aangaande de latere beëindiging van arbeidsovereenkomsten (I) (Contract Clauses on the Termination of Employment Contracts), *Orientatie*, 1998, 203, 212–213.
59. Royal Decree of 25 November 1997, *Official Gazette*, 20 December 1997. For a complete overview of all present collective bargaining agreements dealing with terms of notice for blue-collar workers, see: C. Engels, Contractuele afspraken aangaande opzeggingstermijnen (Contractual Provisions on Terms of Notice), *T.S.R.*, 1998, 127–165.

notification of any authority and without limitation on the duration of the contract. Article 7 of the Act on contracts of employment merely states that the contract of employment is concluded either:

- for specific work;
- for a specific period of time (fixed term); or
- for an indefinite period of time.

The choice between either of the forms of contracts is left completely up to the parties. However, in case the parties do not opt for a contract of employment for an indefinite period of time, a written agreement needs to be concluded. This agreement has to be concluded prior to the employee actually entering into the employment.[60] If no such agreement is concluded or if the agreement is concluded after the employee actually starts the job, the contract of employment is presumed to be a contract for an indefinite period of time. This will have immediate consequences on the termination of the contract by the employer.

Contracts of employment for a fixed term cannot be terminated by giving notice. This kind of contract comes to an end automatically, at the date of expiration provided for in the contract itself. Should the contract of employment for a fixed term be terminated prior to the end of the term, the employer has to pay the employee's salary until the date the term ends under the contract. There is a cap, however, explicitly mentioned in the Act. The termination indemnity the employer has to pay may never exceed the double of what the employer would have had to pay in case of termination of an indefinite contract.[61]

While the Act on contracts of employment does *not put any restriction on the duration of a fixed term employment contract*, it is clear from the Act that the contract of employment for an indefinite period remains the desired contract and the general rule. The Act therefore prescribes that successive contracts of employment for a fixed term are to be considered a contract for an indefinite duration. This assumption can be appealed. The employer can argue that the nature of the work justifies successive contracts or that it had other legitimate reasons for entering into a succession of fixed term contracts.[62] These exceptions to the general rule on a succession of fixed term contracts have to be construed restrictively.[63]

b. Flexibility measures

It has often been argued that employers are reluctant to hire additional workers if their economic future is uncertain. Since termination of employment contracts for an indefinite period requires the payment of large termination indemnities, employers tended to sign fixed term contracts for relatively short terms. Successive contracts were frequent, but normally required more of a justification than mere economics.

A Parliamentary Act of 30 March 1994, allowed for a temporary exception to the stringent rules prohibiting successive contracts of employment. The exception allowed employers to enter into several fixed term contracts of employment in a row

60. Art. 9, Act concerning Contracts of Employment, 3 July 1978.
61. Art. 40, §1, Act concerning Contracts of Employment, 3 July 1978.
62. Art. 10, Act concerning Contracts of Employment, 3 July 1978.
63. Labour Court Brussel, 24 May 1991, *J.T.T.*, 1991, 399.

for a period of time ending 31 December 1997. The impact of the Act on employment was to be measured on a yearly basis.

By Act of 13 February 1998, the system of successive contracts of employment described below was introduced on a permanent basis and was made part of the Act on contracts of employment.[64] The newly introduced measures allow successive contracts of employment without a risk of the contract being deemed a contract of employment for an indefinite period of time.

Two different avenues are available, one that requires government authorisation, one that doesn't.

A maximum of *four successive contracts* of employment can be concluded without authorisation and/or notification if:

- the minimum duration of each contract is three months and
- the total duration of all contracts does not surpass two years.

With government permission, successive contracts of employment for a fixed term can be concluded, provided:

- the minimum duration of each contract is at least six months and
- the total duration of all the contracts does not surpass three years.

To obtain government approval, the need for such an arrangement has to be justified.

3. INDIVIDUAL LABOUR RELATIONS

Certain issues mentioned under the heading of 'Labour market regulations' belong equally under the present chapter.

Successive fixed term contracts of employment are now permitted. However, an employer cannot force an applicant to accept such terms of employment. The consent of both parties is required.

With regard to *termination of contracts of employment*, it was mentioned that high-level white-collar workers can contractually agree to shorter terms of notice than those they would normally receive from the courts if no stipulation on terms of notice were part of the individual contract of employment. Again this measure of flexibility requires genuine consent between the parties involved.

A. Flexibilisation of Working Time Regulations

Working time regulations in Belgium are extremely complex. The relevant rules are scattered over numerous legal provisions which make their application in practice far from easy.

Since the beginning of the 1980s, the government has understood that the strict rules adopted to protect individual employees against abusively long working hours more than a decade earlier might no longer be in line with contemporary business requirements. Unemployment and the growing need to remain competitive

---

64. Art. 10 bis, Act concerning Contracts of Employment, 3 July 1978.

internationally forced the Belgian government to look into certain experiments with regard to working time.

The Hansenne (working time) experiments – Royal Decree of 1982

By Royal Decree of 30 December 1982, the government (the then Minister of employment was Michel Hansenne, acting President of the International Labour Organisation) introduced a set of measures allowing flexible use of working time.[65] Intended as experiments, the measures were only allowed for a two-year period under the Royal Decree.[66]

Annualisation of working time – Social Recovery Act of 1985

The 22 January 1985 Social Recovery Act introduced another form of flexibility. Daily (8 h) and weekly (40 h) working time limits could be exceeded provided that there was a legally binding collective agreement which established the following:

- the average weekly working time, as well as the total number of hours over a period of maximum 12 consecutive months;
- the number of hours during which work can be performed, below or above the daily limit, without, however, exceeding 2 h a day and without exceeding a daily working time of 9 h;
- the number of hours during which work can be performed, below or above the weekly limit, without, however, exceeding 5 h a day or 45 h a week.[67]

As of 1st January 1999, the weekly limit of 40 h was lowered to 39.[68]

New working time arrangements – the inter-industry collective bargaining agreement and the Parliamentary Act of 1987[69]

On 23 April 1996, an agreement was reached in the National Labour Council to formalise what was known as the Hansenne experiments. The agreement called for a new Act, to be voted by Parliament, which would allow enterprises in general to

65. Royal Decree respecting Experiments in the Arrangement of Working Time in Undertakings for the Purpose of Redistributing the available Working Time, 30 December 1982, no. 179, commonly referred to as the Hansenne Experiments.
66. C. Engels and B. Brooks, Trade Unions in the 1980s, Some Lessons for the Future, *Industrial Research Centre Monograph*, The University of New South Wales, 1990, 9.
67. See: R. Blanpain and C. Engels, Belgium, in: *Legal and Contractual Limitations to Working Time in the European Union*, R. Blanpain, E. Köhler and J. Rojot (eds.) Leuven, Dublin, Peeters, Office for Official Publications of the European Communities, 1996, no. 14, 216–217.
68. Royal Decree in order to determine the Application of the Reduction of Working Time stated in article 48 of the Act of 26 July 1996 to Stimulate Employment and to Safeguard the competitive Position, 11 December 1998, *Official Gazette*, 17 December 1998.
69. Collective Bargaining Agreement no. 42 concerning the introduction of new working time arrangements in the enterprises, rendered generally binding by Royal Decree of 18 June 1987, *Official Gazette*, 26 June 1987 thereafter amended. Act, concerning the introduction of new working time arrangements in enterprises, *Official Gazette*, 12 June 1987, hereafter amended.

work for 12 h a day, for economic reasons, and would allow Sunday work, night work for men, etc. if a collective agreement were concluded to that end.

For reasons of competition, agreements first have to be reached at industry level. If after 6 months of negotiation such an agreement cannot be reached, then negotiations can start at enterprise level. There are some safeguards built in: if a trade union delegation exists within the enterprise, all trade unions which have a representative in the delegation must agree. If there is no such delegation the work rules in the enterprise have to be modified to reflect the changes. Only if there is a complaint from an employee or a trade union will the matter be taken up by the joint committee of the sector. The local arrangement in that case may be rejected by the majority of the members of the joint committee (which operates on industry level and is composed of representative employers' associations and trade unions). If all employer or trade union representatives reject the proposal, it is invalid. Other conditions are: the agreements must have a positive impact on employment (a rather vague notion), and employees must be informed beforehand of the proposed changes. These reforms were adopted in the 1987 Act (above) and the framework for a national inter-industry-wide collective bargaining agreement was concluded to that end (No. 42). By mid-1992, some 27 collective bargaining agreements concluded by the sectoral joint committees or subcommittees were in force. Most of them were rendered binding by Royal Decree and thus applicable to all employees within the scope of the joint committee or subcommittee. Only 3 out of the 27 were not.[70]

Just to give one example of flexible working time arrangements that can be introduced on the basis of these legal measures, one could look at the *collective bargaining agreement of the joint committee no. 218*, that is applicable to *all white-collar workers* that do not belonging to any other specific or defined sector of industry. The joint committee no. 218 is extremely important not only for the number of white-collar workers who belong to it, but also because many service industries, including computer industries, belong to this joint committee.

The joint committee no. 218 reached a collective bargaining agreement on 29 September 1988, implementing the above mentioned national measures. The sector level collective bargaining agreement provides for a number of flexible arrangements that can be introduced by the employer without even having to modify its work rules. It allows the introduction of further flexible arrangements, but only after following an elaborate procedure.

1. Working Time Arrangements Explicitly Provided for

The following flexible deviations from the normal rules on working time can be introduced on the basis of sector level collective bargaining agreements.

a. *Sunday work*

Each enterprise may employ workers for six Sundays a year. Each worker participating in such a system can be employed during not more than three

70. See: R. Blanpain and C. Engels, Belgium, in: *Legal and Contractual Limitations to Working Time in the European Union*, R. Blanpain, E. Köhler and J. Rojot (eds.) Leuven, Dublin, Peeters, Office for Official Publications of the European Communities, 1996, no. 35, 227.

Sundays a year. Compensatory rest needs to be taken for 50% of the time worked on a Sunday.

b. 10 h a day/4 days a week

A 10-h-day working time arrangement can be introduced on the condition that the workers work at maximum 4 days a week, excluding Sundays.

The enterprise can ask the workers to work a fifth day, provided:

- the weekly limit of 50 h is respected;
- the worker will not be called into work for a period of less than five hours at a time;
- the worker is entitled to additional compensatory rest as follows:
  1 h for working time above 40 and up to and including 44 h a week;
  2 h for working time above 44 and up to and including 48 h a week;
  3 h for working time above 48 and up to and including 50 h a week;

The collective bargaining agreement allows enterprises to make amendments to the above working time regime of 10 h/4 day work week within the following limits:

- at least one 10 h day;
- for the total of 4 working days, working time needs to equal at least 36 h;
- at least 5 h work any time the worker is called in;
- compensatory rest, as indicated above.

c. 12 h a day/3 days a week

The enterprise may introduce a working time arrangement that includes 12 h working days in a three-day work week. If a 12 h day falls on a Sunday, weekly working time is set at 28 h. This arrangement entitles the worker to a full time salary. It cannot be introduced for a cycle of shorter than two weeks.

A two-week cycle looks like this:

- first week: 12 h Saturday and Sunday;
- second week: 12 h Saturday and Sunday + 8 h on Monday

A three-week cycle looks like this:

- first and second week: 12 h on Saturday and Sunday
- third week: 12 h on Saturday, Sunday and Monday.

Saturday and Monday can be replaced by any other day of the working week.

The collective bargaining agreement requires the employer to inform the workers in writing and in advance of the kind of system it wants to introduce and the reasons justifying it. In the absence of a works council or a trade union delegation, the information needs to be provided to the employees personally. New work time arrangements have to be agreed upon with the employees personally. Company work rules are automatically adapted.

At no point may the number of hours actually worked above the average weekly working hours (multiplied by the number of weeks already worked in the same year) exceed 65 h. Once this point is reached workers have to take immediate compensatory time off.

2. Other Working Time Arrangements Not Explicitly Provided for in the Sector Level Collective Bargaining Agreement

If the employer wants to introduce a different flexible working time arrangement the procedure summarised below to be followed. The procedure is elaborate and requires the intervention of the industry wide joint committee.

(1) Each worker must be provided with the project of the new working time arrangement, mentioning at least:
- working hours;
- work schedules;
- breaks and rest periods;
- method of payment of the remuneration;
- impact of the arrangement on the employment situation.

(2) For 8 days following the communication of the project, the workers may formulate remarks in a register provided by the employer.

(3) After 8 days, the employer sends the register to the president of the joint committee.

(4) The president must acknowledge receipt and send a copy of the project and register to the worker and employer representative organisations in the joint committee.

(5) For 1 month following acknowledgement of receipt, the organisations represented in the joint committee and the workers may forward their remarks to the president of the joint committee.

(6) In the absence of remarks in the register or forwarded to the president during the 1 month period, the president must notify the employer thereof within 8 days. The new arrangement may then enter into force.

(7) If there are remarks, the president must notify the joint committee and the employer thereof within the same 8 day time period.

(8) If the president fails to carry out either of the notifications referred to under item (6) and (7), the new arrangement enters into force at the end of the 8-day period.

(9) The joint committee has a period of 2 months as from the communication of the file by the president to render a motivated opinion.
The joint committee must verify whether the project for the new working time arrangement was concluded in accordance with the regulations.
The project is rejected in the following two cases:
- if the majority of the members of the joint committee so decides;
- if all the members representing either the employers or the workers so decide.

(10) The president must notify the employer of the decision of the joint committee within 8 days.

(11) Failing such notification, the new arrangement enters into force 2 months and 8 days after the communication of the file to the joint committee.

Shift work with night work – inter-industry collective bargaining agreement of 23 March 1990[71]

This agreement is applicable to employers and workers involved in systems of continuous, semi-continuous and fixed night work (enterprises working 24 h a day) between 11 p.m. and 6 a.m.

In principle, only employees with an individual contract of employment for an indefinite period of time may perform under these kinds of working-time systems. Participation is voluntary. Employment contracts for a definite period of time or for clearly specified work are allowed only when this is customary for the sector, the enterprise or the category of workers concerned. The same applies to temporary work lasting more than 6 months (extension of this maximum period is possible through collective bargaining).

The above-mentioned working-time systems are the result of a collective bargaining agreement with the trade union delegations represented in the enterprise. They do not apply to new sections added to the enterprise, to workers not previously employed in the company, or when a whole new enterprise is created.

A 50-year-old employee with more than 20 years of seniority may request, for serious medical reasons, not to participate in any of the above mentioned systems of working time. The request should be made in writing. An employee over 55 years of age may make the same request, but without giving medical reasons. The employer has a 6-month period to satisfy the request and to provide the employee with another job in accordance with his/her skills. If the employer is not able to satisfy the request, the employee may terminate the employment relationship. In this case, he/she has a right to supplementary unemployment benefits for a 5-year period, paid by the employer. Apart from medical reasons, the same request can be made for other compelling reasons. Pregnant women are granted the same rights. Collective Bargaining Agreement No. 46 also deals with transportation, remuneration, weekly working time, compensatory rest, rights of trade union delegations, training, hygiene, occupational safety and medicine, and social infrastructure.

Many provisions allow for collectively bargained alterations at the level of the sector and/or the enterprise.[72]

Night work – the Act of 27 February 1997[73]

The principle prohibition of night work and the exceptions to it, are referred to below. However, the Act of 27 February 1997, introduced a system whereby other deviations from the prohibition of night work are made possible. Such deviations can be the result of Royal Decrees (none up to now). However, deviations

71. Collective Bargaining Agreement, no. 46 concerning accompanying Measures for Shift Work with Night Performances, as well as for other Forms of Work with Night Performance, 23 March 1990, rendered generally binding by Royal Decree, 10 May 1990, *Official Gazette*, 13 June 1990.
72. See: R. Blanpain and C. Engels, Belgium, in: *Legal and Contractual Limitations to Working Time in the European Union*, R. Blanpain, E. Köhler and J. Rojot (eds.) Leuven, Dublin, Peeters, Office for Official Publications of the European Communities, 1996, no. 36, 227–228.
73. *Official Gazette*, 8 April 1997.

from the prohibition on night work can also be the result of bargaining, at least in cases where

1. night work is performed in successive shifts;
2. the work requires a permanent presence; or
3. companies deal with products that spoil easily.[74]

Such bargaining can take place with the workers representatives or, should there be no employee representative bodies, with the workers themselves.

B. Night Work for Women

1. European Background

The European Union has tackled the problem of night work for women indirectly from the angle of equal treatment, namely on the basis of Article 5 of the Directive (76/207/EEC) of 9 February 1976. Indeed, according to a judgement of 4 October 1989, the *Tribunal de Police* (local criminal court), Illkrich (France) referred a question on the interpretation of Article 5 of the 1976 Directive to the Court for a preliminary ruling. The question arose in the course of criminal proceedings brought against a Mr. Stoeckel, the manager of SUMA S.A., who was charged with having employed 77 women in night work contrary to Article L-213-1 of the French *Code du Travail*. This question was all the more delicate since French legislation on night work resulted from the ratification of ILO Convention No. 89, containing a prohibition of night work for women in industry.[75] The six Member States Belgium, France, Greece, Italy, Portugal and Spain denounced ILO Convention No. 89 in February 1992.

The means of reconciling the international instruments emanating from the ILO, on the one hand, and the supranational norms emanating from the Community, on the other, concerning night work for women and equal treatment of men and women, lies in Article 234 (2) of the EEC Treaty. Pursuant to this Article, the Member States concerned shall, to the extent that the international agreements are not compatible with the Treaty, 'take all appropriate steps to eliminate the incompatibilities.'

In the particular case in question, restructuring of the enterprise concerned had been negotiated between the employer and the trade unions and an agreement had been concluded to introduce shift and night work, to avoid some 200 redundancies. The agreement concerning night work applied to female workers.

In the proceedings before the *Tribunal de Police* Mr. Stoeckel maintained that Article L-213-1 of the *Code du Travail* contravened Article 5 of the 1976 Directive concerning equal treatment of men and women.

The French Government argued that the prohibition of night work for women was in keeping with the general aim of protecting female employees and with social

74. Art. 37, Labor Act, 16 March 1971, as amended by Act of 27 February 1997, *Official Gazette*, 8 April 1997.

75. See: M.A. Moreau, Travail de nuit des femmes, observations sur l'arrêt de la CJCE du 25 juillet 1991, *Droit Social*, 1992, 174–185.

considerations, such as the risk of assault and the greater burden of household work borne by women.

On the issue of protecting female employees, the Court held that it was not evident that, apart from cases of pregnancy, the risks incurred by women in such work were broadly different in kind from the risks incurred by men. As far as the risks of assault were concerned, the Court ruled that, given the assumption that the risk was greater at night than by day, suitable measures could be adopted to deal with them without jeopardising the fundamental principle of equal treatment of men and women.

With regard to family responsibilities, the Court reiterated that the Directive did not seek to settle questions as to the organisation of the family or alter the allocation of responsibilities between partners. Turning to the numerous derogations from the prohibition of night work to which the French Government had referred, the Court held that they were inadequate to give effect to Directive 76/207/EEC, since that Directive did not allow any general principle excluding women from night work; the derogations could, indeed, be a source of discrimination. Therefore, the Court ruled as follows: Article 5 of the 1976 Directive is sufficiently precise as to impose on the Member States the obligation not to stipulate in law the principle that night work by women is prohibited, even if that provision is subject to exceptions, where night work for men is not prohibited.[76]

A question to the Court for a preliminary ruling on the interpretation of Article 1–5 of Council Directive 76/207/EEC was raised in criminal proceedings brought by the French *Ministère Public* and the *Direction du Travail et de l'Emploi* against Jean-Claude Levy, who was summoned for having employed 23 women on night work contrary to Article L 213-1 of the French *Code du Travail.*

In its judgement of 25 July 1991 in the Stoeckel case, the Court held that Article 5 of the Directive was sufficiently precise to impose on the Member States the obligation not to lay down by legislation the principle that night work by women was prohibited, even where subject to exceptions, where night work by men is not prohibited. It followed that the national court had to ensure the full effect of that rule and not apply any contrary national provision.

In the present case, the question for a preliminary ruling was basically whether the national court had the same obligation where the national provision, which was incompatible with Community rules, was intended to implement a convention such as the ILO Convention, concluded by the Member State concerned along with other Member States and non-Member States prior to the entry into force of the EEC Treaty.

In determining whether a Community rule could be contravened by a prior international convention, it was necessary to consider whether the convention imposed on the Member State carried obligations of compliance which might still be insisted on by non-Member States who were parties to the convention.

In that respect the Court held that although it was true that equality of treatment for men and women constituted a fundamental right recognised by the Community legal system, its implementation, even at Community level, had progressively required the intervention of the Council by means of directives and that those directives recognised temporarily certain derogations from the principle of equality of treatment.

---

76. COJ, 25 July 1991, *Ministère Public v.* A. Stoeckel, no. C 345/89, *ECR*, 1991, 4097.

In those circumstances, it was not sufficient to cite the principle of equality of treatment to prevent Member State compliance with obligations in that field under a prior international convention, where observance of those obligations was protected by the first paragraph of Article 234 of the Treaty.

In the present case if, through developments in international law, the prohibition of night work for women provided by the ILO Convention was repealed by subsequent conventions binding the same parties, the provisions of the first paragraph of Article 234 of the Treaty would not be applicable. In that case nothing could prevent the national court from applying Article 5 of the Directive and disregarding contrary national provisions.

However it was not for the Court in delivering a preliminary ruling, but for the national court, to determine obligations under a prior international convention on the Member State concerned and to define the limits in order to determine to what extent those obligations precluded the application of Article 5 of the Directive.

The court ruled as follows:

> '*The national court must ensure full respect for Article 5 of Council Directive 76/207/EEC of 9 February 1976 on the implementation of the principle of equal treatment for men and women as regards access to employment, vocational training and promotion, and working conditions and not apply any contrary provision of national law unless application of such a provision is necessary to ensure compliance by the Member State concerned with obligations resulting from a convention concluded prior to the entry into force of the EEC Treaty with non-Member States*'.[77]

2. Belgian Situation

The difference in treatment of male and female employees has been lifted as a direct consequence of the case law of the European Court of Justice (see *supra*).

In principle, at present night work, understood as work performed between 8 p.m. and 6 a.m., is prohibited both for men and for women.[78]

A list of 21 exceptions to the principal prohibition of night work is still contained in the Act.[79] However, the exceptions that previously only applied to male workers now apply even-handedly to male and female workers.[80] A few modifications have been introduced through the new Parliamentary Act of 27 February 1997.

While the legislator still emphasises the general prohibition of night work, it is clear that the actual application of all the provisions of the Act allows for night work in many cases, provided the workers' representatives accept the introduction of a system of night work in the company, or in the absence of such employee representative body, if the employees themselves agree with it directly. The whole issue

77. COJ, 2 August 1993, *Ministère Public v.J.C. Levy*, no. C158/91, *ECR*, 1993, 4287.
78. Art. 35, Labour Act, 16 March 1971, *Official Gazette*, 30 March 1971, often amended thereafter.
79. Art. 36, Labour Act, 16 March 1971, as amended by Act of 27 February 1997, *Official Gazette*, 8 April 1997.
80. Art. 36, Labour Act, 16 March 1971, *Official Gazette*, 30 March 1971, often amended thereafter. See also on this subject: C. Engels, Working Life and Family Life – Policies for Harmonization – Belgian report, in *Working Life and Family Life – Policies for their Harmonization. The 1994 JIL Comparative Labor Law Seminar*, JIL report no. 4, The Japan institute of Labour, Tokyo, 1995, 44–45.

of night work will be one of these areas where protective legislative norm setting may be deviated from, either by collective or even by individual agreement.

C. Derogation from the Protective Legislation

The Belgian working time regulations were described as being very strict. Weekly working hours are set by legislation and by sector level collective bargaining agreements 38 h a week in general. As of 1 January 1999, the official figure of 40 hours for a working week is replaced by 39 h.[81]

However, working time is one of those issues for which the government has allowed negotiated deviations from the general prohibition for quite a number of years. This system of deviations is often referred to as a form of *controlled flexibility*, in as much as

- quite often the employer and the employee cannot bargain on the issue, but the employer will have to bargain with the trade union representing the employees in order to conclude a Collective Bargaining Agreement; and
- deviations from the principle rules are allowed, but only within certain limits.

The 1987 Act dealing with the introduction of new working time arrangements is a typical example of controlled flexibility. As explained, deviations from the regulations were allowed. However, collective bargaining at sector level often determined how far they could go and how deviations were to be implemented. In certain sectors of industry the sector level collective bargaining agreements prevented that similar, but more far reaching agreements were reached at enterprise level, while other collective bargaining agreements allowed that an employer might want to introduce additional flexibility in working time arrangements in light of the particular needs of its business. In the latter case some sector level collective bargaining agreements require the employer to go through an approval procedure before the joint committee of the industry to which they belong (see above). The Act of 27 February 1997 that modified the legal provisions on night work also allows deviations from the text. The Act that recently came into force allows the Crown to determine when and under what conditions night work could be allowed. If there is a trade union delegation within the company, a collective bargaining agreement at enterprise level can provide for the introduction of night work. Prior consultation with employee representatives, within the works council or the trade union delegation, concerning the introduction of night work and the accompanying measures is necessary.

In the absence of a trade union delegation, night work can be introduced by following the same procedures that are applied to modify the company work rules.[82] The fact that the company work rules have been modified and allow for night work does not imply that the workers who are employed in the company need to accept work at night. The participation in a working time system that involves night work still depends on the consent of the individual worker.[83]

Another example of possible deviation from mandatory regulations can be found in the area of dismissals of high-level white-collar workers. The Act on

81. See *supra*; Royal Decree, 11 December 1998, *Official Gazette*, 17 December 1998.
82. Art. 38, Labor Act, 16 March 1971, as amended by Act of 27 February 1997, *Official Gazette*, 8 April 1997.
83. See: M. De Gols, Nachtarbeid (Night Work), *Oriëntatie*, 1997, 206, 215–216.

contracts of employment (3 July 1978) now allows for white-collar workers earning more than a set threshold amount on an annual basis to come to an agreement with the employer on the term of notice to be respected by the employer in case of dismissal. Prior to 1994, the year the law was modified, such contract provisions were considered null and void and contrary to mandatory provisions for the protection of the individual employees.[84] The Belgian Supreme Court confirmed this principle even in cases where the contract included a term of notice at least as beneficial as the application of the mandatory legal provision.[85]

The new legal provision does not allow the individual and the employer to come to *any* sort of agreement with regard to the term of notice. The parties can neither agree that the employer does not have to respect any term of notice at all, nor that the employer only needs to respect a minimal term of one week or one month. The law still sets a minimum form of protection. The term of notice the parties contractually agree on needs to be no less than three months of notice per period of seniority begun with the same employer (see *supra*).

4. COLLECTIVE LABOUR RELATIONS

A. Decentralisation of Collective Bargaining

1. The Parties to Collective Bargaining

The issue of collective bargaining is regulated by the Parliamentary Act of 5 December 1968.[86]

This Act determines who can be a party to collective bargaining agreements. First of all, as far as the workers are concerned, only the most representative trade union organisations have the right to conclude legally enforceable collective agreements. The criteria for representativity are of the same nature as those already applicable to the works council, the safety and health committee, the joint committee and the National Labour Council:

- they must have an inter-occupational character;
- they must be established at the national level;
- they must be represented on the Central Economic council and the National Labour Council; and
- they must have at least 50,000 members.

In accordance with these criteria, the most representative central workers' organisations are the Confederation of Christian Trade Unions, the Belgian General Federation of Labour and the federation of Liberal Unions of Belgium. Workers' organisations affiliated with or forming part of these central organisations are also considered representative. In the discussions in Parliament and by some authors, this provision has been criticised because of the privileged status it gives to some

84. See: Supreme Court, 14 January 1991, *J.T.T.*, 1991, 176; Supreme Court, 24 September 1994, *J.T.T.*, 1990, 489; Supreme Court, 9 June 1986, *Arr. Cass.*, 1985–86, 1369.
85. See: Supreme Court, 8 October 1975, *Arr. Cass.*, 1976, 166.
86. Act concerning Collective Bargaining Agreements and Joint Committees, 5 December 1968, *Official Gazette*, 15 January 1968, often amended thereafter.

organisations. If, for example, in a certain industrial branch or factory, a particular trade union represents a majority of the workers but is not affiliated with one of the three national confederations, this trade union would not be able to conclude a collective agreement, at least not a legally binding agreement under the Collective Bargaining Act of 1968. It would, at most, be able to conclude a convention carrying moral weight.[87]

Both individual employers and employers' associations can be parties to a collective agreement. The criteria of representativeness mentioned above for workers' organisations normally apply to employers' organisations as well, with the obvious exception of requiring at least 50,000 members. However, an employers' association – in any branch of activity – that does not meet these criteria may be declared representative by the Crown, and in fact some representative employers' associations are not affiliated to an inter-occupational organization. Moreover, certain middle-class organisations are considered representative in accordance with the Act of 6 March 1964, 'to provide for the institutional structure of the middle-class.' It should be remembered that only the most representative organisations have a seat on the National Labour Council and on the joint committees in which national agreements are concluded.

The 1968 Act establishes that the delegates of the organisations are presumed to have the competence to conclude an agreement on behalf of their organisation, and that such a presumption is irrefutable. This is an attempt to solve the problems arising out of the fact that some negotiators have no power to conclude an agreement. The law promotes the principle of good industrial relations, that representatives should be able to discuss and negotiate with representatives of management capable of decision-making, thus giving them access, as such, to real decision-making. Nowhere, however, is it clearly stated just who is a delegate of the organisation, nor exactly what indicates that he/she should be recognised as such.[88]

This means that union delegates are not competent, as such, to conclude a collective agreement on behalf of their trade union. Indeed delegates only represent the unionised members in the enterprise and not the trade union. The same must be said about the employees' representatives in the works council or the committee for safety, health and embellishment of the place of work. Works councils, as well as health and safety committees, are independent bodies which neither represent the employer, the employees, the trade unions, nor the enterprise. Employees' representatives are not considered to be delegates of the trade union, in the legal sense, for the purpose of concluding collective agreements within the meaning of the 1968 Act. Altogether, one cannot exclude the possibility that these representatives are in fact engaged in bargaining and the conclusion of collective agreements. But such agreements would not be covered by the 1968 Act. Theoretically there is always the possibility that the trade unions would give the union delegates or employee works council or committee members a legal mandate to conclude collective agreements on

87. See: R. Blanpain and C. Engels, Belgium, in: *International Encyclopaedia for Labor Law and Industrial Relations*, R. Blanpain (ed.), The Hague London Boston, Kluwer Law International, s.d., no. 555, 268.

88. See: R. Blanpain and C. Engels, Belgium, in: *International Encyclopaedia for Labor Law and Industrial Relations*, R. Blanpain (ed.), The Hague London Boston, Kluwer Law International, s.d., no. 556, 268–269.

their behalf. In fact this does not happen and agreements have to be signed by a trade union official.[89]

All this implies that only trade unions can validly conclude collective bargaining agreements. The applicable legislative measures do not allow any deviation. Neither the works council (which is composed of both employer and employee representatives), nor the trade union delegation (only trade union representatives from within a company) can therefore enter into collective bargaining agreements that are enforceable. All this implies that trade unions remain central to the whole issue of collective bargaining.

2. The Level at Which Collective Bargaining Takes Place

Collective bargaining in Belgium takes place at the various levels of industrial relations. It takes place at national, inter-industry level in the *National Labour Council*. Collective Bargaining Agreements concluded within the National Labour Council are almost always rendered binding by Royal Decree and are then applicable to all employers and employees of the private sector. The total number of agreements so concluded is about 65.[90] They relate to issues such as the competence of the works council,[91] collective dismissals,[92] equal pay,[93] recruitment and selection of employees,[94] introduction of new working time arrangements,[95] parental leave,[96] etc. This form of rule making was even used to implement European Union directives into Belgian law, such as the acquired rights directive[97] and the European Works Council Directive.[98]

The collective bargaining agreements concluded in the National Labour Council tend to address broader issues or establish frameworks to be further elaborated at the level of the sector or the individual company. Sector level collective bargaining takes place in the *joint committees of industry* set up per sector of industry. Mostly these joint committees are set up separately for blue and white-collar workers so that bargaining for each group also takes place separately.[99]

---

89. See: R. Blanpain and C. Engels, Belgium, in: *International Encyclopaedia for Labor Law and Industrial Relations*, R. Blanpain (ed.), The Hague London Boston, Kluwer Law International, s.d., no. 558, 269–270.
90. See: R. Blanpain and C. Engels, Belgium, in: *International Encyclopaedia for Labor Law and Industrial Relations*, R. Blanpain (ed.), The Hague London Boston, Kluwer Law International, s.d., no. 539, 258–259.
91. Collective bargaining agreement no. 9, 9 March 1972, rendered generally binding by Royal Decree 12 September 1972, *Official Gazette*, 12 September 1972, hereafter often amended.
92. Collective bargaining agreement no. 10, 8 May 1973, rendered generally binding by Royal Decree 6 August 1973, *Official Gazette*, 17 August 1973, hereafter often amended.
93. Collective bargaining agreement no. 25, 15 October 1975, rendered generally binding by Royal Decree 9 December 1975, *Official Gazette*, 25 December 1975.
94. Collective bargaining agreement no. 38, 8 May 1973, rendered generally binding (articles 1–6) by Royal Decree 6 December 1983, *Official Gazette*, 11 July 1984, hereafter amended.
95. Collective bargaining agreement no. 42, 2 June 1987, rendered generally binding by Royal Decree 18 June 1987, *Official Gazette*, 26 June 1987, hereafter amended.
96. Collective bargaining agreement no. 63, 13 April 1997, rendered generally binding by Royal Decree 13 April 1997, *Official Gazette*, 29 May 1997.
97. Collective bargaining agreement no. 32bis, 7 June 1985, rendered generally binding by Royal Decree 25 July 1985, *Official Gazette*, 9 August 1985, hereafter often amended.
98. Collective bargaining agreement no. 62, 6 February 1996, rendered generally binding by Royal Decree 22 March 1996, *Official Gazette*, 11 April 1996.
99. See: R. Blanpain and C. Engels, Belgium, in: *International Encyclopaedia for Labor Law and Industrial Relations*, R. Blanpain (ed.) The Hague London Boston, Kluwer Law International, s.d., no. 551, 265.

More than 100 joint committees exist in Belgium. On the average they conclude about 700 collective bargaining agreements per year.[100] This means that wages and working conditions in the different industries are to a large extent set at sector level. Pay scales and job classification systems are the result of sector level collective bargaining as well.

Below this, collective bargaining takes place at the level of the *individual enterprise*. In 1995, 3041 agreements were registered with the Ministry of Labour. Five were concluded in the National Labour Council; 837 in the joint committees and 2199 concluded at enterprise level. According to the Ministry of Employment and Labour, the subjects addressed were:[101]

Subject	*Joint committee*	*Enterprise*	*Total*
Wages/working conditions	78	114	192
Wages	20	24	44
Meal vouchers		123	123
End/year/bonus	20	3	23
Other bonuses	17	17	24
Conventional pre-pension (Ç. No. 17)	97	459	556
Restructuration	1	173	174
Half-time-prepension (C. No. 55)	22	71	93
Pre-pension/55 years (C. No. 60)	55	26	81
Applying a C/pre-pension	1	64	65
Collective dismissal	1	109	110
Representation/employees	13	17	30
Social elections		8	8
Working time	19	40	59
Reduction/working time	3	6	9
New working time regulations	3	100	103
Shift work		23	23
Part-time work	3	15	18
Part-time (Art. 11 *bis*)		104	104
Long-term-unemployed	82	76	158
Redistribution available work	6	148	154
Promotion/employment (C. No. 60)	196	394	590
Social funds	121		121
Various	62	90	152
Total 1995	842	2199	3041

100. See: R. Blanpain and C. Engels, Belgium, in: *International Encyclopaedia for Labor Law and Industrial Relations*, R. Blanpain (ed.) The Hague London Boston, Kluwer Law International, s.d., no. 526, 251.

101. See R. Blanpain and C. Engels, Belgium, in: *International Encyclopaedia for Labor Law and Industrial Relations*, R. Blanpain (ed.), Kluwer Law International, The Hague, Boston, London, no. 552, 266–267.

Since the second half of the 1980s there is a clear shift towards sector level and enterprise collective bargaining. However, this is a controlled form of decentralisation whereby collective bargaining agreements concluded at national or sector level often provide for further implementation and concretisation at the lower levels of industrial relations.

As already mentioned, there is government intervention in collective bargaining as well. The Parliamentary Act of 26 July 1996 on the promotion of employment and the safeguarding of the competitivity of the Belgian enterprises is characterised by dramatic government intervention in collective bargaining. The government wants to control the wage evolution and at the same time stimulate employment. The following scheme has been established:

a. Collective bargaining on wages, including the impact on jobs

The competitiveness of Belgian industry is the point of departure. Wage development has to be controlled and this is done in relation to three reference states, namely Germany, France and the Netherlands. These are Belgium's most important trading partners. The strategy goes as follows:

1. Inter-industry level

Twice a year (before 31 January and 31 July) the Central Council for the Economy and the National Labour Council report on the evolution regarding employment and wage cost in Belgium and the three countries of reference.

- Yearly (before 30 September) the Central Council presents a technical report on the maximum available room for labour cost expansion, including the possibility for real wage increases.
- Every two years (before 31 October) the social partners conclude an inter-industry agreement, including measures to promote employment and maximum wage cost development. This agreement takes into account forecasts in the countries of reference, but will guarantee as a minimum a foreseeable indexation to the cost of living and the barometric augmentations.
- In case no such agreement between the social partners can be reached within a period of two months after the technical report has been published, the government provides for mediation between the social partners.
- In case this does not succeed, the government itself establishes the maximum allowable wage increase.

Failing a collective agreement, the government can also take measures relating to employment such as:

- redistribution of available work (diminish working time, part time, interruption of the professional career, measures for youth);
- a more flexible organisation of the labour market.

2. At sectoral, enterprise and individual level

At sectoral level, before 31 March, and at enterprise level, before 31 May of the first year of the inter-industry collective agreement, collective agreements can be concluded relating to employment and wage cost development. The latter has to respect the maximum development compatible with a minimum cost of living as a barometic augmentation. In doing so, the cost of living mechanism and the economic potential of the sector are taken into account.

Maximum wage cost development has to be respected by the agreements concluded at inter-industry, sectoral, enterprise and individual level.

The employer who does not respect these prohibitions is penalised.

A Superior Council for Employment shall before 30 November of every year give recommendations regarding the collective agreements at inter-industry or sectoral level if the measures proposed regarding employment are insufficient. The Government can take the necessary measures on the basis of these recommendations.

The collective agreements at inter-industry or sectoral level need to contain a mandatory clause providing for an adjustment mechanism in case it appears *de facto* that wage cost developments in Belgium or in the sector are higher *than those in the countries* of reference. If the social partners do not act, the government will. A strict timetable is also provided.

If the employment development is weaker than in the three countries of reference, the social partners or the government are allowed to take additional measures.

b. Promotion of employment

The envisaged measures relate to:

- full pre-pension;
- part-time pre-pension;
- employment plans in the enterprises (financial incentives);
- annualisation of working time;
- part-time;
- temporary work; and
- reduction of working time.

c. Some figures

For the present two-year period, sectoral employment agreements could be concluded until 15 May 1997. Negotiations took place in 116 of the 164 joint committees and sub-committees. This led to 85 agreements covering 1,444,050 employees or some 70 per cent of the private sector workforce. An analysis of 70 sectoral agreements shows that the following measures were retained:

Interruption/career	51 agreements	1,180,000 employees
Part-time pre-pension	42 agreements	860,000 employees
Training	43 agreements	900,000 employees
Part-time	28 agreements	700,000 employees
Flexible working time	13 agreements	30,000 employees
Reduction working time	9 agreements	350,000 employees[102]

102. See R. Blanpain and C. Engels, Belgium, in: *International Encyclopaedia for Labor Law and Industrial Relations*, R. Blanpain (ed.), Kluwer Law International, The Hague, Boston, London, s.d., nos. 526–527, 47–48.

It is clear from the above that the framework that was set up stimulates to a very large extent lower level collective bargaining.

The same approach is found in the inter-professional agreement that the social partners concluded in December 1998. This agreement is not as such enforceable in court. It highlights the social partners' ambition for the two-year period to come. In the inter-professional agreements, the social partners also offer 'suggestions for future actions' to the government. In the recent past the social partners have had difficulties reaching such agreements.

In the December 1998 agreement, the social partners at national level directed a number of requests to the sector level collective bargaining partners, dealing among other things with:

- investment in training and continued training, especially with regard to low-skilled jobs,
- bridge pension systems, allowing for 'quasi retirement' for employees that have not yet reached legal retirement age,
- terms of notice for blue-collar workers, aimed at increased job security,
- removing existing inequalities (male/female) from job classification systems.

It is clear that the emphasis is once more put on the decentralised level of collective bargaining.

B. Relationship between Individual and Collective Bargaining

The Act of 5 December 1968 on Collective Bargaining Agreements and Joint Committees[103] regulates the relationship between individual and collective bargaining agreements, providing for an explicit ranking among the various sources of labour law in Belgium. This hierarchy addresses not only the relationship between collective bargaining agreements and individual arrangements between employer and employee, it specifies the relationship among the collective bargaining agreements concluded at the various levels of the Belgian system of industrial relations.

Article 51 of the 1968 Act establishes a list of the legal sources which regulate the employment relation in hierarchical order. The sources of obligations arising out of the employment relation between employers and workers shall be as follows, in descending order of application:

1. the law in its peremptory provisions;
2. collective bargaining agreements declared to be generally binding, in the following order:
   a) agreements concluded in the National Labour Council;
   b) agreements concluded in a joint committee;
   c) agreements concluded in a joint sub-committee;

103. Act concerning Collective Bargaining Agreements and Joint Committees, 5 December 1968, *Official Gazette*, 15 January 1968, often amended thereafter.

3. collective bargaining agreements which have not been declared to be generally binding, where the employer is a signatory thereto or is affiliated to an organisation which is a signatory to such an agreement, in the following order:
   a) agreements concluded in the National Labour Council;
   b) agreements concluded in a joint committee;
   c) agreements concluded in a joint sub-committee;
   d) agreements concluded outside a joint body;
4. an individual agreement in writing;
5. a collective bargaining agreement concluded in a joint body but not declared generally binding where the employer, although not a signatory thereto or not affiliated to an organisation signatory thereto, is within the jurisdiction of the joint body in which the agreement was concluded;
6. company work rules;
7. the supplementary provisions of the law;
8. a verbal individual employment contract;
9. custom.

It should be stressed that an individual labour contract which is implicitly modified by a collective agreement shall remain unchanged if the collective bargaining agreement ceases to be in force – unless there is a stipulation to the contrary in the collective agreement itself. In this case the legislator has opted for the so-called 'incorporation' theory by which the individual normative part of the collective agreement is incorporated into the individual labour contract when the collective agreement ceases to be in effect.[104]

The hierarchy established under article 51 of the Act on Collective Bargaining Agreements does not however prevent individual bargaining or collective bargaining at a lower level of industrial relations, not even concerning areas covered by the higher level collective bargaining agreement, unless of course the collective bargaining agreement explicitly precludes this.[105]

For certain areas, sector level collective bargaining agreements do not allow any bargaining at enterprise level or any individual bargaining. The introduction of new working time regimes, discussed above, comes to mind.

Should the higher level collective bargaining agreement not prevent lower level bargaining, the Act holds that those provisions resulting from lower level bargaining that are contrary to the provisions established in a higher level bargaining agreement will be null and void.[106]

If the lower level agreement (collective or individual) establishes better terms and conditions than the higher level agreement, this is not considered contrary to the lesser, higher level provision. It is always possible under Belgian law, unless stated otherwise, to deviate from norms established at a higher level to the advantage of the employee.

---

104. See R. Blanpain and C. Engels, Belgium, in: *International Encyclopaedia for Labor Law and Industrial Relations*, R. Blanpain (ed.), Kluwer Law International, The Hague, Boston, London, s.d., nos. 584–585, 279–280.

105. See: R. Blanpain and C. Engels, Belgium, in: *International Encyclopaedia for Labor Law and Industrial Relations*, R. Blanpain (ed.) The Hague, London, Boston, Kluwer Law International, s.d., no. 549, 264–265.

106. Arts 9 e.s., Act concerning Collective Bargaining Agreements and Joint Committees, 5 December 1968, *Official Gazette*, 15 January 1968, hereafter often amended.

5. THE DRIVING FORCES OF DEREGULATION

The deregulation or re-regulation in Belgian labour law does not have one single cause. Looking at the issue of night work and the abolition of the difference in treatment between men and women, one could say that the change in law was directly caused by the case law of the European Court of Justice in respect of equal treatment between men and women.

Other forms of flexibility have been introduced to reduce unemployment and keep the economy competitive by keeping costs down.[107] This certainly holds for the whole set of regulations and rules dealing with working time. The same can be said about the relaxation of the rules on successive contracts of employment for fixed duration and the rules making termination of contracts of employment easier and less costly.

The same goals of reducing unemployment and keeping the economy viable have led to a whole new set of rules and regulations.

6. EVALUATION OF CURRENT DEREGULATION AND LABOUR LAW REFORMS

Introducing flexibility into Belgian labour law, and particularly into areas such as working time, did not always come about through deregulation, understood as doing away with excessive forms of regulation. The most obvious forms of flexibility introduced that dealt with working time were the result of re-regulation. This means that other ways of regulating working time were introduced. The Belgian government and legislature did not want a full scale return to unbridled capitalism where employees and employers bargain on equal footing, with minimal labour law to back up workers.

Whenever regulation of certain issues was relaxed, other forms of regulation were provided. The re-regulation was aimed at finding a way better adapted to regulating matters, instead of abolishing regulations all together.

The government understood, for example, that working time regulations had become outdated and required an approach more closely related to the different sectors of industry than a unified national approach. Nevertheless this approach does not give employers absolute freedom of action. A counter balance either sets standards to be established at the sector level of the industry or allows an employer to introduce flexibility on the condition of entering into a collective bargaining agreement with all the worker representatives in its company.

Deregulation is certainly not the hallmark of Belgian labour law. While certain areas of the law have been re-regulated, others have become subject to even more regulation. This is certainly true for the area dealing with equal treatment where the European Union influence was of overriding importance. The changes in

107. See for example: M. De Gols, Partage du temps de travail, 'flexibilité, expérimentation sociale ... crise ou mutation des principes dans l'organisation du travail?' (Sharing of Work, Flexibility, social Experiments. Crisis or shift in the Principles regarding the Organization of Work) in *100 ans de droit social belge* (100 Years of Belgian social Law), Brussels, Editions Bruylant, 1986, 415, 424; H. Lenaerts, Het sociaal recht na de golden sixties: een zilveren jubileum, in *Sociaal Recht: Niets dan uitdagingen* (Social Law: always a Challenge), W. Van Eeckhoutte (ed.), Mys & Breesch, Gent, 1996, 845, 857.

the existing regulations on night work were directly caused by European Community case law.

In the same way, worker privacy was the subject of more regulations. Again, the EU directive on data protection had an important influence.

Finally, there is a whole area of labour law, social security law and related matters that has increasingly become the subject of regulation, not deregulation. The whole area of employment stimuli has been gradually expanding. The government has even intervened in areas that used to be considered out of its direct reach such as wage setting and bargaining. A special Parliamentary Act was passed on July 26, 1996, on the promotion of employment and the safeguarding of the competitivity of Belgian enterprises.[108] The principle aim of the Act is to keep the Belgian economy competitive by preventing labour costs from increasing more than in the neighbouring countries. For every two-year period, the social partners can determine what will be the maximum wage increase. For the 1997–1998 period the wages could not increase more than 6.1%. In principle, the range of the maximum wage increase per two-year period is to be set by the social partners. In the absence of an agreement on this topic, the government intervenes, as it did in setting 6.1% for the first period of the salary freeze or wage restraint measures (1997–1998). Under the threat of government intervention, the social partners set the level of permissible wage increases for the period 1999–2000 at 5.9%.

7. THE ROLE OF LABOUR LAW IN THE 21st CENTURY: DO WE NEED A NEW CONCEPT OF LABOUR LAW?

Unemployment is the key issue facing governments and nations. The competitiveness of our economies is crucial in this respect. In order to be able to survive in the increasingly competitive global environment, adjustments to these new realities need to be made.

It is not possible to return to the capitalism that ruled at the turn of the 20th century. However, the labour law regulations and all the costs attached to them that were affordable during the golden sixties and seventies, can hardly be sustained now. Furthermore, the regulations introduced then are frequently no longer in tune with the present economic situation and requirements.

The area of working time has been progressing in the direction required to satisfy the needs of our contemporary economies. Flexibility will be a key word. This concept is not equivalent to the abolition of all worker protection, however. While protection against excesses and unacceptable working conditions are still indispensable and will remain so, the very stringent and inflexible rules of the past are not necessary to guarantee this.

In general one can say that some flexibility has already been introduced into Belgian labour law. At the same time a lot remains to be done. While the issue of temporary work agencies and interim labour has been dealt with, the rules that are applicable in determining when and under what conditions interim labour can be used are still, in theory, rather strict. Such restrictions seem hardly necessary.

---

108. See: R. Blanpain and C. Engels, Belgium, in: *International Encyclopaedia for Labor Law and Industrial Relations*, R. Blanpain (ed.), Kluwer Law International, The Hague, Boston, London, s.d., 47 e.s.

Closely tied to this problem is the issue of putting workers at the disposal of other employers with a delegation of some part of the employer's normal authority. Recent legislative measures have made it even more difficult to lawfully put permanent workers at the disposal of another employer. The practice has become quasi-impossible from a legal point of view, even though it is widespread and in line with real business needs.

There is no justification for keeping such restrictive laws on the books, and certainly not to pass even more stringent laws. The same also holds with regard to the (quasi) monopoly the government services have with regard to fee-charging private employment placement. An additional boost to get rid of such regulations has been given by the European Court of Justice.

The difference in protection of white and blue-collar workers is enormous and not justifiable. Its continued existence hinders mobility of workers.

All this brings us to an even more fundamental question. Should labour law as a body of protective legislation continue to apply in the way it does to only one section of the working population. Should the *summa division* between subordinate employment and self-employment continue to exist? In light of the proposed ILO Convention and Recommendation on Contract Labour the question seems to be particularly relevant. The ILO's intention is to introduce a third category of workers in between the subordinate worker and the self-employed worker. This third category is the contract worker.[109] Given the fact that it is already difficult to distinguish between the existing two categories, one questions the usefulness of introducing yet another and even more unclear factor to make the distinction between the various categories of workers. One wonders whether it would not be better to abolish these distinctions all together and to provide all those who are engaged in work a basic and standard form of protection?[110]

109. See C. Engels and L. Salas, Cause and Consequence, What's the Difference in Respect of the EC Transfer Directive, in *Labor Law and Industrial Relations at the Turn of the Century, Liber Amicorum in Honour of Prof. Dr. Roger Blanpain*, C. Engels and M. Weiss (eds.) The Hague, London, Boston, 1998, 275, 279–281

110. See: C. Engels, Contract labour, de afhankelijke zelfstandige of de zelfstandige afhankelijke (Contract Labour: the dependent Independent or the independent Dependent), in *Liber Amicorum Prof. Dr. Roger Blanpain*, Brugge, die Keure, 1998, 261–266.

2. Deregulation and Labour Law: French Report

Marie-Ange Moreau

French labour law was created at the end of the 19th century around the principle of workers' protection, and the construction of strong and rigid mandatory rules guaranteed by law.

Collective bargaining is regulated by the principle of 'favourability', which means that only clauses more favourable for the worker than the law will be introduced into a collective agreement. Traditionally, in many areas of labour law containing mandatory regulations, there was no flexibility, no possibility for the parties via collective agreements or contracts to introduce clauses less favourable than law.

But starting with the economic crisis of 1973, first the legislators and then the trade unions were obliged to consider changes within the labour law to allow for some flexibility. The first such change was the regulation of fixed-term and temporary contracts. The first law was passed in 1979 and many reforms were discussed from 1979 to 1990.

The organisation of working time was the second move towards flexibility. Collective bargaining was opened in 1984 on the flexibility of working time, with the goal of redistributing working hours between the employed and the unemployed. But the collective bargaining failed, because the trade unions refused to accept the introduction of any flexibility in the calculation of working hours, for example, to calculate on an annual rather than a weekly basis. The first law to introduce some flexibility, referred to as the 'loi Seguin', was passed in 1986 and reformed in 1987. It was the first advance in France towards flexibility in the area of working time. Faced with the employers' demand for flexibility and growing unemployment it was only after 1993 that the trade unions, with great reluctance, overcame their objections to flexibility in working time.

Today French Labour Law is under attack but it is not possible to use the term 'deregulation' as it was in Great Britain in Mrs. Thatcher's years. French social politics continue to guarantee workers' protection and the respect of collective bargaining.

But there are more and more areas where flexibility is being introduced.

The Ford model on which French and other western labour law was based is passé, and the fundamentals of our labour law are called into question with regards to individual and collective relations.

For 10 years, in the face of economic crisis, rising unemployment and the pressure exerted by employers' lobbying and an international/European currency, many laws to allow for more flexibility have been introduced.

R. Blanpain (ed.), Deregulation and Labour Law, 43–58

The French legislator wanted **to maintain a high level of social protection, and at the same time, offer the possibility of flexible management to employers**.

These contradictory aims lead to paradoxical situations in the evolution of French labour law: the guarantee of workers' protection is still strong and explains the different limits placed on an employer's decision-making, including the extensive limits established by the courts, and those of the employee and union representation within large companies. For example, in 1987, at the same time that the legislators agreed to exceptions concerning working time, they also re-enforced the trade unions' control and imposed the conclusion of collective agreements to introduce exceptions to the law of the 39 h work week.

In 1993 judiciary controls on collective dismissals has grown significantly.

For 10 years, the judges have also imposed on the employer the obligation of information when it decides to cancel an advantage accepted as practice or contained in an informal agreement. The economic reasons for an employer's decision are not questioned, but it is required, before cancelling the advantage, that workers and their representatives be informed some time in advance.

That case law is a good example of the mixture of worker protection and flexibility and it is possible to find it in many areas of labour law.

The move towards flexibility is offset by another development at the international and European level: France has ratified many ILO Conventions and generally speaking, French labour law has a higher level of worker protection than the international conventions.

The European laws have a stronger impact on French labour law. The European legislation has obliged French legislators to rewrite some laws, particularly in the area of health and security within the enterprise, and to introduce new rules on gender equality. The French regulation of women's night work was voided in 1991 by the EEC Court, not to introduce more flexibility, but to end different rules governing men's and women's night work.

The European directives are a factor in the *transformation of laws* to attain conformity within the European Union, *but not of deregulation*: a 'no-regression' clause forbids any reduction in national protection.

More generally, the *strengthening of fundamental rights within the European Union* applies to all countries since the Amsterdam Treaty with its references to the Charter of Fundamental Rights signed by the Community in 1989 and to the European Social Charter (1961) acts as a bulwark against deregulation.

These fundamental rights are protected by the European Court of Justice and will be, after the complete ratification of the Amsterdam Treaty, a definitive basis for national labour laws in Europe, even in countries with their own social charter embedded in the constitution. The adoption of these fundamental social rights should be a condition in negotiations for the entry of Eastern European countries into the European Union.

The transformation of labour laws is not only a result of international environment and unemployment; many changes come from new methods of management and organisation within the firm: the introduction of new technologies, work by computers out of the plant, end of the Ford model, networking firms, tertiarisation of activities, outwork enterprise, subcontracting, and, especially inside international firms, increased risk of an enterprise's delocalisation.

All of these factors exist within developed countries and create a real challenge for trade unions, both national and international.

In France, it is another paradox that despite the growing crisis within the unions, they win new powers of regulation through collective bargaining. The trade unions are negotiating inter-, professional agreements which become laws, thus more and more creating the model for laws. Moreover, the trade unions' force traditionally was better organised at the professional sector level (niveau de la 'branche professionnelle'). Because of the decentralisation of collective bargaining, the professional sector level is no longer as important. The most important level for collective bargaining, especially for negotiating working time, is now the enterprise. And it is easier to negotiate flexible rules at that level than at the professional sector level.

In the area of the labour contracts, traditional rules are maintained but there is also a search for new flexibility: the labour contract is becoming a management tool for the employer who can introduce flexibility clauses. But these clauses fall under the judge's control, in particular for issues concerning breaches of fundamental rights or individual or collective liberties.

Paradoxes also arise *between the new flexibility and new ways of workers' protection*.

And in the middle, the *judge*, who has had a new role in labour relations for 10 years, systematically obliges the employer to inform and to warn workers and their representatives. The judge also reviews the regularity of employers' decisions based on economic factors, particularly in cases of collective dismissal. There is a link between the spectacular increase of the judge's arbitration and the introduction of more flexibility in France.

The judge is becoming a virtual player in labour relations.

As in other countries, the words 'flexibility' and 'precariousness' are used in relation to levels of protection under previous labour law and can be viewed as relative rather than objective.

For example, in France it was always possible to breach the labour contract, employment is never terminated during a worker's life, as in Japan. The degree of flexibility can be measured by the obligations imposed on the employer when dismissal is decided. In the case of working time, flexibility is not a question of minimum or maximum working hours in a day (European imperative standards), but in the calculation of working time on a weekly or yearly basis.

The minimum standards are not called into question in France, just the way they are applied.

The concept of precariousness is also a question of reference. Full-time work or non-fixed-term contracts should be the standard. Precariousness is also used in reference to duration of work or to resources of the worker (i.e. poverty level or 'working poor'). The term is used in both senses in France.

Consequently, it is useful to examine within both individual and collective relations the degree of flexibility and precariousness resulting from French labour regulations, in order later to be able to compare French developments and those in other countries.

1. FLEXIBILITY IN INDIVIDUAL LABOUR RELATIONS

The search for flexibility by small and large enterprises in a globalised market is present from the beginning to the end of the labour relationship and renders more precarious the labour law protections. Many are the areas where flexibility and precariousness increase, but workers' guarantees are also increasing.

1.1. Areas with Flexibility and Precariousness

This search for flexibility in the management of the workforce is organised in the labour market (which is still national and not European), with great freedom for the firm, because the employment service is organised but not monopolised by the state, and private employment businesses are allowed. Areas of flexibility can be found in all steps of the organisation of the workforce.

1.1.1. The border of subordination

The most important problem is now to re-draw the contours of the employment contract in the face of independent contracting and contracting for services. Hierarchies are very difficult to maintain when the worker with special qualifications and new technologies is free to organise his job.

The 'loi Madelin' was voted in 1994 and establishes that every person who is incorporated is not necessarily a worker, even if he works within a 'juridical permanent link' with another enterprise. This new formula is completely obscure and removed from labour law's protection many small enterprises where there is just one person who works for himself (for example, driver, road haulier, housekeeper, etc.). The labour inspector may decide they are 'workers' and redefine the situation to apply labour law, by the addition of facts that prove that the contractor is in permanent dependence of the main enterprise.

There is an interest in increasing the area covered by labour law to include activities which are performed in 'economic dependence' or which are done for 'the profit of another'. Some prefer to increase the area of independent activities by applying the criteria of the employer's intent. The difficulty in finding a good analysis is the same in Germany, Sweden and the Netherlands.

Subcontracting is traditionally outside of the range of labour relations, the rules of commerce apply when defining the relation between two (or more) enterprises.

In France strong regulations govern subcontracting and illegal work. A subcontractor must be independent in order to make a profit with its services. It is forbidden to externalise an activity by contract just to avoid giving collective advantages to the workers or to lower the cost of work ('marchandage', article L 125-1 labour code).

In many European countries illegal work is regulated as a means of labour market regulation. But there is no link among the workers of subcontractors, even if they are working for the same contractor. When there is a chain of subcontractors, labour law is not applied to the workers. Rules originating from European directives might regulate the security on a building site. But the autonomy of the subcontractor is the result of commercial freedom to negotiate the commercial contract. In consequence, the management of firms established under international subcontracting offers double flexibility: flexibility in the choice of the law and flexibility in the choice of subcontracting.

Some international firms today negotiate a 'charter' to oblige all their subcontractors to respect the social rights of their workers, especially fundamental rights (i.e. guarantee against child work). These Charters are sought by firms to give them a good image, especially in light of media coverage. It is a first step towards regulation of a common social statute for subcontracted workers. But it is a unilateral norm introduced into the various commercial contracts as a social obligation.

The impact of the labour market may be found in the regulation of dispatching workers: in France, the right to hire workers is left to the employers, the employment agency (ANPE) controls the labour market but without exclusive rights in recruitment. However, it is not permitted to transfer workers to another site for the purpose of some benefit. Making profit on the workforce is prohibited. Two possibilities only are open to employers: to lend workers without any profit (for example, inside a group, to a good client) or to call on temporary workers under mandatory regulation, i.e. workers from the strongly regulated temporary agencies (cf. *infra*).

1.1.2. Flexibility introduced in the employment contract

In France, the employment contract is of indeterminate duration and it imposes on employer and worker alike the respect without modification of the stated duties. If the employer wants to change usual working conditions, the worker must comply, refusal to do so can mean dismissal without severance pay. If the employer wants to change an important condition of the contract, such as pay, qualification or place of work, the worker may refuse and the employer must stick to the contract without any modification, with the exception that he may dismiss the worker for reasons of redundancy, if the grounds for the change are related to economic factors.

If there is a mobility clause, a clause that allows the modification of the job (for example within a shop), or a clause giving the right to change working time (night/day, Saturday/Sunday), the worker has accepted the right of the employer to make modifications and may not refuse the modifications.

Nowadays, employment contracts are more and more sophisticated, and include many clauses giving flexibility. But since 1993 the judges review contracts for violation of fundamental rights and liberties (article 120-2 of the labour code) and to establish that the provisions have a basis in real economic interests on the part of the enterprise.

1.1.3. Flexibility given by fixed-term contracts and temporary contracts

French law strongly regulates fixed-term and temporary contracts which put the worker in a precarious situation and are only to be made under exceptional circumstances. The law was established in 1990 and the French labour ministry announced a reform in November 1998. The aim of the legislator is to guarantee protection to the worker during the contract and to regulate and limit the use of fixed-term and temporary contracts. The legislation is almost the same for both types of contracts. The main difference is that in the case of temporary contracts, the employer is the temporary agency and the worker is not working for his employer but for his employer's contracting agency according to the provisions contained in the contract. The form of these contracts is regulated by law: certain provisions must be included, the choice of a fixed-term contract must be justified according to an accepted list of reasons, and should not be used for work that is permanent in nature.

These contracts have a maximum duration of 18 months, except in cases of replacement when the term equals the time of replacement. At the end of the contract, the employer may end the relationship without any reason (just the term) and without any compensation. In some cases, the worker will have a 'precariousness compensation' (6% of the pay).

The list of the reasons justifying fixed-term contracts is finite: temporary increase of activities, replacement (maternity, illness, etc.), access to employment within the law's limitations for some specific groups of the unemployed (youth without qualifications, people over 50 years, women with children and so on), seasonal work, work in some areas where fixed-term contracts are the custom (cf. list).

The practice of fixed-term contracts is widespread and everybody knows that the stated justifications are not always real: if the worker can prove that the reason stated in the contract is not true, he systematically wins his trial, the contract is rewritten and compensations are given to the worker (after 2 years in the firm, at the very least, 6 months pay). But very often, there is no trial at the end of illegal contracts, and labour inspectors, trade unions, works councils aware of the use of illegal fixed-term contracts only act if the percentage of workforce affected is too high. This laxity is the result of the present level of unemployment in France.

The law is strict, the judges are strict, and the multiplication of fixed-term contracts is forbidden when the job is, in fact, ongoing in nature. Some employers' associations regularly ask to lengthen the term to 5 years but it has not been accepted by the ministry.

Fixed-term and temporary contracts are a means of flexibility and are a widespread cause of precariousness. On the other hand much hiring today is done under fixed-term or temporary contracts and consequently, they have helped to bring down unemployment.

In 1996, the temporary work grew quickly because temporary agencies offered good rates and referred workers with high qualification, even in new sectors (for example hospitals).

But some sectors use temporary workers as a permanent workforce (the automobile sector uses between 20% and 30% temporary workers). The growth of temporary work is worrying and the labour ministry will propose some reforms in 1999 to prevent the structural and illegal use of temporary and fixed-term contracts in order to reduce the precarious situation of those workers, generally young people, unqualified workers, women, and the long-term unemployed.

1.1.4. Precariousness through part-time work

Part-time work is the subject of frequent discussion in France. For many years it was 'reserved' to women: some women wanted to work part-time, to combine their professional life and their family life, but many of them had no qualifications (60% at the minimum wage) and no choice to refuse a part-time job. Until 1993, employers in the private sector refused to introduce part-time work, especially for white collar workers. But in 1993, the social insurance contributions were reduced for part-time workers (30% less) and consequently the increase of part-time work has been spectacular: 7% in 1990, 17% to 18% in 1998. This government aid has now been stopped because of the law of 13 June 1998, reducing working time to 35 h/week (cf. *infra*).

Part-time work refers to a variety of situations: it could have been chosen or imposed; the contracts can be fixed-term or permanent; working time can be calculated on a weekly or yearly basis; wages can be above or below the poverty level, etc.

Many problems involving the 'new poverty' have appeared in France: the 'working poor' are often women and part-time workers.

The organisation of part-time work is also a problem and the law of 13 June 1998 prohibits the imposition of more than one break of more than 2 h each day for a part-time worker to counter the common practice in supermarkets where part-time employees have 2 h breaks in the morning and in the evening. Even if the employer must give many guarantees to the part-time worker (period with or without work, equality with full-time workers), the part-time workers are often, though not always, in a precarious situation.

People entering the labour market are also in a precarious situation and for nearly 20 years the legislator has provided for special contracts for the young and unemployed. These contracts allow for exceptions to fundamental rules of labour law, especially to regulations on minimum wage. Various programs of government incentives have been tried with limited results. Generally, these special contracts are fixed-term but the worker may leave the job if another employer offers him a permanent contract.

It is difficult to remove flexibility and precariousness in 'employment laws' which are really 'unemployment laws': precarious contracts are a step towards continuous employment. But, the problem is not to enter a labour market completely built on precariousness and flexibility.

The hope in France and especially at the Labour Ministry is to reduce this precariousness with the introduction of the 35-h-week on 1 January 2000 and the resulting reorganisation of working time.

1.2. Increase of Some Guarantees

Developments in French labour law have not only focused on increasing flexibility but also continue to lower unemployment and guarantee fundamental rights. A review of the guarantees given to the workers since 1990 follows.

1.2.1. Guarantees to combat unemployment

The French High Court has held that employers must play a greater role in keeping workers employed. That principle has had many applications.

(1) In 1992, the Court of Cassation held that the employer had a 'duty of adaptation': the worker must acquire through training an adaptation of his qualification and of his knowledge during the time of his contact to enable him to perform the job. This training must provide an adaptation to new technologies or reorganisation and be commensurate with the worker's abilities. The employer must not dismiss a worker for insufficient or antiquated skills before such vocational training has been offered.

(2) Also in 1992, the High Court established a duty of finding another job inside the enterprise or inside the other companies of the group, before deciding redundancy: the duty to make an offer obliges the employer to know which jobs are free at all work locations in the group, and to propose these jobs, even if they are different, at another location, at a lower pay, etc. The worker has the choice to take the job or not.

The duty of adaptation and the duty of finding another job have revolutionised the management of the workforce in France.

In 1993 a requirement was added to the 'loi Aubry', following the European directive on collective dismissals (February 1975), the duty to include within the corporate restructuring plan a special plan with a list of the jobs proposed to the workers to avoid or to reduce the number of dismissals. The case law, especially from

1996, has reinforced this duty of finding another job: the judges ask for precise offers, the number of jobs, their locations, their qualifications. The employer must prove he made the maximum effort to find new jobs in the enterprise or in the group. The plan has to be in relation with the size of the firm. If the plan is insufficient or if the measures to limit the effects of collective dismissals are inadequate, the plan is null and void and the employer must reemploy the workers included in that redundancy. The sanctions are heavy and have brought on problems and discussions, but the results are clear: the plans are very sophisticated and limit the social effects of restructuring.

The same duty of finding a new job has been extended to sick workers when the plant doctor decides that the worker can't go on at the same job or under the same conditions. The employer has one month to find another job which complies with the doctor's orders, or to compensate the worker, or, if it is impossible to find an adequate job, to dismiss. This duty has existed since 1981 with regard to unfitness after an occupational illness or accident and has been extended since 1992 to other situations.

1.2.2. Protection of fundamental rights

The main guarantee given to workers is to declare null and void a dismissal; such cases are growing in number:

- all the decisions founded on discrimination are, of course, null and void,
- dismissal after occupational illness or accident during the period of sick leave,
- dismissal during maternity leave or caused by maternity,
- dismissal of worker's representatives without labour inspector's authorisation,
- dismissal founded on exercise of the right to strike,
- redundancy without an adequate plan.

In other cases, when dismissal has no real or just cause, the worker may obtain compensations and redundancy payment, but may never work again in the enterprise. When the dismissal is declared null and void, the worker may work again at the same job or at a job similar to the one he had before the dismissal.

Not only must the labour contract be in accordance with fundamental rights and liberties, the charter of discipline within the enterprise must also respect these fundamental rights. The judge reviews the regulations as well as the employer's disciplinary powers which have to be used in the 'interest of the enterprise' and not arbitrarily.

There is in French labour law a resistance to flexibility. The balance between flexibility and protection, as it is reflected in individual labour relations, will be more favourable for workers when the economic crisis diminishes and employment grows.

2. FLEXIBILITY IN COLLECTIVE LABOUR RELATIONS

Since 1987, collective labour relations in France have changed to introduce, by collective bargaining, flexibility in labour relations.

In the same period, employers began to suppress many benefits given to the workers during the heady years of growth. The High Court had to rewrite the guarantees given to workers and the limits on flexibility imposed on employers when these regulations had been introduced by an unnegotiated collective statute or by collective bargaining (a special case because of the favourability principle).

The favourability principle is the basis of collective bargaining legislation since 1950: collective agreements had to be more favourable than the law; between contract and collective agreements; the more favourable clause was applied; and decentralised bargaining had to be more favourable than the national one.

The favourability principle was useful during the years of growth, but during the crisis, the collective benefits given by collective agreements became too costly, and a real need to rewrite collective agreements to introduce new balances appeared.

The legislator accepted the introduction of new procedures (1) in order to cancel benefits and change collective agreements, even 'in pejus', but tried in exchange to give new guarantees to trade unions.

The option to negotiate collective agreements 'to the bottom' was new to France in the 1990s. Consequently, the introduction of flexibility and the review of collective agreements created the need to find actors to negotiate, inside trade unions as well as outside (2). Perhaps a new threshold will be cleared with the introduction of the law on working time (3).

2.1. Introduction of New Procedures

New procedures are established either by the legislator or by case law: the juridical system applies differently in the case of unnegotiated norms and collective agreements.

2.1.1. Flexibility in the cancellation of benefits under unnegotiated norms

The High Court and the legislators alike consider that the employer must be able to cancel the benefits given to workers, without any review of the economic reason, if the benefit in question is neither contractual nor negotiated as part of a collective agreement. Many benefits are merely the result of custom or a decision of the employer, especially in small enterprises where there is no union representation. When the benefit is discussed by the works council, the agreement is generally considered as an 'atypical agreement', without any value for collective bargaining, which was reserved until 1996 to trade unions (cf. *infra*). For 10 years many benefits of this type were cancelled: informal breaks during working hours, grants and bonuses, break rooms, parking fees paid by the employer, use of minitel and use of phone for private calls, etc...

The High Court requires employers to inform each worker of the cancellation, to inform employees' representatives, giving the possibility to open negotiations, and to let some time pass between the announcement of the cancellation and its implementation (3–6 months). If this procedure is followed, the benefit is considered cancelled and the worker must accept it. It is a way to give financial flexibility to the employers. Some collective agreements offer even greater guarantees for the maintenance of benefits, for example a waiting period of 15 months, mandatory collective bargaining during that period, and the maintenance of 'individually granted benefits'. There is also a movement to introduce flexibility in collective bargaining.

2.1.2. Flexibility in collective agreements

Recent years have been characterised by the development of derogatory clauses ('accords dérogatoires') and by the introduction of the option to revise collective agreements. In France, collective agreements are signed by representative trade unions. Five national trade unions are presumed representative, even if they have just one worker inside an enterprise (CGT, FO, CFDT, CFTC, CGC).

National representative trade unions or their subsidiaries negotiate collective agreements without any formality or any majority. They just have to choose a union representative. This rule of representation was made to encourage the conclusion of collective agreements more favourable than law.

But the legislator, in 1982 and 1987, agreed to validate in the area of wages and working time collective agreements which contained clauses different or less favourable than the standards fixed by law i.e. derogatory. A new statute was passed which applies to collective agreements that depart from the law: they may be signed by a representative trade union but the other trade unions within the enterprise may veto the agreement if they received a majority of votes during the last elections at the enterprise.

The right of veto allows important trade unions or a group of trade unions to prevent the introduction of a collective agreement which alters the repartition of wage increases or working hours.

The use of this right of veto is very difficult because in France the trade unions do not work together and it is very difficult to find a majority of votes within such pluralism.

Many agreements of this kind were concluded on working time to allow a calculation on a yearly and not a weekly basis. The calculation on a yearly basis allows for high periods (40–48 h/week) and low periods (under 39 h/week) without compensation after 39 h of work i.e. overtime pay, limitation of overtime work at 130 h/year for each worker, special rest periods for overtime.

This calculation on an annual basis is very useful for seasonal activities or for enterprises with fluctuations in their activities. It is a way to adapt to the variations of the market and offers great flexibility in the organisation of work. But it also leads to significant change in the workers' private life.

In 1992 the legislator also allowed for the revision of collective agreements without terminating the collective agreement. This revision could be negotiated by a trade union that had not been part of the preceding negotiations. For example, if a collective agreement is signed by the CFDT, some time later the FO can sign a revision of that agreement, even if the revision is less favourable than the original agreement. In this case, the right of veto is open to the trade unions which represent the majority (same calculation of majority).

The law on the revision of collective agreements allows employers' associations more flexibility to reorganise firms along the lines of an international currency. Starting in 1990 negotiations became a trade-off ('donnant-donnant'): the cancellation of a clause on a special allowance was traded for more vocational training, better protection against illness was traded for new working time etc.

Especially in the restructuring of groups, the negotiation is between flexibility and deregulation.

But many agreements on working time aim at more flexibility in order to avoid redundancy. In France the issues of redundancy, social plans to limit or avoid collective dismissal, and new organisation of working time with more flexibility are strongly linked. The labour ministry asked labour inspectors to help enterprises reach an agreement with trade unions to lower working time (by 10% less, to limit the number of dismissals and to hire new workers, all in exchange for government subsidies ('loi de Robien', 11 June 1996). In 1996 many enterprises followed these recommendations, because the subsidies were substantial.

The new law of '35 h' is, like the 'loi de Robien', too expensive for the State.

The French legislator believes that if employers and trade unions accept the introduction of new forms of organisation, more flexibility, and the cancellation of benefits (in exchange for other benefits or not), it will be good for a firm's economic performance and thus for employment.

The legislator has given the unions a mission to bargain the transition to a more competitive organisation.

This principle is no longer a point of discussion but the problem remains that collective bargaining often takes place in the context of restructuring and redundancy, and against the background of a crisis in the trade unions. Union representatives are not always in a position to bargain with force because they do not always enjoy the support of the majority of the workers. The decentralisation of collective bargaining is a factor in adapting to the enterprise's economic reality but traditionally, the trade union's force was higher in the professional sector ('branche professionnelle'). The aim of the legislator is for decentralisation to provoke greater sharing of working time (cf. *infra*). For this new actors are needed to negotiate more flexibility in working time.

Some flexibility in labour relations is unavoidable when adapting to the economic evolution internationally. It is not possible to maintain an inflexible labour market when the firm's market is continually changing with globalisation.

The problem is to fix the limits of that flexibility and the guarantees given to workers.

2.2. Recognition of New Actors

In 1995 an inter-professional agreement ('ANI') was negotiated by the employers' association CNPF and the five national representative trade unions to energise collective bargaining and revise the conditions of negotiations to ease the social dialogue.

The trade unions accepted to open to elected representatives the right to negotiate, especially to members of works councils in enterprises where there was no union representation (generally small ones without union presence).

The law of 12 November 1996 introduced the option to allow works council members to negotiate collective agreements if a previous professional sector agreement made allowances for it. For the agreement to take effect, it had to be validated by a special commission whose members were chosen from within employers' associations and national representative trade unions.

In a case decided 25 January 1995 the courts also accepted that a worker be given a special warrant by a trade union to negotiate collective agreements.

The Constitutional Council ('Conseil constitutionnel, 6 November 1996') held that the decision was constitutional. If the right of workers' participation was protected by the Constitution, the monopoly on collective bargaining was not. The Council asked that the new actors, like union representatives, be protected against dismissal in order to guarantee fair negotiations.

It is difficult to evaluate the consequences of the presence of these new actors: only a few sectors with generally small enterprises have accepted the opening of collective bargaining to works council members, and numerous mandates have been given to workers to negotiate on working time issues. Trade union controls are very strict. The law allows for negotiations within small enterprises but doesn't offer a lot of guarantees to the worker representatives who face their employers.

Some people think only the trade unions will be able to stay the tide of deregulation and flexibility because of their independence and their strength. Nevertheless, implementation of new working time regulations through collective bargaining should lead the country to a new competitiveness and to growth in employment.

Less rigidity and more flexibility may reduce individual benefits but increase collective benefits. The increase in the number and the change in the quality of the actors is thus in the general interest.

2.3. The Law of 35 h

The French law of 35 h was adopted 13 June 1998 only after a great fight with the employers' association CNPF which did not want to reduce working time.

The text is quite complex but the aim of the law is to oblige businesses with more than 20 employees to reduce working time to 35 h per week after 1 January 2000 (2002 for smaller businesses).

Starting immediately, companies could negotiate a collective agreement to prepare for this reduction, induced by government subsidies to those companies which reduced their working time by 10% before 1 January 2000 and which hired for at least 6% of the hours.

The challenge is to provoke the social partners to negotiate the reorganisation of the firm for more competitivity and a better use of the free time given to the workers. The law leaves open to the social partners whether working time should be calculated on an annual basis or not.

In all, it is a good opportunity for employers to increase flexibility in working time.

The law does not impose regulations on pay scales. At present, collective agreements that have been signed allow for a very small reduction in pay (1–3%) through different measures, but especially through a two-year moratorium on wage increases.

Difficult problems have emerged: the organisation of working time reduction for white collar workers, the negotiation of the repartition of working time for greater competitivity, limiting the cost of the reduction, increasing worker creativity and work quality in the new organisation, etc.

There are also many legal questions. The most important is whether it is possible to impose a pay reduction on workers: pay scales are part of the work contract and case law says that employers must not modify contractual remuneration. In addition, the contract takes precedence when it is more favourable than the collective agreement. The workers could therefore refuse the reduction in working time as found in the collective agreement since it means a reduction in pay. The collective agreement could have the absurd effect of leading to the dismissal of workers.

Some hold that workers may not refuse the pay reduction because the ratio pay/working time is more favourable for them.

The discussion is heated and nobody knows what the High Court will decide.

It is advisable to negotiate a good pay/working time ratio, to propose new possibilities to workers in the use of their free time (vocational training throughout their working life, a four-day work week, cumulation of free time over many years, etc.), and to respond to workers' wishes (which can be very different between men and women, young and old, blue collars and white collars, etc.).

Another problem touches on the respect of the private sphere, in particular for white collar workers. The European directive of 19 November 1993 imposes a weekly break of 24-h plus 11-h. Can white collar workers be called at home during this break? Can they be obliged by contract to come to the firm during the break? For what reason? For which job? Article L 120-2 of the labour code forbids the infringement on personal freedom not justified by the interest of the enterprise and allows the courts to limit these practices.

Interpreting the European directive to require a strict respect of the break period is one way to protect the private sphere. But the answers to the questions are not clear.

There are also difficulties in the organisation of white collar work. Their working hours are not usually counted and they were paid at a fixed rate based on a global evaluation. But for the last two years labour inspectors and judges have been strict in verifying that the working time of white collar workers is below the maximum (48 h/week) and that the pay evaluation reflects the real working time.

The introduction of the 35-h week for white collar workers will be difficult because a lot of them work a 48-h week and more. Exceptions in the law only apply to top management and open questions of definition.

A lot of collective agreements give vacation to white collar workers to compensate for the working time (up to 22 days each year), with the possibility of saving these vacation days on an account for use for vocational training or sabbatical. The main difficulty is to verify white collar working time, particularly if they work at home at night (via computers, mobile phone, etc.).

With collective bargaining, there is a *chance for a cultural revolution inside the enterprise*: some are reflecting on their economic and social aims, and the possibility of profiting from increased hiring to bring about the growth of the group or the enterprise; others have decided to limit the consequences of the law and are waiting for 1 January 2000. A future law will establish the definitive framework of the reduction in working time, using the collective agreements to do so.

The legislator's will is to promote decentralised collective bargaining and to encourage the process in small enterprises. The agreement on the 35-h-week will then be negotiated as before by union representatives or, if absent, by a mandated worker under the direction of a trade union. The mandate has to be precise. Works council members may negotiate only if a professional sector level agreement provides for it.

The result of those negotiations will be very interesting: we have only seen the beginning of the collective bargaining process and the real debate has not started because emotions are still running high on the subject.

Internationally we are looking at a *poker game*: if the enterprises arrive at a more competitive organisation to optimise their economic abilities, the effect on employment may be real. But many employers say that the costs will be too heavy in the face of the European and international currency.

3. EVALUATION

It is very difficult to evaluate the situation because French labour law is full of paradox and is in transition.

The trust in collective bargaining to manage the need for flexibility, created by the pressure of international competition and by the variations in the market, certainly is justified. The unions carry a huge responsibility in their fight to maintain jobs and the quality of working life both inside and outside the plant.

The trade unions have understood the necessity to negotiate issues effecting the work place in order to maintain good levels of employment, a trade union view that is quite new in France.

Antoine Jemmaud has identified three phenomena in France:

(1) affirmation of a real right of employment with new and original rules,
(2) flexibility in the use of the workforce, in individual and collective relations,
(3) strengthening of the rights of the person.

The trend in France is to introduce procedures which permit more flexibility. At the same time the workers continued to be protected by labour law, fundamental rights, by the force of the employment contract, even in the case of fixed term or temporary contracts, by the courts and by the role of the unions in collective bargaining.

One cannot speak of deregulation since collective bargaining agreements and contracts are still in force to regulate labour relations. Certain regulations to protect the worker will be rewritten in the new economic environment.

The problem is to determine ***the limitations of a 'useful flexibility'* in regard to the private sphere, employment security, poverty, and health equality**.

In fact, these are neither individual nor collective considerations but concern society as a whole. The State is always present in labour relations, but the state's actions must be completed and carried out by the social partners.

There is nothing new in the recognition of the inter-relatedness of certain labour regulations (ex: organisation of rest periods, calculation of working time on an annual basis, especially for part-time workers), with the general interest and societal problems on a whole.

It is possible to say that each enterprise's organisation *has direct consequences on employment or on poverty levels: this closeness is new in France*. It is very difficult to manage in the interests of both employers and trade unions.

In France, the term 'entreprise citoyenne' ('citizen enterprise') is used to express the idea that the enterprise has a public function in direct relation to general problems such as unemployment, demographics, exclusion, poverty, etc.

But it is better to talk about a '*social citizenship*' in order to develop the abilities of the social partners, workers, employers, trade unions and other representatives and their contribution to the problems which are so linked to the organisation of work.

It is not easy to envision new concepts of labour law since demands are always changing and consideration must be given to action taken by the ILO, etc.

It is useful to consider ways to *reinforce international protections* in the face of international management methods: more effective ILO conventions and fundamental rights, social clauses in international treaties, charters or international collective agreements in multinational groups to protect fundamental rights.

The question of flexibility or deregulation of labour law is a national problem since our labour law, even within the context of the European Union, is national.

Supra-national regulations limit deregulation and management's use of the workforce: the European directives and the Charter of social fundamental rights have created a set of uniform rights to protect workers and to give a fair chance to firms on the European market.

In North America, the social clause in NAFTA guarantees fundamental rights, especially trade union freedom.

French *labour law has to be adjusted to fit the flexibility and the mobility of international firms.*

National considerations are relative, international ones are universal.

BIBLIOGRAPHY

General books on Labour Law, written by G. Couturier (PUF, 2t.), G. Lyon-Caen, A. Supiot, J. Pelissier (Dalloz), J. E. Ray (Liaisons sociales), A. Mazeaud

Special issues

- La négociation collective: nouveaux horizons, nouveaux problèmes, *Droit social*, décembre 1997
- La réduction du temps de travail, *Droit social*, septembre 1998
- Négocier et appliquer les 35 heures, *Liaisons sociales*, suppl. no. 12754, 30 septembre 1998

Articles and specialised books

G. Borenfreund, La représentation des salariés et l'idée de représentation, *Droit social* 1991, p. 685

G. Borenfreund, Le droit du travail en mal de transparence, *Droit social* 1996, p.461

G. Couturier, Quel avenir pour le droit du licenciement? perspectives d'une régulation européenne, *Droit social* 1997, p. 75

G. Couturier, Plan social et mesures de reclassement: l'apport de la loi du 27 janvier 1997, *Droit social* 1997, p. 223

M. Despax, De l'accord à la loi, *Droit social* 1987, p. 184

A. Jeammaud, Le droit du travail en changement. Essai de mesure, *Droit social* 1998, p. 211

A. Lyon-Caen, Les droits fondamentaux et l'Europe des droits du travail, in A. Nayer, *Droit du travail: effectivité, efficacité?* éd. La Chartre, Bruxelles, 1996, p. 145

A. Lyon-Caen, Le rôle des partenaires sociaux dans la mise en oeuvre du droit communautaire, *Droit social* 1997, p. 68

G. Lyon-Caen Quel avenir pour quel droit social? *Cent ans de droit social belge*, Bruxelles, Bruylant, 1986, p. 879

M. A. Moreau, Travail de nuit des femmes, observations sous CJCE – 25 juillet 1991, *Droit social* 1992, p. 174

M. A. Moreau Le droit social communautaire à la recherche d'une mémoire, *Mélanges Savelli*, P. U. Aix-Marseille, 1998, p. 153

M. A. Moreau and G. Trudeau, La clause sociale dans l'accord de libre-échange nord-américain, *RIDE* 1995, p. 393

M. A. Moreau and G. Trudeau, Le droit du travail face à la mondialisation de l'économie, *Relations industrielles*, 1998, vol. 53, no. 1, p. 55

M. A. Moreau, P. Staelens, G. Trudeau, Nouveaux espaces economiques et distorsions sociales (alena, cee, eee), *Droit social* 1993, p. 686

M. L. Morin, La loi et la négociation collective: concurrence ou complémentarité, *Droit social* 1998, p. 419

P. Rodière, *Droit social de l'Union européenne*, LGDJ, 1998

P. Verge and G. Vallee, *Un droit du travail?, essai sur la spécificité du droit du travail*, éd. Yvon BLAIS, Québec, 1997

S. Simitis, Le droit du travail a-t-il encore un avenir?, *Droit social* 1997, pp. 655–668

S. Simitis and A. Lyon-Caen, L'Europe sociale à la recherche de ses références, *RMUE* 1993, no. 4, p. 109

A. Supiot, *Critique du droit du travail*, PUF Paris, 1994

A. Supiot et al., *Transformations du travail et devenir du droit du travail en Europe: Rapport pour la Commission européenne*, juin 1998

A. Supiot, direc., *Le travail en perspectives*, LGDJ, Paris, collec. Droit et société, no. 22, p. 630

B. Teyssie, Remarques sur le droit du travail, *Etudes en l'honneur de A. Colomer*, Litec, 1993, p. 495

Ph. Waquet, Le juge et l'entreprise, *Droit social* 1996, p. 472

3. Deregulation and Labour Law in Germany

Detlev Joost

I. INTRODUCTION

In my country, the deregulation discussion has a long story with small results. It is a typical feature of German labour law that the number of legal rules has always increased and that the area for exercising individual freedom of contract has been reduced. In the second half of the century the *Wirtschaftswunder*, a long-term economic boom, has led to many regulations containing benefits for the employees, the government perhaps assuming that the economic boom will never end. Germany was thus given one of the highest social standards in the world, the employees having a strong protection by labour law.

Things have changed. The country suffers from severe economic problems; the unemployment rate is alarmingly high (see below in Section 1.1); the national debt is exceeding 2.3 trillion DM (2.3 *Billionen* DM). Unemployment appears to be the most urgent problem. It is partially caused by Germany's reunification in 1990, but the roots lead back to the sixties. Whole branches of industries vanished or came into severe trouble for years and decades: textile industry, shipyards, steel industry, coal mining, a long list.

The economic problems, leading to high unemployment, have induced the deregulation discussion. Deregulation in this sense means abolishing regulations in order to lower labour costs, increase incentives to engage employees and create new jobs. The target is not the modernisation of regulations due to a change of the surroundings of labour.

The paper refers only to labour law. Of equal importance is the sector of social law, e.g. unemployment insurance. These regulations have quite often been changed in order to keep the social systems stable. Nevertheless they are regarded to be in the fundamental crises: expenses too high, revenues too low, an increasing number of payees and a diminishing number of payers.

II. STEPS OF DEREGULATION

1. Labour Market Regulations

1.1. Employment placement services

Originally there had been for a long time a state's monopoly in employment placement services, ruled by the *Arbeitsförderungsgesetz* (Act for the Promotion of Labour) and

R. Blanpain (ed.), Deregulation and Labour Law, 59–68

executed by the *Bundesanstalt für Arbeit* (Federal Employment Office). This monopoly has been abolished in 1994 by the Act for the Promotion of Employment.

Since then we have a dualism. The *Bundesanstalt für Arbeit* is still active as a service for employment placement and is still the main mediator. The private fee-charging service is legalised, but the activity requires a permit. The permit has to be given if the person is eligible.

The change has been caused by the opinion of the government that the monopoly is not the best way to fight against unemployment. The time since the change has taken place is too short to judge the results.

1.2. Temporary work services

The temporary work service is conducted by the *Arbeitnehmerüberlassungsgesetz* since 1972 (Law on Temporary Employment Service). The service provided by private persons is legal, but there are many restrictions imposed by the law.

The person needs a permit by the *Bundesanstalt für Arbeit*. The permit can only be denied, if the person is not eligible or violates the law.

The person has to play the full role of an employer with all legal employers duties. Thus the employee gets a solid employment.

Fixed-term contracts between the person and the employees are generally prohibited.

The contract has to contain certain minimum conditions.

The legally allowed working-time for a single third party (hirer) is limited.

At the end of 1995 6,231 persons had a permit for a temporary work service. The number of employees was 162,275. These are the legal figures. It is assumed that there is a fairly high percentage of undetected illegal services. Authorities believe that the illegal sector is 6–10 times higher than the official.

The Law on Temporary Employment has been deregulated several times.

The legally allowed working-time for a hirer has been raised up to now 12 months.

No permit is required if an employer with less than 50 employees hires out for no longer than one year in order to prevent dismissals or short-time work.

1.3. Fixed-term contracts

We have estimated about 1.6 million fixed-term employment contracts. These contracts have been a great problem at all times. Under the rule of our general civil law, the fixed-term contract between employer and employee is legal without any restrictions. The time limit can be a week, a month, a year, five years or whatsoever. A restriction has not been imposed by law but by judicial decisions. The courts have assumed that fixed-term contracts violate the Dismissal Protection Act unless the employer has a good reason for the time limit. If he lacks a good reason the contract is valid for an unlimited period.

In order to improve employment the *Beschäftigungsförderungsgesetz* of 1985 (Act for the Promotion of Employment) has eased the making of fixed-term contracts. The act was originally only valid till the end of 1989 but has been extended twice till the end of 1995 and now 2000. In 1996 the possibilities for fixed-term contracts have been expanded. The main principles are:

- The fixed-term contract is legal up to two years (originally only 18 months) even if there is no good reason for the limitation.
- Within two years the contract can be renewed up to three times.
- For employees over 60 years the fixed-term contract is legal without any restrictions.

1.4. Dismissal regulations

The dismissal of employees is governed by the *Kündigungsschutzgesetz* (Dismissal Protection Act) since 1952. This act changes the general civil law, under which contracts of employment can be terminated by the employer without having a good reason for the dismissal. The most important items of the Dismissal Protection Act were until 1985 resp. 1996:

- A legal dismissal requires a good reason. The reason can originate in the person of the employee (e.g. contagious disease), his behaviour (e.g. theft) or in operational reasons (e.g. lack of orders). In case of operational reasons the legal dismissal is additionally on condition that the employer has sufficiently given respect to the social circumstances of the employees concerned. These circumstances can be (examples): age, obligations to provide maintenance, length of service, chances to get new employment and so on.
- The protection is on condition that the contract has existed longer than six months. During the first six months the employer can even under this act terminate the contract without having a good reason to do so. This period is a so-called *Probezeit* (trial period).
- The Dismissal Protection Act is only valid for enterprises with more than five employees. Part-time employees were counted as normal employees till 1985. A firm e.g. with five full-time employees was not, a firm with six part-time employees, each with a working-time of ten hours, was under the act, despite the first firm having a working time of (5 × 40) 200 h per week, the second only 60.

The protection against dismissal is widely regarded as a main cause for unemployment. The government therefore has made several issues on deregulation.

- In 1985 the last of the items mentioned above was changed by the Act for the Promotion of Employment in order to improve part-time employment. Employees with a working-time up to 10 h per week or 45 h per month are not counted any more. After this change both firms in the above-mentioned example were free of the Dismissal Protection Act.
- A second more important step was taken in 1996 with the *Arbeitsrechtliches Beschäftigungsförderungsgesetz* (Act on Labour Conditions for the Promotion of Employment). This act has changed several regulations. The most important are:
  - The level for the applicability of the Dismissal Protection Act is now more than ten employees per firm. This legal change will probably refer to add. 5 % of all employees. Before the change an est. 25 % of all employees were not under the Dismissal Protection Act.
  - In case of a dismissal due to operational reasons, the social circumstances which have to be observed by the employer when choosing an employee for

dismissal are restricted. Only age, length of service and obligations to provide maintenance are to be weighed. All other social circumstances are no longer of any importance. Thus the judgement of the employer whether the dismissal is legally effective shall be of higher precision.

Very unclear is an all-new rule, which has been created recently by the Act for the Promotion of Labour (see below 1.6.). It says that employers shall give priority to operational measures in order to avoid dismissals. What this means is hard to tell. Under the Dismissal Protection Act a dismissal is anyway not effective if it is not necessary. Above all the legal consequence is unclear if the employer fails to do what he should do. Perhaps the dismissal is not effective; perhaps there is no direct consequence at all.

1.5. Part-time employment

Part-time employment is widely considered as an effective weapon against increasing unemployment. With the Act for the Promotion of Employment of 1985 steps have been taken to abate legal discrimination of part-time jobs, in order to give incentives for this form of employment. The main rules are:

- The principle of equal treatment is applicable. The employer must not treat a part-time employee unlike a full-time worker except if he has a good reason.
- In case of job-sharing there is generally no obligation for an employee to replace another in case of absence (e.g. illness).

1.6. Contract of integration

A special problem is the phenomenon of long-term unemployment. This has often been considered by the government. One idea is the *Kombi-Lohn*, which means to let the wages be partially paid by the employment office. This is not yet effective. But the government has taken a similar step. In 1997 the *Sozialgestzbuch III* (Act for the Promotion of Labour) has newly created the so-called *Eingliederungsvertrag* (contract of integration). If the employer hires a long-term unemployed person, the employment office can promote this relation. Employer and employee can enter into a contract of integration with the consent of the employment office. The contract is a fixed-term contract with a minimum of two weeks and a maximum of six months. The employer has the obligation to give the employee the chance of qualification with the target of entering upon an ordinary employment contract. The employment office can pay the employer a non-repayable grant and has to refund all payments of the employer for times without work performed (esp. continued payment in case of illness).

2. Individual Labour Relations

2.1. Working-hour regulations

Working-hour regulations have always been a central aspect of both legislation and collective bargaining. Since 1938 the *Arbeitszeitordnung* was effective. It has been succeeded in 1994 by the *Arbeitszeitgesetz* (Act on Working-hours). The general maximum of working-hours is still 8 h per day. As the Saturday is regarded as a working day, the general maximum per week is 48 h. This contains no change compared with the former *Arbeitszeitordnung*. The new act supports flexibility:

- The working-hours can be prolonged up to 10 h per day if the average of eight hours is not exceeded within six calendar months or 24 weeks. Special regulations apply to works in the night-hours.
- The maximum can be exceeded in cases of emergency.
- The employment office can allow a higher maximum in some cases.
- Collective agreements can provide other rules, e.g. prolongation up to 10 h per day for a maximum of 60 days per year.
- The work on Sundays and public holidays in generally prohibited. But there is a wide catalogue of exceptions.

2.2. *Women's night work*

The *Arbeitszeitgesetz* has abolished the former ban on women's night work in 1994. The reason has nothing to do with deregulation but refers to the constitutional principle of equal rights for women and men.

2.3. *Continued payment of wages*

One of the most important steps towards deregulation was the alteration of the continued payment of wages during illness of employee. Under the previous law the employer was obliged to continue payment for six weeks in every case of illness, the level being 100% of the wages. In 1996 the level was reduced to 80%. The reduction is accompanied by the right of the employee to get 100% if he resigns one day of paid vacation per five days of illness. The legal minimum of paid vacation is four weeks, the real paid vacation by collective or individual contract is for nearly all employees higher; 50% of the employees reach six weeks. This has to be stressed in order to judge the discussion on this step of deregulation (see below IV.).

2.4. *Derogation from legal norms through collective bargaining agreements*

Under our constitution the parties to a collective agreement (unions and employers associations) have the right to settle labour conditions without interference by the legislation. Therefore in a wide area legal norms on labour law can be changed by collective agreements. The possibility of derogation from legal norms is no major problem. The real problem is to which extent the unions are inclined to sign an agreement which grants a smaller protection to the employee than the law.

On the level of the firm there is no possibility of derogation from legal norms except when the management enters an agreement with a trade union (which is possible; so-called firm collective agreement). The works council (shop stewards committee) does not have the power to change the conditions fixed by labour law. It acts within the range given by the law.

The derogation by individuals' consent does not play an important role. Despite some legal rules underlying contractual amendment, here the interesting regulations are cogent (*ius cogens*). This applies for instance to the Dismissal Protection Act. The reason is that it is legally assumed that the employee does not sign the contract in full freedom but is often confronted with a more or less dictate by the employer. Still many aspects of labour law are discussed whether the freedom of contract could and should have a stronger impact on labour conditions.

3. Collective Labour Relations

3.1. Decentralisation of collective bargaining

It is widely assumed that decentralisation might be of help in the battle against unemployment. But there are some heavy obstacles on this way.

3.1.1. Company bargaining

As mentioned above (see section 2.3.) the management can enter a collective agreement. But this decentralisation refers only to the firm as one party of the contract. The other party has to be a union. A union is only legally acknowledged if it represents the employees of more than one firm. This is not fixed in the law but is prevailing opinion in science and courts decisions. Thus the union as one party will always consider the needs of all employees including those working in other companies.

3.1.2. Transfer to works councils

This is a very important item in the current discussion. The opinion is often expressed that it would be a great advantage if labour conditions could be fixed 'near to the plant'. For a collective bargaining it would be necessary to install the works council, a very important institution in Germany, as a party for such bargainings. And that precisely is the problem. Under the *Betriebsverfassungsgesetz* (Works Councils Constitution Act) the works council cannot deal with labour conditions that are in fact or at least usually settled by the unions. The unions have strict priority. Agreements between the management of the firm and the works council on subjects that are in general handled by the unions are legally void. This applies even if the agreement with the works council is more favourable for the employees. Steps by the government to change the preventing law have not been taken and not even considered. Some authors hold that the law should at least be interpreted in a way that favourable conditions for the employee bargained by the works council are valid. A major problem in this discussion is that the unions have a constitutionally guaranteed field of activity while the works councils have not. The works councils do not even occur in the text of the constitution. Therefore it is widely assumed that the works councils cannot be made a rival to the unions without violating the constitution.

3.2. Individual bargaining

This is a very interesting item in the discussion of deregulation. The relation between the trade unions, i.e. the collective agreements and the individual, i.e. its bargaining, is strongly regulated by the law. Under the *Tarifvertragsgesetz* (Collective Bargaining Act) the collective agreement applies only to the members of the union which entered the contract. Outsiders are free to agree with e.g. lower wages or longer working-hours or even both.

For the members of the union the collective agreement is *ius cogens*. By individual contract e.g. lower wages cannot be agreed with. This regulation only serves the protection of the employee against exploitation. Therefore the employee can enter an individual contract containing (for him) better conditions compared with the collective agreements, e.g. higher wages or shorter working-hours.

In many cases it is hard or even impossible to tell from an objective point of view whether the conditions made by the individual contract are favourable for the employee or not. Let us look e.g. at the relation between wages and working-hour. If the collective agreement contains a maximum working-hour of 35 h per week and hourly wages of (x), is it favourable or not for the employee to agree with 40 h and hourly wages of $(x+y)$? In 1984 it was suggested to interpret the principle of freedom of contract in a way that in such cases, when the agreed condition is neither definitely favourable nor unfavourable but in a certain sense neutral, the decision should be left entirely to the employee (*Joost* ZfA 1984, 173, 182 f.). This has in the meantime become the prevailing opinion and is a small piece of deregulation.

But major steps in order to strengthen the individual contract have not been taken. The main reason is the fear that any deregulation could end in a modern form of exploitation.

3.3. Cost reduction for newly founded firms

Under the Works Councils Constitution Act from 1972 in case of changes in operations the works council can demand a *Sozialplan* (social compensation plan) which means that the employer has to make payments to the employees in order to compensate economic disadvantages caused by the changes in operation. These costs can sum up to several 100,000 DM or even several million DM. If the employer does not enter the social compensation plan voluntarily it can be made effective against his will by decision of a conciliation committee. In order to promote new foundations of firms the law was changed in 1985 by the Act for the Promotion of Employment so that a social compensation plan is not necessary if the changes of operation take place during the first four years after the foundation. As dismissals of groups of employees are regarded as change of operation, newly founded firms have no extra costs when dismissing employees during the first four years. The idea is that they will not hesitate to engage employees during this unsafe period.

III. THE DRIVING FORCES OF DEREGULATION

The main cause of deregulation measures is the high unemployment rate. Unemployment has increased throughout the last decade and has reached a definitely high level. The statistics for August 1998 show a total of more than 4 million unemployed, which is a rate of more than 10%. These are only the official figures. Estimates of experts say that the real rate of unemployment is much higher. The last elections (September 1998) show how dramatic the problem is. Most statements say that the defeat of the Christian-Democratic Party with chancellor *Kohl* is due to the unemployment problem and the lack of a convincing concept to overcome the problem. Pressure from global competition appears to be only part of the unemployment problem.

The European Council Directives have had no impact on the above mentioned measures of deregulation. Decisions of the European Court of Justice have in many ways altered the labour law but were not especially effective regarding deregulation.

IV. EVALUATION OF CURRENT DEREGULATION AND LABOUR LAW REFORMS

Deregulation is not at all a universal phenomenon in labour law. In total we can only see few and small steps in the direction of deregulation. These steps cannot be regarded as part of an overlapping concept how labour law should be reformed with clear targets and clear actions. It is merely a matter of single actions not really bound together.

Unsurprisingly we find some fields of labour law where regulations have been increased. This applies e.g. to the following areas.

- The effects of a transfer of plant to another owner on labour conditions is ruled by law since 1972 (with amendments 1980) without the parties having the freedom of contractual alteration. All employment relations are transferred by law to the buyer, the working conditions remaining the same. Conditions set by collective agreements are further on valid. Dismissals due to the transfer are illegal. These regulations are partially imposed by a European Council Directive. They can be considered as the most important regulations in our present labour law.
- The transformation of companies is accompanied by several important regulations in order to give the concerned employees protection. E.g. the works councils have special rights; the regulations on transfer of plant are applicable; the dismissal protection is strengthened; regulations on co-determination are upheld in case the transformation changes the legal requirements.
- Until 1988 the executives of the plant or firm were not represented by the works council or a similar institution. Since then they have a representation of their own (*Sprecherausschuß*), which is widely a copy of the general works council.
- The regulations against employment discrimination have been strengthened, partially due to a European Council directive and a decision of the European Court of Justice.
- The Act on the Proof of the Important Conditions of a Labour Relationship of 1995 requires that the employer either enters a written contract which lists up ten main conditions of the contract or gives the employee a signed paper with this contents no later than one month after the beginning of the employment. This act was caused by a European Council directive.

The general reactions to deregulation are very controversial. In general the unions point out that acts of deregulation simply destroy the necessary protection of the employee and do not lower the unemployment rate. Deregulation is often considered as a capitalistic rollback. The few steps taken by the government in recent years have all been refused by the unions. Nevertheless the unions certainly fight against unemployment. Their concept is to reduce the working-hours for all employees. They have entered a battle to install collective agreements with a maximum of 35 h per week and were successful. Recently claims towards 30 h per week have been made.

The employers' associations welcome the deregulation steps but think they do not go for enough and get stuck halfway. Main targets are the dismissal protection, the co-determination and the regulations on transfer of plants, which are considered as an obstacle for necessary restructuring of companies.

In the political arena the discussion is equally controversial. The above-mentioned steps of deregulation have all been taken by a government led by the Christian-Democratic Party. Incoming chancellor Gerhard Schröder from the Social-Democratic Party has announced before the successful elections in September 1998 that he will immediately withdraw the reforms referring to the Dismissal Protection

Act (see above II.1.4.) and the reduction of continued payment of wages in case of illness (see above II.2.3.). These reforms are considered as socially unbalanced. The political struggle shows once more that deregulation is not nourished by a long-aimed concept or even a vision but is mainly based on the consideration with which steps can be taken having the next election in view.

V. THE ROLE OF LABOUR LAW IN THE 21st CENTURY

Are the ideas of the past senile? Do we need a new concept of labour law being confronted with an economy, which changes with a breath-taking speed? No and yes:

No Labour law, understood as a law for the protection of the employee, is conceptionally based on the historical European experience that under the reign of freedom of contract an untamed capitalism tends to brutal exploitation. Nothing justifies the assumption that the results will be better under the conditions of globalism and fast-changing economies. A merely market-oriented labour law means in the end: no labour law.

Yes The neglect of market rules has led to a situation where a workable employment market does not exist. The social ideal to grant the employee an ever-increasing protection leaves him in the end unemployed – and thus totally unprotected. It is necessary to realise again that the market is ruled by incentives and that different goals cannot always be reached at the same time. The discernment has to be strengthened that labour law can no longer be an experimental field of social idealism beyond the market. The changes in economy will reveal this realisation quite merciless.

Does this mean that we have only the choice between a labour law as we know it combined with an ever-increasing unemployment rate and a return to market-oriented principles which give the employee no stronger protection than he achieves by individual bargaining? In an interview *Milton Friedman* gave recently to a German newspaper, he said that the unemployment in Germany would be homemade and due to governmental control. The ability of employers to hire and fire should be improved. Dismissal protection, paid vacation, unemployment insurance, health insurance and social security pension insurance would sound good but would above all create unemployment. Germany would have the choice: Either to work six months per year only for the taxes and produce an army of unemployed (remember *Karl Marx*, who entitled the unemployed as industrial reserve army). Or to shorten governmental expense and influence, lower taxes and stimulate the market to create jobs.

Is that the only choice? Perhaps there is a way in the middle. A new concept has to reconsider the necessary balance between freedom and equality. In labour law freedom refers to the individual freedom of contract allowing labour conditions to be adapted to personal needs, skills and circumstances. Equality refers to the social protection, which is needed for all employees because of their state of dependence. Social protection will be of no smaller importance in the century that lies ahead of us and cannot be discarded. But market-reactions should play a far more important role in considering and revising regulations set by labour law. Especially rules which prevent employers from creating jobs should be abolished if they are not definitely necessary.

This refers, among others, to the important phenomenon of the second wage. The low or high costs of labour are undoubtedly the main factor for employment and unemployment. The additional costs for the employer not expressed by the normal wages are now up to 100% of the normal wages. This second wage consists of a various range of payments, e.g. paid vacation, holiday allowance, Christmas benefits, 13th monthly salary, continued payment in case of illness or motherhood, paid educational leave, paid household day, etc. Ca. fifty per cent of these costs are imposed by governmental acts, the other half is based on collective or individual agreements. Many of these costs could be abolished or at least decreased to diminish the total costs of labour efficiently. As the saying is: *Man kann des Guten zuviel tun* (you can do too much of the good).

4. Deregulation and Labour Law in Italy

Michele Tiraboschi

DEREGULATION AND LABOUR LAW: AN HISTORIC-CONCEPTUAL FRAME OF REFERENCE

The subject of this national report is the analysis of the connection between *deregulation* and *labour law*. The main objective is not simply to describe the more recent evolution in Italian employment law and the most relevant factors driving the change in progress, but to look at the effects that these modifications have on capitalistic production and, in particular, their shape in juridical terms. Through the evaluation of emerging tendencies and reforms that have recently characterized Italian labour law – moving towards a progressive deregulation of employment relations – I will try to answer questions that, today more than ever, are central to our field. The questions challenge, if not the theoretical bases, at least the necessity of many rules that constitute the normative body of labour law. The questions are direct but at the same time complicated and radical: what is the future and the role of labour law in the 21st century? Do we need a new concept of labour law? To answer these questions from a perspective that allows a comparison between different legal systems, we need to clarify what we mean exactly by 'deregulation' and 'labour law', in such a way as to avoid answers that are ideological and pre-determined.

It is necessary to point out, first of all, that the term 'deregulation' can be translated with different words in Italian which then correspond to different legal concepts. Some Italian scholars, for example, use the expression 'delegification' to refer to the inversion of the trend that has brought about a wide 'juridification' of employment relations through coercive and mandatory rules to protect subordinate work (see Ferraro, 1990, 149). Used in this sense the term 'delegification' is not a correct translation of the word deregulation. It is true that from a technical and formal point of view the term delegification is part of the most comprehensive concept of deregulation, but a part cannot express the whole. In fact, the term delegification simply indicates the relationship between legal sources at different levels, and more precisely, the process of devolution of regulations of specific subjects or institutions from a legislative source to a lower source (i.e. regulations or collective agreement). By translating the term deregulation with the word delegification we actually indicate a juridical operation of a rather limited range, thereby sacrificing and losing the complex meaning of the term.

Equally limited is the doctrinal trend which suggests translating the term deregulation to indicate a broad but generic philosophical concept which supports a

R. Blanpain (ed.), Deregulation and Labour Law, 69–96

reduction of the area covered by state regulation, i.e. the area in which all forms of behaviour are regulated in order to satisfy public interest (for this perspective see Tremonti, 1985, 107). Again the translation of the term deregulation risks being partial and misleading even if it well represents the ideological and cultural meaning behind the word. Defined in these terms, the analysis of the connection between deregulation and labour law allows only for a superficial interpretation of the changes that have recently affected Italian labour law. It is, in fact, a perspective of research that focuses attention only on the flexibilisation of employment relations, but does not contribute to a consideration of the real causes that have affected the evolution of Italian labour law. The fact that human behaviour is not subject to state regulation does not mean that such behaviour ceases to be relevant from a juridical point of view. Simply, these acts or facts have their source of regulation in private (individual or collective) autonomy. It should be noted that deregulation does not involve fewer juridical rules, but rather more correctly, fewer State rules to the advantage of a wider normative authority of private (individual or collective) autonomy. It has been rightly pointed out in this regard that when private rule, more or less broadly, substitutes the public one, the number of necessary negotiations increases because each case requires adjudication instead of being able to refer to a single rule fixed for every case by a public source.

It is surely more useful to use the term deregulation in the broad and undetermined sense, subject to precision during analysis. From this point of view the concept of deregulation must be compared with a concept of juridification. To reflect on the reasons that have brought about the juridification of employment relations actually means questioning the reasons that have brought about the construction of the rules set up which constitute labour law. This analysis could then lead us to understand, with a better critical knowledge, the present trend widespread in all systems towards the deregulation of employment relations.

In this connection, it is useful to question and resolutely reject the validity of an interpretation that, very simplistically, identifies labour law as an instrument of protection of the weaker party (the worker) as compared with the great contractual power of the employer, an interpretation that then leads to individualising, in the present process of deregulation of employment relations, the effort to loosen some of the stiffness and constraints on the competitiveness of enterprises in the international scene and/or contribute to the creation of new employment opportunities at a time when there are alarming rates of unemployment. The historic perspective reveals a profile often neglected by labour law doctrine, and that still points to labour law as a means of weaker party protection. As a reaction to a new organisation of production methods and circulation of wealth, the employment relations regulation was not, in fact, able simply to turn into a unilateral means of protection and emancipation of a party characterised by social under-protection and economic dependence. Although not always supported by values and/or homogenous political, economic and social objectives, right from the beginning the State's regulatory intervention in the process of industrialisation never assumed any unidirectional aspect. Beyond the contingent motivation (declared or real) of each single given norm, the discipline of employment, as a matter of fact, assumes importance right from the start, not only under the traditional framework of worker protection, but also under the concurrent and certainly no less important context of the conservation of social peace and existing order, of the health of the young and of the integrity of descent, of the rationalisation of the production system, of the regulation of the forms of competition among entrepreneurs, etc. The product of the juridification of employment relations is therefore, undoubtedly, a *distributive* right of protection and resources, but also, at the same time, a right of *production* i.e. a discipline of roles and of the means of production in an industrial society.

Of particular note, from this point of view, is the historic evolution of the discipline of employment placement and the progressive suppression of private intermediary and speculative centres of employment. In an employment market profoundly modified, marked by chronic imbalances between demand and request of employment and destined to be regulated exclusively by the blind game of contrary forces, it was, in fact, inevitable that the control of hiring and occupation flows in general ended up representing a formidable instrument of power capable of influencing not only the results of the process of capitalistic production, but even earlier, influencing the same political–institutional balances of different national systems. Chiefly in those countries in which the industrialisation process delayed development, and conversely, where the tone of the union debates tended to undermine the very foundation of the emerging capitalistic society, the question of state control of placement became a true and proper 'question of sovereignty' to the point of legitimising the State's direct intervention in the economy, in contradiction to, only apparently, the free-trade principles then dominant. The growing power of the working coalitions on an issue so strategic to the 'wealth of a nation' – to use Adam Smith's expression – like that of control (monopolistic) of one of the factors of production could not do other than represent a head-on challenge of the sovereignty of the emerging national State, laboriously still trying to free itself from the pre-capitalistic super-structure and from the encrustation of the *ancien regime*. The union's capacity, real or only potential, to influence the process of creation and distribution of wealth and to affect the political–institutional balances of the State, either by control of the employment market or through reformist and revolutionary stimulus, put the question of 'economic sovereignty' as a necessary and unfailing complement of the political and territorial sovereignty.

It is precisely with reference to the question of control of the employment market – referred to by employers as an instrument for establishing economic power and the acquisition of labourers, and referred to by unions as a privileged channel of establishing an opposing union power – that determines the deep fracture between Continental European countries and Anglo Saxon countries. While the former – chiefly Italy – represent a tradition more or less markedly '*étatiste*' that in the name of the supremacy of the State has led to a progressive and massive juridification of employment relations through the intervention of the unbreakable rules of law and the State's monopoly of the juridical production. The latter, proving themselves, even with specific differences, to be '*stateless societies*', limit public intervention in the employment market to those few essential rules in order to ensure the ideal development of the capitalistic system of production, assuming a position of neutrality as regards the free flow of economic factors and of conflicts of interest that pass through the social body.

In the evaluation of the reasons for this deep fracture, it is impossible to indicate with any degree of precision the role assumed by the ideologies and by the ideals of justice and solidarity as regards the weight of the economic and social conditioning that have accompanied, in the diverse systems, the emerging process of industrialisation. Of particular concern is the risk of evaluating past events and institutions by applying paradigms and classic models of the present to the point of misinterpreting the events and the defining processes intrinsically connected to them. Nevertheless, in our opinion, without wanting to propose a purely deterministic view of history and of the movements of ideas,[1] two factors in particular can explain more than others why in Anglo Saxon countries 'economic sovereignty' is not considered a fundamental element for the full affirmation of political and territorial sovereignty with an affect on juridical rules of relations between capital and employment in general and on the process of casting of intermittent work through agencies in particular. In the first place, as has rightly been pointed out,[2] the true peculiarity of the Anglo-American experience is having exorcised the revolutionary violence of the union movement right from its beginnings. Whereas in other countries it has lived for a long time with the institutional practices of the unions and of the workers movement, only to fizzle out much later and not without first giving rise to deep fractures and lacerations in the social body over the processes of legitimisation of the forms of production of wealth and of appropriation of the 'result' of the work of others. The union movements in Britain and even more so in the USA were in effect well free of the destructive practices of Luddism, from the political suggestion of Cartism and from the utopia of revolutionary socialism, thus orientating themselves towards a new unionist creed that with *self-help* participated in the optimism of the Victorian society. In this particular cultural context, union control of the employment market was seen not as a destructive force against the political–institutional order of the modern State, but rather, together with strikes and collective agreements, as a spontaneous industrial demonstration and, at the same time, a factor of regulation of the competition and rationalisation of the capitalistic system of production 'upon which (...) the maximum productivity of the community as a whole depends'.[3] But even more decisive in this regard, because it also explains the peculiar behaviour of Anglo-American unionism, is the circumstance[4] that both in Great Britain and in the USA the process of industrialisation happened spontaneously and was, right from its conception, firmly in the hands of a bourgeoisie that, on the one hand, forcefully reclaimed full freedom of action and autonomy from the State and that, on the other hand, rapidly abandoned the establishment of the *ancien régime* in the centre of political and economic power. In these countries the control of production and of the appropriation of the value-added created by the work of others is achieved independently of the State and entirely entrusted, even when passing via the *laissez-faire* individual to the collectivity, to the self-regulating capacity of the market. In Continental European countries industrialisation occurs under the intervention of the State and through public control of economic and social factors, often overwhelming, as in the case of Italy, and not without profound tensions and social conflicts that upset the fragile politico–institutional balance of the emerging capitalistic society. Apart from rare cases, these countries respond with a notable delay to the demands of industrialisation and try, nevertheless, to bridge the gap with Great Britain and the USA, progressively increasing the intensity and the role of the State's intervention in the economic and social sphere. For these countries it was obligatory that the

1. Still valid, in this regard, is the teaching of Max Weber (see *Economia e società*, Ed. Comunità, Milano), that shows well that a unidirectional relation of cause and effect does not exist between the juridical system and economic system, but rather complex interrelations that do not allow identification of necessary laws and deterministic models of development of each system.
2. See P. Craveri (1990), voce *Sindacato (storia)*, in *Enc. Dir.*, vol. XLXX, Giuffrè, Milano, 661.
3. S. Webb, B. Webb (1926 ma 1897), *Industrial Democracy*, Longmans, Green and Co. Ltd., London.
4. Well shown by G. Baglioni (1974), *L'ideologia della borghesia industriale nell'Italia liberale*, Einaudi, Torino, 40–48.

'economic sovereignty' and, consequently, the control of the employment market and of the production and distribution mechanisms of wealth, became instruments for the complete affirmation of political and territorial sovereignty both internally (as opposed to a wide process of private normative protection) and externally (in comparison and competition with other nations).

It is precisely these justifications for the juridical approach to employment relations that now explain the tendency toward deregulation. The recent and numerous changes in the mechanisms of production and circulation of wealth that have established the definitive separation between the limits of the State and those of the market,[5] now render impractical any project of law meant to combine political–territorial sovereignty and economic sovereignty. In countries with an '*étatiste*' tradition, the internationalisation of the economy and the globalisation of the market greatly accentuate the incapacity of the local and national protagonists to control this socio-economic phenomenon and with it, the crisis of the State–Nation. The greater ease with which the '*stateless societies*' have adapted themselves to the changes of the economic market testifies to the present ineptitude of the imperative rule of law in the form of juridical innovations and highlights at the same time the greater flexibility of jurisdictional controls and/or of the market in adapting the right solutions to the recent changes in economic–productive structures. It is certainly not the case that now, faced with the internationalisation of the economic markets, the competition between different national labour laws has progressively led to, in various countries and juridical systems, the takeover of the public monopoly on placement, and contextually, to the removal of the principle constraints that prevented the legalisation of the administration of labour. The rules of competition based by now on a supra-national scale have, in fact, brought about a progressive loosening – or, in any case, a 'circumvention' – of all those displays of the State's sovereignty that, in one way or another, represented an obstacle to the production and circulation of wealth, proposing again in new terms the old problem of legitimisation of the forms of acquisition of the value added by the labour of others, a problem that seemed definitively resolved with the creation of the normative model of the subordinate employment contract for an indefinite period. Even when it does not translate into an escape into the 'submerged' and informal economy, the alteration of the traditional forms of acquisition and use of the work force is, by now, a constant of the modern processes of production of wealth. Very indicative in this respect is the gradual 'legitimization of negotiation formalities originally undervalued to the extent of even being considered illegitimate',[6] such as the ever more marked trend to adopt 'formulas and institutions belonging to commercial law'.[7] If the social parties and national governments do not seem presently capable of controlling the economic–productive structure and, at the most, limit themselves to look for 'palliatives to resist change and contain the effects to the social level',[8] the same supra-national protagonists are still far from identifying efficient instruments of regulation of the market and the

5. The point is well shown, among others, by S. Cassese (1993), *Oltre lo Stato: i limiti dei governi nazionali nel controllo dell'economia*, in F. Galgano, S. Cassese, G. Tremonti, T. Treu *Nazioni senza ricchezza. Ricchezza senza nazione*, il Mulino, Bologna, 35.
6. G. Ferraro (1998), *Dal lavoro subordinato al lavoro autonomo*, relazione AIDLASS su *Impresa e nuovi modi di organizzare il lavoro*, in corso di pubblicazione.
7. S. Simitis (1997), *Il diritto del lavoro ha ancora un futuro?*, in *Giornale Dir. Lav. Rel. Ind.*, 609.
8. R. Blanpain (1998), *Il diritto del lavoro nel XXI secolo: l'era dei lavoratori dal 'portafoglio' creativo, in Dir. Rel. Ind.*, n. 3, 333.

economy and, in most cases, are limited to merely taking note of the changes in progress.

Not even in largely homogenous areas like the European Community is there any movement towards the elaboration of a regulative outline for alternative juridical models of the subordinate employment contract for an indefinite period. The efforts of the European Union in this field have not, in fact, gone further than a Directive on the protection of the health and safety of temporary workers[9] and the weak and fruitless proposals of the Directive on the subject of temporary work as regards the elimination of distortions in competition and the risks of social *dumping* resulting from the different social costs connected to the different national regulations of the forms of temporary work.[10] In comparison to these tenuous attempts at discipline of a contractual scheme alternative to those of an undefined and stable period that testify unequivocally to the persistent weakness of the European process of social integration, it has been the Court of Justice that has assumed a role of substitution, supplying a significant contribution towards the modernisation and harmonisation of the national employment markets. As shown by the events surrounding the invalidation of the Italian public monopoly of employment placement in light of the Community anti-monopoly norm,[11] the Court of Justice has contributed to an increased use of market criteria in a subject area – that of regulation of employment relations – traditionally void of such logic. In fact, though changes have occurred in the economic–productive structure, there is still today strong national resistance on the regulative level that, in line with the original constitutive character of the discipline of employment relations and of the criteria for the legitimisation of the acquisition of the value added through the work of others, operates to keep the subject of labour within the competence reserved to the State legislator.[12] Nevertheless, in the global market 'keeping the national protective rules stationary without controlling the rules of running such a market means risking self-destruction: that is to say it can render invalid the competitiveness of the economic system and cause the progressive impoverishment of entire national collectives'.[13]

The uncertain results of the transition process from an economy regulated by national protagonists to a system of production and circulation of wealth governed by supra-national regulation contributes to nurturing the emergence of informal practices and *sui generis* of using the labour of others, so much so that a thin correlation is made between the globalisation of economies and the progressive 'informalisation of employment relations'. The convergence in the practice of the use of labour, according to some authors,[14] leading to the loosening of dependent work protection in response to market pressures appears therefore to be more the fruit of competition between different national labour laws than the result of a conscious process

9. Directive n. 91/383/CEE.
10. See, among others, M. Jeffery *The Commission Proposals on 'Atypical Work': Back to the Drawing-Board... Again, in Industrial Law Journal*, 1995, 296.
11. See Court of Justice, causa C-55/96, Job Centre.
12. See T. Treu (1997), *Politiche del lavoro e strumenti di promozione dell'occupazione: il caso italiano in una prospettiva europea, in M. Biagi (a cura di), Mercati e rapporti di lavoro. Commentario alla legge 24 giugno 1997 n. 196, Giuffrè, Milano, 3 e ss. (e ora in Scritti in onore di Giuseppe Federico Mancini*, Giuffrè, Milano, vol. I, 597 e ss.).
13. See T. Treu (1994), *L'internazionalizzazione dei mercati: problemi di diritto del lavoro e metodo comparato*, in Studi in onore di R. Sacco, Giuffrè, Milano, vol. I, 1117 e ss.
14. D. J. B. Mitchell (1999), *E' in atto un processo di convergenza?*, General Report on Forum 5 of the Bologna Meeting of the IIRA, September 1998, in *Dir. Rel. Ind.*, 1999/1, forthcoming.

of harmonisation guided by supra-national protagonists and finalised to conciliate competitiveness with social justice.[15] The better the resistance to favour the evolution of economic–productive relations, the more risk there is of destructuring employment relations.[16]

The above should help understand that the regulation of employment relations is not responding exclusively to a *ratio* of pure protection of the weaker party as a result of the disorder and failures of the free market in the process of industrialisation. Presented in terms of facing off the advantages of the free market and the constraints of law, the issue of the deregulation of employment relations is not only badly posed and misleading but also historically incorrect. Firstly, because the 'advantages' of the free market versus the effect of public intervention are not at all clear. No particular proof exists showing that the deregulation of employment relations can, *per se*, bring about a reduction in unemployment or an increase in competitiveness in enterprises; on the contrary, it seems well illustrated that an excessive precariousness in employment relations, besides destroying stable work posts, ends up in the long run proving itself to be counter-productive for the entire production system, leaving the enterprises without a qualified and reliable work-force. From this perspective of more importance are the structural policies of employment; industrial, financial and public spending management policies; the rules that discipline international commerce or the access to the system of credit and to the capital market or, the local policies of support of the productive and social tissue, well represented in our country by the experience of the 'territorial pacts' and by 'area contracts'.

In Italy the deregulation of employment relations has not been guided by the legislator but accomplished in an underground way, thereby showing the uselessness of the imperative rule of law to govern. This explains the elevated levels of illegal work and the conspicuous move away from dependent work towards self-employment and irregular forms of work. Faced with the complex transformation of the economic, political and social reality of our country, the question, cyclically posed, is no longer whether or not the juridical–institutional balances and the normative order of Italian labour law have, by now, reached the fatal level of safety or saturation beyond which it is no longer possible to proceed.[17] Unless one is prepared to admit – or concede, at least temporarily – a progressive reversal of the levels of dependent work protection, the real problem would appear to be another, i.e. how to establish a limit, and especially, through which instruments the State (legislator, magistrate, public administration) can today push on towards the rightful and irreversible recovery of underground and atypical work, so as to then avoid running the risk of breaking the fragile balances upon which we base the entire socio-economic, and thus contributing to further marginalising large strata of the productive forces of the country. The answer to this question is certainly not an easy one and is, to the contrary, made particularly complex by the relentless rules of competition at, by this stage, the supra-national scale, that gradually render ever more 'eccentric' the role of the State, given the decisive and tumultuous process of internationalisation of the economy, of the transformation of the productive process and of the distribution of the

---

15. This was the subject of the 11th International Congress of IIRA, Bologna 22–26 September 1998.
16. See: S. Simitis (1997), *Il diritto del lavoro ha ancora un futuro?*, op cit., where he speaks about a process of *déconstruction du droit de travail.*
17. It is the question that posed by G. Giugni (1982), *Il diritto del lavoro negli anni '80*, in *Giornale Dir. Lav. Rel. Ind.*, 375, as regard the 'labour law of the crisis' of the eighties.

wealth. The crisis of legality that increasingly characterises the modern social State cannot, in fact, be explained merely on the basis of a diffused and vague wish to get away from the laws of the State considered 'inauspicious, confusing and invasive'. More pervasive than the of rejection of the progressive penetration of the State apparatus into civil society is the ineffectiveness of 'State sovereignty over the rules that govern the mechanisms of production and the transfer of wealth (to affect) indirectly but in a decisive way the discipline of work'.[18]

There is truth in the theory formulated at the beginning of the century by Jean Cruet, according to whom 'the law does not dominate society but if anything it expresses it'.[19] This does not, however, change the fact that labour law emerges and develops in contradiction to this assumption as a form of social reform that as such imposes an undeniable effort – a tension – to change society. From this point of view, the increasing social complexity and the changes underway in the economic and productive structures cannot do other than lead to a broadening of these same efforts of public intervention, both in the traditional area of the distribution of wealth and in the new one of support for employment and for the productive system.[20] Consequently, the scales are weighted in favour of those who recognise that labour law develops inside a market economy, that the law is more than *business efficiency*, and therefore, assign to the process of employment relations regulation the necessary means to adapt the imperative of efficiency to social justice and individual freedom.[21]

Against this background, we will go on to develop the theses on the basis of two concrete and complementary developments: (a) the introduction of private mediators in the work market and the recent legalisation of temporary work through an agency, and (b) the proposals of reform of Italian labour law in search of new answers for the 21st century. Before developing this analysis, a brief synthesis of the present evolution of Italian labour law follows.

DEREGULATION AND LABOUR LAW IN ITALY: THE NEW LEGAL FRAMEWORK

After a long period of relative stability, characterised by a progressive expansion of the statutes governing dependent work and the consequent move away from the accepted legal framework of labour, Italian employment law has recently gone through a great metamorphosis (see Biagi, 1998, Id., 1997).

---

18. See T. Treu (1994), *L'internazionalizzazione dei mercati: problemi di diritto del lavoro e metodo comparato*, cit., 1122.
19. J. Cruet, *La vie du droit et l'impuissance des lois*, Flammarion, Paris, 1908, 3 (as cited by A. Supiot, *Du bon usage des lois en maitière d'emploi*, cit., 336), according to whom, it would be interesting to verify the validity of this theory over the Century, there seems to be no doubt about his validity in the subject of labour policy: 'en ce domaine, le constat de l'impuissance des lois est tombé un jour de la bouche même du Monarque: 'Contre le chomage, on a tout essayé ...' en vain! La cause dès lors semble entendue et le consensus établi: on ne crée pas d'emploi par décret; les lois ne pouvent rien à l'empli, qui procède en dernière instance d'un certain état de l'économie. Le droit de l'emploi ne pourrait guère que mettre en oeuvre les dures lois de l'économie, leur donner un visage humain pour en assurer mieux l'inexorable application'.
20. T. Treu (1990), voce *Diritto del lavoro*, Digesto, Utet, Torino, IV ed., 1990, estratto, 50.
21. L. Mengoni, in G. Giugni, L. Mengoni, B. Veneziani, *Tre commenti alla Critique du droit du travail di Supiot.*, in *Giornale Dir. Lav. Rel. Ind.*, 1995, 477.

Act no. 196/1997 (the so-called 'Treu Package') and the resulting regulations to implement the act have extended and strengthened the range of atypical forms of work: fixed-term contract, part-time work, temporary work through an agency (dispatching work), apprenticeship, training contract, work experiences, job internships (borse lavoro) and public works jobs (lavori di pubblica utilità). Act no. 59/1997 (the so-called 'Bassanini Law') and the subsequent Legislative Decree no. 469/1997 have thoroughly redesigned the boundaries between the public and private areas in labour market management and employment services, thus eliminating the rigidity and inefficiency of the public monopoly of placement. Already well implemented or at least on the way to being completely defined are measures to support research and technological innovations, financing of entrepreneurial development in depressed areas or in areas of urban decay, the reorganisation of incentives for hiring and geographical mobility, improving infrastructures through qualified public investment, the reorganisation of the professional training system and, in particular, of continued training as an instrument to raise employability and the quality of the worker pool. Ready for definitive take-off are new instruments of huge importance for local development such as the so-called 'area contracts' (*contratti d'area*) and 'territorial pacts' (*patti territoriali*), and only now are we beginning to appreciate the enormous impact and the future development of a previous reform: the so-called privatisation of public employment initiated by the Legislative Decree no. 29/1993 and implemented through the Legislative Decree no. 369/1997 and the Legislative Decree no. 80/1998 (on this point see, in general, Treu, 1998).

Concerning deregulation of individual labour relations, three main points should be emphasised:

1. The growth of the independent contract, self-employment subcontracting, insourcing and outsourcing;
2. Frequent derogation from legal norms set by protective labour legislation through the use of collective bargaining agreements; and
3. The flexibilisation of working-hours regulations.

With regard to the first point, the most impressive form of indirect deregulation is the explosion in the use/abuse of contractual schemes that, from a formal point of view, are not subordinate, but that guarantee the use of union workers without applying labour regulations. We call this form of work *quasi-subordinate* or *co-ordinate* and it represents a third category. This third legal scheme of private autonomy can easily escape the reach of employment law, and it is not easy for the courts to requalify this form of work as subordinate employment. We presently have around two million workers engaged under this contractual scheme that bypass legal and collective rules. Other ways to contravene labour law include commercial contracts such as fictitious trainer contracts, franchising, sub-contracting and, in general, all kinds of out- and insourcing. This is the way to side step the rules on dismissal.

In order to control the undermining of labour law, there are more and more cases in which the legislation allows derogations from legal norms set by protective labour legislation through the use of collective bargaining agreements. This is particularly true in the use of atypical forms of contract. From a legal point of view fixed-term contracts, temporary employment through an agency and part-time work are still considered exceptions to the rule of the open-ended and full-time contract. However, collective bargaining has the power to enlarge the use of all kinds of atypical forms of contracts and thus to get around dismissal law. In this context, it is relevant to look at the procedure adopted to request a derogation from legal norms set up by protective labour legislation:

(a) first of all, in addition to the original justifications established by the legislator, the collective agreement can identify additional circumstances that allow for an atypical contract;
(b) in doing so, the collective agreement must establish the maximum percentage of fixed-terms contracts, temporary employment through an agency, part-time contracts, apprenticeships and so on allowed in any undertaking;
(c) this is only possible in the case of a collective agreement signed by a representative trade union.

Through collective bargaining it has even been possible to introduce new legal schemes never experimented with previously like job-sharing and labour-on-call. Quite recently, with a simple circular, the Minister of Labour accepted job-sharing or labour-on-call especially when they are allowed by collective bargaining. So, through collective bargaining it has been possible to experiment with small doses of regulated flexibility in order to remove the principal obstacles in the functioning of the regular work market and develop a favourable climate for the creation of new employment.

From this perspective – creation of new employment – the debate is now concentrated on flexibilisation and reduction of working time. Working time regulations in Italy have been based for a long time on a 1923 royal decree limiting working hours to 8 h *per* day and 48 h *per* week. However, further legislation is about to be enacted to implant the EU regulations in this field. It should be emphasised, first of all, that this legislation has never been revised because the social partners have always preferred to regulate working time by means of collective bargaining in order to preserve their bargaining autonomy. Recently, Act 196/1997 introduced new rules. It fixed normal working time at 40 h a week and allowed for national collective agreements to provide for shorter hours and for normal working time to be the average length of work time over a period not exceeding one year. Social partners are requested by this act to negotiate a new draft legislation aimed at transposing the provisions of the EU directive on working time. This new legislation confirms the big role of collective bargaining in introducing further and more convincing regulations.

The debate on the 35-h-week has been of increasing importance recently. Following the French model, a proposal to reduce the work week to 35 h is presently under discussion in the Parliament. The Government is proposing a legislative measure largely based upon contractual agreements. The most recent proposal is to provide some forms of incentives to reduce weekly working time and sanctions on the use of over-time. The 35 h legal working time should be enacted by the next century after a transition phase based on experimental contractual agreements. Small firms could be excluded from the 35 h regime. The aim is only to reduce working time, not to re-organise at plant level.

These and other interventions clearly indicate that labour law, originally intended as a unilateral method of protection established to regulate a unique model of dependent work (i.e. the typical full-time contract for an indefinite period), is today passed over not only by the Italian legislator and but by business, which for a long time has experimented (sometimes on the boundaries of legality) with new contractual schemes of organising work. Particularly symbolic in this respect is the case of temporary work through an agency which has for a long time been experimented with in business (see Tiraboschi, 1994), in spite of a very rigid framework binding this form of work until the recent legalisation through art. 1–11 of Act no. 196/1997 (see para. III).

The reform process does not stop here. The transition from a monolithic and rigid labour law (*il diritto del lavoro*) to more comprehensive and dynamic labour laws – now defined and declined in the plural (*il diritto dei lavori*) – which take into consideration the evolving society and economy, has only just begun. Phenomena noted and constantly quoted by sociologists and economists – like the globalisation of markets and technological innovation, together with the old economic diseases of growth of illegal work and the legal strategies to escape from the rules of dependent work – now impose a new projectile strength that allows a decisive updating of Italian employment law. Paradoxically, the same statistical evidence about atypical and irregular work[22] shows that it is not a lack of work but rather a lack of regulations and contractual schemes able to extract the work from illegality and divide it equally among all those involved in the labour market. In particular, the conceptual distinction between contract of service and contract for services is more and more inadequate in regulating the evolution of the Italian labour market. The jobs of the future require simple and flexible rules capable of dealing with uncertainties during the process of qualification which is a traditional source of contention.

A typical characteristic of the Italian labour market is that the compression of numerous forms of work into the rigid scheme of contract of service and contract for services pushes all the atypical forms of work into a large grey area, very close to illegal work, not to mention the desire to circumvent labour regulations and the need for such forms of work for the maintenance of the business or in the interest of the workers. In order to progress from this problematic and fragmented framework it is necessary to experiment with new ways of making labour law such as the recent circular no. 43/1998 from the Minister of Labour which recognised the legitimacy of a contractual scheme such as *job-sharing*, up until then never experimented with for fear of possible controversies regarding the exact qualification of this form of working relationship (remember that part-time is still forbidden under Italian labour law). The circular demonstrated that it is not necessary to wait for Parliament to act to regulate new work schemes, but that in some cases, administrative intervention clarifying the limits and the fundamental rules of the contract is sufficient.

This does not mean removing the fundamental protection of labour law. But experimentation with 'regulated flexibility' (*flessibilità normata*) in small doses can contribute to the removal of some of the obstacles hindering the regular work market, while offering a favourable climate for the creation of *new* employment and for the channelling of supply and demand which, today, is dispersed and fragmented due to a lack of adequate information and instruments to evaluate the work-force (see Treu, 1997). From this perspective, the recent legalisation of temporary work through an agency and the end of the State's monopoly of placement are symbolic for the future development of Italian labour law and, because particularly representative of the Italian climate, merit a closer look.

22. In this context suffice it to say that the Italian Institute for Statistics (ISTA) has recently shown that in Italy there are approximately 5 million irregular workers engaged in the underground economy corresponding to about 23 percent of the Italian workforce.

THE ABOLISHMENT OF THE STATE'S MONOPOLY IN EMPLOYMENT SERVICES AND THE LEGALISATION OF TEMPORARY WORK THROUGH AN AGENCY IN ITALY, BETWEEN EXPERIMENTATION AND SOCIAL CONCERTATION

It should be pointed out at the outset that the recent legalisation of temporary work through an agency cannot simply be interpreted as either a process of deregulation of the Italian labour market or as a new attitude of the Italian Government faced with a drastic reduction in labour standards. Taking into consideration the ineffectiveness of regulation on the public employment service and the conspicuous presence on the Italian labour market of a sprawling illegal network made up of private agencies and co-operatives acting as intermediaries, Act no. 196/1997 represents an attempt to re-regulate a sector which has remained for too long outside the law (Tiraboschi, 1997). The introduction of temporary work through an agency into our legal system represents an opportunity to clarify once and for all the difference between the illegitimate intermediary in the hiring of labour (still illegal under article 1, Act. no. 1369/1960) and legitimate intermediary justified by recent movements in the labour market and in the organisation of work. The objective of the Italian Government is to reshape some of the guidelines of labour law to make them compatible with the ever-increasing economic constraints.

The procedural technique adopted by the Italian legislator is noteworthy. Act no. 196/1997 reflects the previous agreement between the Government and the social parties (see Employment Pact of 24 September 1996 and prior to that Agreement on the cost of labour of 23 July 1993). The *legalisation* process follows a period of indispensable social *legitimisation.* In fact, as demonstrated by comparable experience, only social legitimisation can grant a stable juridical framework and real possibilities for future development in this area (compare, for example, the French case with the German one).

Naturally, the will to reach social consensus has given way to some (perhaps excessive) compromises and limitations. But it should be pointed out that this act is for the most part experimental: after two years of enforcement, article 11 provides for a meeting between the Government and the social parties in order to introduce, if necessary, corrections and revisions. In any case, the more contested points are left to the process of collective bargaining. This will involve the social parties that have the power to implement and effect changes in the labour regulations, especially to determine when and where temporary workers can be employed and what percentage they represent of the total number of workers of the user employer.

1. Agencies Authorised to Supply Temporary Labour Services

Article 2 of the Act lays down very strictly who is authorised to supply temporary agency labour. As in France, Germany and other European countries the supply of labour cannot be performed freely by anyone who wishes to engage in this area, but is permitted only to an 'agency' specifically authorised by the Ministry of Labour to do so. It is important to point out that the activity of supplying labour can be performed only by 'legal persons' and not by individuals. These legal persons must be registered as a company on a special list created by the Ministry of Labour.

Registration as an agency is subject to evidence that the applicant has met specific requirements:

- the legal form must be that of an enterprise/undertaking (the notion of enterprise/ undertaking includes co-operatives, but additional requirements make it very difficult to use a co-operative in labour supply. See below);
- the name of the enterprise must include the words 'enterprise for the supply of temporary labour';
- provide capital of not less than 1 billion Italian lire and for the first two years of activity a guaranteed deposit of 700 million Italian lire; from the third year, in place of the deposit a bank or insurance guarantee for not less than 5 percent of the turnover in the previous year, net of the value added tax and in any case not less that 700 million Italian lire;
- presence of the registered office or branch within the territory of the Italian State;
- identification of the activity of supply of temporary workers as the sole business on the hypothesis that 'mixed' enterprises (supply and placement of workers) can be less easily controlled and more subject to abuses and potential fraud;
- availability of offices and professional skills appropriate for performance of activity of supply of labour;
- guarantee that the service is available throughout the national territory and in not less than four Regions.

Special provisions pertain to the personal qualifications of directors, general managers and managers:

- absence of criminal convictions: for crimes against the state, crimes against the public trust or against the public economy, for the crime of association of a mafia-like character (under article 416-bis of the Penal Code) or of unpremeditated crimes carrying a penalty of imprisonment for not less than three years for crimes or misdemeanours under laws aimed at the prevention of accidents at work or under laws on labour or social security;
- not subject to preventive measures: special surveillance by the police, interdiction to reside in one or more municipalities other than that of legal or habitual residence as provided for under Italian law.

Authorisation to supply temporary agency labour may also be granted to a workers' co-operative which, in addition to meeting the conditions required for other companies, must have at least fifty members and, among these, as financing member, a fund for the development of co-operative; and it must employ non-partner-employees for a number of days not exceeding one third of the days of work performed by the co-operative as a whole. In this case, however, not the worker-partners but *only* the workers employed by the co-operative can be supplied by the co-operative as a temporary labour. This provision is highly controversial since it seems to be in opposition to the general principle governing workers' co-operatives under which priority and preference in job opportunities are given to partners, not to non-partners. Authorisation may also be issued to companies directly or indirectly controlled by the State with the aim of promoting and providing incentives for employment.

2. The Contract for the Supply of Temporary Workers

The contract for the supply of temporary workers (*contratto di fornitura di lavoro temporaneo*) is a commercial contract through which an agency authorised by the Minister of Labour supplies one or more workers employed by the agency for either a specific mission or for an indefinite period to be at the disposition of a firm – or a public administration – who benefits from these workers 'in order to satisfy the need for temporary work' (art. 1). This contract is the pivotal element on which the entire trilateral legal scheme rests in the sense that it connects the three parties involved, directly by identifying the legal relations between the agency and the user, and indirectly by specifying the kind of work, the duration, the remuneration and so on. This explains why, although it is a normal commercial contract, the Italian legislation has put a lot of emphasis on its regulation. The protection of the worker derives from the regulations which govern the contract, and especially from the division of the rights, the powers, the obligations and the responsibilities between the agency and the user.

As a general rule, the supply of temporary workers is still forbidden:

- for jobs of 'low professional content' identified as such by the national collective agreement of the industry to which the client organisation belongs, signed by the 'comparatively representative' trade union organisations;
- to replace workers exercising the right to strike;
- in production units in which, during the previous twelve months, there have been collective dismissals involving workers assigned to the tasks to which the temporary labour refers, except in the event that it is to replace absent workers with the right to retain their job;
- in production units in which there is a suspension of relations or a reduction in hours with the right to 'wage integration' (a kind of unemployment pay) involving workers employed on the tasks for which the supply of temporary services is requested;
- to client organisations that do not demonstrate to the Provincial Labour Office that they have carried out the risk assessment required by Italian law;
- for work that requires special medical surveillance and for particularly hazardous work identified by decree of the Minister of Labour and Social Security and issued within sixty days of the present Act taking effect;
- in agriculture and construction temporary work supply contracts can only at the present time be introduced on an experimental basis following an agreement on the areas and models of experimentation between the employers' organisations and the trade unions 'comparatively representative' at the national level.

The law (article 1) provides that such a contract can be made:

(1) 'in cases of replacement of absent workers'. In comparison to Act no. 230/1962 on fixed-term contracts, this is a possibility of using temporary work through an agency to substitute for absent employees, including those who do not have the right to maintain their job. Under Act no. 230/1962, the use of temporary work in the form of fixed-term contracts was allowed only in order to substitute for workers with the right to maintain their job. If the collective agreement, legitimised by Act no. 56/1987, allows for the possibility to establish fixed-term contracts to substitute for those absent without the right to maintain their job, the type of contract chosen by the user can depend solely on financial considerations. The business must decide between the inferior cost of fixed-term contracts and the relevant advantages gained through agency employment in terms of the quality of service of highly skilled and well-trained workers.

(2) 'in cases of a temporary need in an area requiring qualifications not covered by the firm's ordinary production organisation'. This offers an exception to Act 1369 of 23 October 1960 outlawing intermediaries in the hiring of labour and banning labour-only sub-contracting. Therefore, these cases must be interpreted in a restrictive sense. In particular, this second case does not seem to allow for the use of temporary work through an agency in order to satisfy a boom in production which is not manageable using the ordinary production organisation. In other words, the concept of a 'need in qualifications not covered by the firm's ordinary production organisation' must be expressed in an objective sense rather than referring to the skills and specialisations present in the firm. This interpretation conforms with the philosophy behind the Act: temporary work through an agency should not be considered an *alternative* to regular employment, but constitutes a *complementary* instrument. For these reasons one cannot agree with authors who consider that the new norm allows in principle for a company to understaff the business, filling gaps with temporary employees. The high cost of temporary work through agency renders this strategy of HRM irrational rather then illegal from a juridical point of view;

(3) 'in the case provided for in the national collective agreement negotiated for the industry to which the client organisation belongs and signed by the comparatively representative trade unions'. Attention should be paid to the new formula 'comparatively representative unions' which reflects the increasing problem of a number of unions co-existing in the same industry, equally claiming to represent employees. This formula should empower the Government and local authorities to select those unions which, in the context of a specific sector/branch, are more representative than others, in comparative terms representing (not necessarily organising) more workers than others. It is unlikely that this legal solution will be able by itself to solve the problem of union representation. One should add that it is necessary to develop appropriate legal mechanisms to test in more effective ways the ability of trade union organisations to represent workers not affiliated with them as well.

The contract for the supply of temporary workers must be in written form, the worker who provides his/her work to the client organisation is deemed to have been employed by the latter under an open-ended employment contract. Any clause intended to limit, even indirectly, the right of the client organisation to employ the worker at the end of the contract for temporary work is null and void. Further, a copy of the contract for temporary workers must be sent by the supplying agency to the Provincial Labour Office responsible for the territory within ten days of its signing.

3. The Contract Between the Worker and the Agency

The temporary agency employment contract is the contract by which the temporary employment agency employs the worker. The worker may be employed under a fixed-term contract, i.e. for a specified time corresponding to the duration of the work for the client organisation. The worker may also, at the discretion of the temporary work agency, be employed on the basis of an open-ended contract, i.e. for an indeterminate time. Once employed, the temporary worker is required to carry out his/her activities in the interest and under the direction and control of the client organisation. The exercise of disciplinary power still belongs to the agency, on the assumption that the employment relationship is established between the agency and the worker. Nevertheless, Act 196/1997 provides that the client/user company shall report to the agency on possible violation of work duties by the worker for possible disciplinary action. Commentators have underlined that this solution seems to be rather complicated, a consequence of the 'triangular' arrangement characteristic of the temporary agency work.

In the case of employment for an indeterminate period, the worker remains at the disposal of the agency even in periods when he/she is not working for a client organisation. In this case, the contract between the employee and the agency shall make provisions for an income guarantee for periods in which no work is performed ('availability bonus'). As far as the application of statutory or collectively agreed employment protection standards is concerned, the temporary work agency workers are not considered part of the workforce of the client/user firm, with the exception of health and safety provisions. The temporary work contract must be in written form and a copy must be given to the worker within five days of the start of activity with the client organisation. In absence of a written contract or indication of the start and finish of the job at the client organisation, the contract for temporary employment converts into a contract for employment binding the agency for an open-ended period. However, the stated period of initial assignment may be extended, with the consent of the worker and in writing, in those cases and for the duration provided for in the national collective agreements for the category.

If the work continues beyond the specified time, the worker is deemed to have been employed in an open-ended relationship by the client organisation after the expiration of the specified time of temporary services. Thus, if the temporary work continues beyond the term initially agreed upon or subsequently extended, the worker has the right to an increase of 20% in daily pay for each day of continuation of the relationship for ten days. This increase is chargeable to the agency if the continuation of the work has been agreed upon.

Temporary workers must be employed with pay and other terms and conditions of employment equal to those to which employees at the same level of the client organisation are entitled. The principle of parity of treatment between permanent and temporary workers is found in the legislation of many European countries. However, the collective agreement of the industry to which the client organisation belongs can identify modalities and criteria for determination and payment of wages and salaries in relation to the results achieved in implementing programs agreed upon between the parties or linked with the economic results of the organisation.

4. The Legal Statute of Temporary Workers

The great difficulties of providing effective protection of the individual and the collective rights of groups involved in the supply of temporary work have consistently paralysed the process of legalising this option. These stem not from the temporary and intermittent type of work in a user company, but from the structural and programmatic separation between the (holder of the) *contract* and the (real user of the) *working relationship.* In fact, for the temporary worker, an employment contract that involves two potential employers (the agency and the final employer), can mean a contract with 'no stated effective employer' (Siau, 1996, p. 16) or, in any case, with no visible control over the power and responsibilities connected to the use of a dependent work force.

A particularly indicative example can be taken from the British experience. The deep uncertainties shown by the case law with regard to the contract between the intermittent worker and the temporary work agency, together with the difficulty of integrating the requisites of continued seniority required by British legislation, have made labour law to protect dependent employment relationships substantially irrelevant for the majority of this kind of worker. There is a real danger that in this and other cases the worker is demoted 'from subject of rights to transitory object' (Ghezzi, 1995, p. 229).

To face up to the danger of masking the real relationships of production and, consequently, that of a substantial undermining of workers' rights, the legislator has introduced a series of corrections to guarantee, although only in an indirect way, the rights of temporary workers: rigorous selection of those qualified for the supply of temporary work (art. 2); limitation of the cases of a legitimate appeal to the supply of temporary work and reference, for the non-disciplined cases, to the provisions of Act no. 1369/1960 that today still represent the general rule with respect to the qualification of the interposing phenomena (art. 1, 10); clear and unequivocal division of the responsibilities and obligations of the assignor and the assignee with regard to the protection of the health and safety of temporary workers (art. 6, 1), to social security benefits and contributive and welfare services (art. 9, 1), and to the transfer to the worker of wages (art. 6, 3), to the damages caused to third parties by temporary workers during their mission (art. 6, 7), to accident and professional diseases insurance (art. 9, 2), etc.

Coupled with these 'indirect' guarantees of protection of temporary workers' rights – purely instrumental, most of the time, to safeguard steady work and full-time employment – is Act no. 196/1997 with some important provisions for 'direct' protection of individual and collective temporary worker's rights which can be considered a sort of real 'statute' of temporary workers. The 'duplicity' – factual, if not juridical because of the negotiated agreement – of employers with whom the worker has to interact does not allow for an effective assimilation of the temporary work supplier's rights with those of the workers already employed, whether under standard or atypical contracts. Instead, precise specifications (if possible through the stipulation of a collective agreement for temporary work agencies' employees, cf. art. 11, 5) regarding the active and passive legal position of the worker, both in the supplier agency and the user enterprise, is required.

A fundamental frame of reference in adjusting the general regulations to the particularities of this situation should be based on the principle of equal treatment, or of not distinguishing between permanent workers of the user enterprise and temporary work suppliers. In the relationship between the temporary work agency and the user enterprise, the principle of equal treatment should modify the character of manpower supply as mere speculation on other people's work (art. 3, Act no. 1365/1960), and with regard to the individual worker's legal position, guarantee a good social integration of the worker into the collective of the user enterprise. Weighted according to collective relationships, the principle of equal treatment allows for the expression of the intermittent work force's concerns that coincide with those, usually prevalent in union dynamics, of the permanent personnel either of the temporary work agency or of the user enterprise, avoiding both the dangerous phenomenon of social *dumping* and a polarisation of interests between different groups of workers present in a given production context.

For these reasons, in spite of the rubric of article 4 that refers to the economic conditions of the temporary worker, it seems reasonable to assume by equal treatment not only that which is economic but also normative. In this sense the social parties have expressed themselves in the 1993 and 1996 Agreements which provide temporary workers, as evidenced by the same accompanying report of Bill no. 1918/1996, with 'conditions of full parity with the employees of the user company'. Article 4, para. 2 states, however, that the worker temporarily assigned to a user enterprise must be 'paid out a wage not inferior to the one the employees at the same level of the user enterprise are entitled to receive', without any specific referral to remuneration, while article 1, paragraph 5, lett. (c) and article 3, paragraph 3, lett. (f) require that both the supply contract and in the temporary work contract specify the place, the working hours, 'and the economic and normative remuneration of the working services'.

Practically speaking, several problems emerge, especially with reference to inconsistent arrangements between the supplier and the user. More problematic is establishing wage levels for tasks and qualifications that, according to the law that legitimises the resort to temporary labour, presumably do not normally exist in the enterprise.

In case of open-ended hiring, the temporary work contract has to provide for a monthly indemnity of 'availability' divisible into hourly shares, and it will have to be paid by the same supplier enterprise during the periods the worker is waiting for assignment (art. 4, 3). The indemnity should conform with the amount agreed upon by the collective agreement and should not be inferior to the minimum fixed by Decree of the Ministry of Labour and Social Security; in the case of part-time work, the amount is proportionally reduced. It is important to note that the indemnity of availability is characterised as a type of minimal remuneration due to the worker hired with an open-ended contract. If, as is the case with short periods of assignment, the remuneration received for the work effectively carried out in the user enterprise does not reach the indemnity level, the supplier enterprise is obliged to increase the remuneration until it equals the indemnity of availability.

Special consideration should be given to the provision in article 3, paragraph 4 according to which the worker '*has the right to supply his work for the whole period of assignment*, except in the case of not passing the trial period or the advent of a just cause for withdrawal from the contract'. In fact, in one way, the right to supply the work for the entire period of the mission represents a guarantee with respect to possible discriminative practices against the worker, although it is easy to imagine how in practice the effectiveness of this provision is greatly weakened because of the relationship of power and economic interest that exists between worker and agency, on the one hand, and between the agency and the user enterprise, on the other.

For these reasons it is not correct to state that article 3, paragraph 4 regulates only the withdrawal for just cause from the contract for fixed-term temporary work, and refers to the general legislation on dismissals in the case of an open-ended temporary work contract. Just cause for withdrawal, dealt with in article 3, paragraph 4, involves malfunctions which affect the contract for the supply of temporary work and therefore, primarily, the relationship between the supplier and the user enterprise. Paradoxically, in the contrary case, the temporary worker employed under an open-ended contract would be entitled to complete his mission even in the presence of a justified reason (subjective or objective) for dismissal, although a just cause for withdrawal from the employment contract is not mandatory. Similarly, the temporary worker, even if hired with an open-ended contract, should be allowed to withdraw freely from the employment relationship by giving his/her resignation during the trial period, even though he/she has received the indemnity of availability in the waiting period before assignment.

The advent of a cause for the legitimate cancellation of a contract for the supply of temporary work will obviously also have effect on the temporary work contract, in the sense that the fortunes of the employment contract are subordinate to those of the contract which join the temporary work agency and the user enterprise. Such a case will imply, as a consequence, the cancellation of the fixed-term temporary work contract that, by definition, is effective for the length of time of the work performed for the user enterprise. There are, however, greater problems concerning the future of the open-ended temporary work contract, even if in this case strong doubts as to the logic and systematic nature can be raised concerning the application of the general legislation of Act no. 604/1966 on the temporary work contract and the subsequent effects.

This subject deserves attentive analysis (also with reference to problems connected with disciplinary action) that cannot be developed during a first consideration of articles 1–11 of Act no. 196/1997. In the following discussion, it should be remembered that the general legislation concerning dismissals is structurally unrelated to the open-ended temporary work contract, on the one hand because it deals with a form of negotiation not related to article 2094 of the Civil Code and, on the other hand, because the withdrawal from the contract with notice is hardly compatible with the assignment period of the worker to the user enterprise.

The question deserves more attentive consideration because the position mentioned above in purely problematic terms is a minority position. With respect to the open-ended temporary work contract, only two premises for cancellation are admissible, both requiring a just cause for withdrawal from the employment contract: the mission interruption for a just cause for withdrawal from the supply contract that reflects (though not automatically, as in the fixed-term employment contract) its effects on the temporary work contract, on one hand, and the groundless refusal of a worker in availability to accept the execution of a mission, on the other. If these considerations prove to be of merit, one can exclude the existence of another possibility for the withdrawal from the temporary work contract. It is not clear, however, what interest a temporary work agency could have in paying a fixed-term worker 'in availability' who, as in this last case, once having accepted the mission, can then freely determine the cessation of the contractual obligation through simple notice.

In this matter, the collective agreement for employees of the temporary work agency (cf. article 11, para. 5) will both regulate the procedures for withdrawal with notice during the periods of availability of the worker hired with an open-ended contract prior to the assignment of a certain mission, and categorise the causes of withdrawal considered justified for the temporary worker's periods of assignment, irrespective of the type of contract under which he was hired. This is the only way, at least in order not to completely ignore the interests of the temporary work agencies (already reasonably limited), to draw up open-ended temporary employment contracts. Thinking differently, the circumvention of the general legislation on dismissals will flow *de facto* from the economic choices made by the supplier enterprises that will probably limit themselves to concluding fixed-term contracts with temporary workers, thus basically excluding the possibility that these workers benefit from a minimum income between one mission and another (this has so far come up in Germany where in contravention to the obligation to hire the temporary worker with an open-ended contract, practice shows a net predominance of precarious and temporary contractual relations).

Aimed at limiting, if not completely excluding, the undeniable risks of 'precariousness' inherent in the situation of the temporary worker is article 5 of Act no. 196/1997 on professional training of temporary workers, in harmony with both the 1996 Agreement for work and the general efforts at reorganising professional training outlined by article 17 of the same Act. Article 5 of the act sets up a Fund aimed at financing the temporary worker's professional training and sustained by the supplier enterprises' payment of a contribution equal to 5% of the remuneration paid to such workers. If states in the collective agreements applicable to the supplier enterprises, the Fund can, moreover, assign resources to support workers' incomes 'in periods of work shortage' (art. 5, para. 4). The implementation of this provision is subject to the issuing of a decree within sixty days from the date when the law goes into force. At this time it can only be assumed that training will occur in the periods which elapse between the several work assignments (see Vittore and Landi, 1997).

With specific reference to professional training as an 'antidote' to precariousness in employment relations, one can only puzzle over the exclusion of workers with limited professional qualifications from the field of application of the act. It is surely paradoxical that these workers in particular – already excluded from the ordinary labour market and, therefore, relegated to the hidden one – will not be able to benefit from those unique professional training initiatives that could contribute to a real elevation out of their precarious *status* (Veneziani, 1993, Treu, 1995). Article 5 is perplexing from the user enterprises' point of view as well. Within the general context of articles 1–11 of Act no. 196/1997, Art. 5 does not in fact guarantee the temporary work agencies any competitive advantage based on the 'quality' of their human resources which time and time again are put at the disposal of the user enterprises. In fact, temporary workers' training, as it is organised, presents itself as a purely coercive measure that does not fulfil a corresponding interest of the temporary work agency to raise the professional level and specialisation of its own employees. It must not be forgotten that all those clauses were intended to limit, even indirectly, the ability of the user enterprise to hire the worker at the end of contract for the supply of temporary work (art. 1, para. 6 and art. 3, para. 6). Even if this provision is justified with respect to temporary employment contracts for a specified period, it is unreasonable if applied to temporary employment contracts for an indefinite period. Paradoxically, a provision conceived in the interest of temporary workers ends up being turned against them since it discourages the establishment of stable relations between user company and workers. A comparison can be made with Spain and Japan. Spanish and Japanese legislation consent indifferently to supplier enterprises establishing fixed-term or open-ended employment relationships with their own temporary workers. In practice, while the Spanish temporary work agencies have immediately tended towards fixed-term contracts, Japanese agencies, putting more stress on training and on investment in human resources, do not hesitate, on the contrary, to hire the huge majority of temporary workers (more than 80%) for an indefinite period (cf. Tiraboschi, 1995). It is easy to predict that, since provisions to sustain employment for an indefinite period are missing, Italian agencies will orient themselves, as the Spanish do, towards the activation of precarious contracts.

If this is to be the orientation of the Italian supplier enterprises, it will be particularly difficult to assign to the temporary worker professional training with a connection between one assignment and another. The lack of juridical stability in employment relations with the temporary work agency will probably make the training process of the work force casual and irregular, both intricate and fragmentary. An analysis of the temporary workers' union rights reveals a noted distinction between the relations in a temporary work agency and those between temporary worker and user enterprise. As far as the forms of representation of temporary workers within the temporary work agency are concerned, there are few regulations which establish *ad hoc* rules or provide for an adaptation of the general rules to the peculiarities of this case. With the result – largely taken for granted – that this primary channel of representation for temporary workers is completely hypothetical and secondary. The formulation adopted by the Italian legislator on this point is quite limiting: 'to the user enterprises' employees have to apply the union rights stated by Act no. 300, 20 May 1970 and following modifications' (art. 7, para. 1). Not only is any co-ordination missing between the forms of representation of the temporary work agency's permanent workers and the temporary workers (for example using a mechanism of polls division with respect to the creation of a RSA) and, within this last category, between workers hired with a fixed-term contract and workers hired with an open-ended contract, but there are also no minimal directions on how to quantify the work force that is, by definition, temporary and fluctuating. Italian regulations typically do not give any consideration to how, concretely, to reconcile the enjoyment of union rights (both active and passive) with a particular type of work and with the phenomenon, typical of the professional supply of manpower, of fragmentation and dispersion of the enterprise collective. The risk is that the important principle affirmed in article 7, para. 1 will remain a dead letter.

The problem of counting the temporary work agency's employees emerges, obviously, with regard to enforcement of the Workers' Statute. Taking into consideration the formulation of Act no. 196/1997, it is beyond dispute that the dimensional requisites of article 35 of the Statute can also be applied to temporary work agencies' employees. With reference to union rights of temporary workers assigned to a user enterprise, article 7, para. 3 of Act no. 196/1997 does not hesitate to affirm that 'the temporary worker, for the whole length of his/her contract, has the right to exercise within the user enterprise the rights to freedom and to union activity, and even to participate in the assemblies of the user enterprises' employees'. If, however, one tries to align the formal provision of the act with union practices, it clearly appears that, in this case as well, the acknowledgement of some rights to the temporary worker runs the risk of being purely theoretical.

From a comparison of the provisions concerning temporary workers' rights included in the national multi-industry Agreement of 20 December 1993 about the creation of unitary union structures, it is possible to infer that a temporary worker can rarely satisfy the requisites stated in the agreement necessary to remain in the enterprise. With particular reference to the delicate question of the right to stand as a candidate, the collective bargaining at industry level which came after the national multi-industry Agreement of 20 December 1993, even if slightly different in wording, has substantially confirmed this interpretation. In C.c.n.l., the eligibility of workers with a fixed-term contract or rather with a *non-open-ended contract*, including temporary workers, is provided for, at least theoretically. But this possibility is generally limited to the condition that, on the date of the elections, the employment contract is for a period which is not inferior to 6 months. The right to stand as a candidate is therefore closed to those workers hired with a contract for a duration inferior to 6 months, and, in another situation, no device is provided to match the temporary/precarious employment period with the three-year office as RSU member.

At the end of the non-open-ended employment contract, the appointed mandate expires automatically. However, even if one were to assert that these rules are not applicable *by analogy* to the temporary labour force, it is, in any case, true that Italian union procedures have shown a total indifference towards the mechanisms of representation of the labour force present inside the company on a merely temporary basis (cf. Tiraboschi, 1996). On this point, a restrictive interpretation prevails that will lead to the exclusion, at the root, both of the right to vote and the right to stand as a candidate to the temporary worker on the presumption that this worker has no contractual obligations with the user enterprise (some have tried to refute this position through the valorisation of the existent bargaining connection, insisting on its application on a theoretical and practical level).

And yet, despite some obvious difficulties, it does not appear that the status of the temporary worker is radically incompatible with the exercise of the right to vote. At the company level, the temporary worker must at least be recognised as having the right to participate in the elections of the representative for workers' safety since article 18 of Legislative Decree no. 626/1994 holds that 'the representative for safety is elected directly by the workers and chosen *among them*', and does not require that the worker be in a position of legal subordination to the user.

Union rights, according to article 7 of Act no. 196/1997, only attain a significant degree of efficiency if they apply to the collective interests of the stable labour force of the user enterprise. User enterprises are required by Article 7, para. 4 to communicate to the unitary union structure, or to plant-level union structures and, in their absence, to the territorial trade associations adherent to the comparatively representative national confederations, the frequency and the reasons for recourse to temporary work rather than the supply contract, as well as, every 12 months, the number and the reasons for the temporary work supply contracts, their length, the number and the qualification of the workers involved.

As already affirmed elsewhere (Tiraboschi, 1996), in order to resolve the delicate problem of representation of the temporary work-force's collective interests, while avoiding tensions and antagonisms between the precarious labour force and the steady one, it must be recognised as part of the general problem of 'participation'. One cannot but agree with those who, faced with 'the mutation that (...) the labour factor is undergoing, both in contents and execution (and in the contractual typologies used)', presses for 'a corresponding process of change and adaptation of union action, in the exercising of its protective function of workers' interests (...) and the opening towards participation models' (on this point see Carabelli, 1996). With reference to temporary work through an agency, the search for adequate channels of communication between the individual and the collectivity cannot be limited to traditional profiles concerning union rights or the access for temporary workers to the functions of representation inside the company, but must reach far beyond, through research and experimentation of new forms of representation and the merging of these, so to speak, disparate interests.

DEREGULATION AND REFORM OF COLLECTIVE LABOUR RELATIONS

In collective labour relations, we cannot speak of a process of deregulation because this area of labour law is still completely unregulated. New pieces of legislation are under discussion and soon we will have an act on collective bargaining and trade union representation. If we look at present practice, it is not possible to speak even of a process of decentralisation of collective bargaining. Rather the key issue is the co-ordination between the three levels of bargaining, inter-confederation, national industry-wide enterprise and plant level.

In the absence of state regulations, a major contribution to the co-ordination of the bargaining system came from the tripartite agreement of July 1993. As agreed in this social pact, the clauses in the national contract governing hiring and firing practices, job classification, working hours, career paths are to be negotiated every 4 years, while wage clauses will be renewed every 2 years. Bargaining will take place at both national and plant level. However, plant level bargaining takes place only every 4 years and only on issues not already regulated by the national contract. This co-ordination supports a trend towards consensual governing of industrial relations and provides at least *de facto* a major control of conflicts.

Collective bargaining, supported by new legislation, will probably continue to be the main instrument in governing industrial relations in the future. It may be a complement but not a substitute for more or less institutionalised forms of joint consultation and workers participation. There is still a wide distrust in Italy regarding participation. Workers, without wishing to create tension and antagonisms between the stable and the precarious workforce, no longer side step the problem of participation. The changes in the workforce press for a corresponding process of change and adaptation within the union in exercising its function of protecting workers interest and opening towards participation models. In this respect the hot issue is the request by the employer associations for lower pay rates in the depressed area of the south of Italy. While CISL and UIL trade union confederations have indicated that they are willing to open negotiations on allowing companies in the south to pay wages below the national minimum rates for a fixed period, CGIL is strongly opposed.

More recently we have experimented with new kinds of negotiation through the introduction of area contracts and territorial pact. These contracts and pacts are broad agreements at local level between companies, trade unions, banks and local authorities to promote economic development and reduce unemployment through a high level of flexibility in regulating employment relationships. The continued control at national level of wages is meant to regulate competition among employers, in the Italian case it has also been an instrument of controlling inflation in order to respect the *criteria* laid down in Maastricht by the E.U.

EVALUATION OF CURRENT DEREGULATION (DRIVING FORCES OF DEREGULATION)

As far as Italy is concerned, all the points indicated in our program apply: countermeasures against unemployment, pressure from global competition, international pressure to harmonise regulation. In employer and in some academic circles there is a strong emphasis on deregulation as an instrument to revitalise the economy and fight the high level of unemployment. Employment legislation is seen more and more as an obstacle to the development of the economy and one of the most important factors that lead to high unemployment. In my opinion, from a position balancing the advantages of the free market and the constraints of law, the issue of the deregulation of employment relations is not only badly posed and misleading but also historically incorrect.

As a reaction to a new organisation of production methods and circulation of wealth, employment regulation was not, in fact, a unilateral method of protection and emancipation of the weaker party of the contract. Not always supported by values and unified political, economic and social objectives, right from the very beginning the state's regulatory intervention in the labour market never assumed a unidirectional aspect. Beyond the contingent motivation of each single norm, the regulation of employment assumes importance right from the beginning not only as part of the traditional framework of worker protection, but also of those concurrent and certainly no less important factors like conservation of social peace, rationalisation of the productive system, regulation of the forms of competition among entrepreneurs. The product of the legislation of employment relations is therefore, undoubtedly, not only a distributive right of protection of resources, but also, at the same time, a right of production, i.e. a discipline of roles and of the means of production in an industrial society.

For these reason I don't think it is correct to speak of a crisis in labour law connected to the recent process of deregulation. In my opinion, labour law is simply an instrument of regulation of society and of the economy and it can work or not work. Probably it is more correct to speak of a crisis of a certain image of labour law, but this is quite different. The emphasis is now not only on the protection of the weaker party but moreover on the rationalisation of the productive system. Labour law as an instrument of regulating the way of working in a capitalistic society is still valid. So we have to find ways to help labour law work better. In this way the stress is more on 'derigidification', simplification, and nationalisation than on a mere deregulation and a return to market rules. In any case the advantage of the free market as regard the substance of the economy and the fight against unemployment is not at all clear. No particular proof exists showing that a deregulation of employment relation can, *per se*, bring about a reduction in unemployment on an increase in competitiveness in enterprises. On the contrary, it seems well-illustrated that the excessive precariousness of employment relations, other than destroying stable work posts, ends up, in the long run, proving itself to be counter-productive for the entire productive system by taking away from the enterprises a qualified and particularly reliable work-force.

From this perspective, what seems to have more importance is not brutal deregulation but structural policies of employment, access to the system of credit and to market capital, locally based policies of support of the local productive and social system, and moreover the rules that discipline international commerce and relations among different national states. I believe that the recent deregulation of labour law and the crisis of legality that characterises Italy, a crisis characterised by the extremely high level of black market work and an informal economy, cannot be, in any case, explained merely on the basis of a diffuse wish to escape from regulation considered invasive and too heavy for the employer. In my opinion it is the recent loss of state sovereignty over the rules that control the mechanism of production and transfer of wealth that affect indirectly but in a decisive way the ineffective discipline of work. So globalisation and internationalisation of the economy are really the most powerful driving force of the process of deregulation.

In this respect I think that not only national government but also international institutions like the European Community are not at present capable of controlling the economic–productive structure, and at the most, limit themselves to finding palliatives to resist change and contain the effects at the social level or are reduced to merely taking note of the change in progress. Not even in large homogeneous areas like the E.C. is there any movement towards the elaboration of a regulative method of alternative juridical models of the subordinate employment contract for an indefinite period. Two years ago I was in a large research group on the transposition in five different countries of the directives on health and safety at work, and the result of this research clearly indicated that the process of transposition led to a process of diversification rather than harmonisation of rules. In reality, even though changes have occurred in the economic production system, on the regulative level there is still today strong national resistance to a supra-national project of re-regulation of the criteria of legitimisation of the acquisition of the value-added through the work of others. Without any form of supra-national control I see, at least in Italy, the start of a process-informalisation from contract toward status. I wonder if the recent changes in the economy will lead us to abandon the traditional distinction between subordinate workers and the self-employed in order to arrive at an essential core of imperative regulations and principles common to all bargaining relationships concerning labour.

THE ROLE OF LABOUR LAW IN THE 21st CENTURY: DO WE NEED A NEW CONCEPT OF LABOUR LAW?

The technique adopted by Act no. 196/1997 for the regulation of temporary work through an agency represents undoubtedly a substantial starting point to begin a more exhaustive reform of Italian employment law and to provide a clear regulation of atypical work forms in general. Given the specific legal and cultural context of Italy, simple deregulation is not possible. On the contrary, it will be necessary to experiment, as we have said, with doses of 'regulated-by-law flexibility' which contribute to the creation of a climate favouring employment and to the recovery of the broad areas of black market work. The Government's commitment, formally affirmed in agreements with the social parties, consists in fact in loosening some of Italian labour law's real rigidities, but without destructuring the market of steady and full-time labour. Within this broad context, characterised by specific bonds of economic and social compatibility, the inevitable problem of redefining the boundary between independent and dependent work cannot be simplistically – and unrealistically – achieved by intervention directed at penalising atypical work, the co-ordinated arrangements and new forms of work organisation. Legislative intervention to establish a typology for a new bargaining scheme (co-ordinated work) does not seem relevant either. The market requires flexibility, simple rules, certainty of the law: a new definition introducing a contractual *tertium genus* would do nothing but foster litigation, uncertainties in definition and an escape into the black economy.

More convincing and realistic is the idea of a *Statute of new work* which, pragmatically, would address the problem of new employment forms from the point of view of protection (and of their remodelling as regards all employment relations), rather than with a view to the creation of formal definitions and concepts. The idea should be abandoned of defining and classifying a contractual reality which rapidly and constantly changes, in order to arrange, on the contrary, an essential and limited core of imperative rules and principles (above all with reference to the Constitution) common to all bargaining relationships concerning labour.

In brief, the *Statute* should be operative at two separate levels but with the aim of sustaining each other. On the one hand, we could conceive a voluntary measure to stimulate certification, in the administrative setting, of the qualification assigned by the parties to a specific labour relationship; on the other hand, in order to make such a measure effective, it will be necessary to move towards a removal of some of the clauses which contribute to promoting litigation over employment relations and the *physical* escape into the black market and the area of atypical employment (as distinguished from the *pathological* escape that, in addition to an erosion of labour guarantees, is also an element of distortion of the competition between enterprises and must therefore be terminated), outlining a new way of fundamentally reducing the distinctions under the present norm and most of all the characteristics which, at the moment, define independent and dependent employment relations. The mechanism of employment relations certification can reasonably work only if, in the interim, the game of convenience (for both parties) is made more balanced. The convenience game is the return of employment relations into a particular bargaining scheme rather than into a new one, only because it is convenient for the parties. From this perspective, a *Statute of new work* could offer the possibility of modulating and graduating (typologically) the protection enforceable in every kind of agreement in conformity with the categories represented by concentric circles which – along with a *continuum* of modalities in work execution – extend from the minimum and imperative protection enforceable for all employment relations, to the guarantees belonging only to dependent work (protection against dismissals).

The issue of employment relations certification as an answer to the swell of legal cases on the subject of contract qualification, does not seem to pose any particular problems, on the condition, obviously, that the bargaining program *ex ante* agreed upon by the parties will be respected during the exercise of the employment relations. In order to foster certification and support the parties' will, it would be useful, moreover, to distinguish between an area of absolute incontrovertibility or of public order (in other words, related to the worker's fundamental rights), and not at the parties' disposal under penalty of relations re-qualification in judicial session, and an area of relative incontrovertibility, administrated by the collective partners during collective bargaining and/or by the same individual partners as established by the employment relation but, in this last case, *only* before the administrative body qualified for the certification (wages over minimum, management of career paths, terms of notice, relationship stability, allowance in case of relationship suspension, working time modulation, etc.).

More critical, undoubtedly, is the part concerned with the remodelling of employment protections for which adequate political and social consent can hardly be realised, but, surprisingly, taboos and ideological difference emerge anew. Nevertheless, it is clear that the regulation of atypical work imposes a rewriting (at least in part) of the traditional dependent work protections, for the corresponding normative realignment of social security benefits, an outlining of a social security regime common to all independent and dependent workers which, granting a basic social-insurance tax revenue for all employment relations, contributes to making less dramatic the qualifying problem of individual work forms for the social insurance providers as well. An intervention of mere regulatory nature into atypical work forms, without a corresponding redefinition of the dependent work statute, will only contribute to making labour management rules more pervasive, and thus stimulating a further escape into the hidden economy and a reaction in the form of labour outsourcing and enterprise relocation.

A serious reform bill cannot, in consequence, ignore this issue. In this connection, frankly puzzling is the ideological preliminary question concerning dismissals posed by some political and trade union forces, referring to a normative and social framework which already provides for broad forms of evasion of the employment stability rule. Apart from black, grey, etc. work, nobody can deny, watching developments in the dependent labour market, for the most part through the legitimate resort to temporary work typologies, fictitious training contracts (apprenticeship, work-training contract) and to independent and co-ordinated work contracts where the rules concerning dismissals are not enforced. Why should we accept this hypocrisy, if only to not touch on the dismissal issue, instead of following a policy aimed at effectively re-launching the open-ended labour contract and youth employment? There is no shortage of ideas about these matters. Apart from the prohibition of discriminatory dismissals or for illness or maternity, one could cease enforcing rules concerning individual dismissals without impairing the protections of the adult labour force firmly inserted in a business context (a) for those workers in their first working experience with an open-ended dependent employment contract and not over the age of 32; (b) for all new hiring, during the first two years of work, in provinces where the average yearly rate of unemployment, according to the broadened ISTAT definition, recorded for the year before hiring, reaches the level of at least 3% with reference to the national average as it results from the same record; (c) for those workers who have less than two years' seniority of service with the same employer.

There is no shortage of ideas. What is missing is the capability (the courage?) of abandoning old schemes and consolidated paradigms which do not correspond anymore to the reality that we would like to regulate (on this point see Blanpain, 1998).

BIBLIOGRAPHY

G. Baglioni (1974), *L'ideologia della borghesia industriale nell'Italia liberale*, Einaudi, Torino, 40 e ss.

M. Biagi (1997), *Mercati e rapporti di lavoro,* Giuffrè, Milano.

M. Biagi (1998), *A love-hate relationship: regulating non-standard work in Italy*, in The Role of Private Agencies, Leuven, 1–2 April 1998.

R. Blanpain (1998), *Il diritto del lavoro nel XXI secolo: l'era dei lavoratori dal 'portafoglio' creativo*, in *Dir. Rel. Ind.*, no. 3, 333.

U. Carabelli (1996), *Le RSA dopo il referendum, tra vincoli comunitari e prospettive di partecipazione,* in *Diritto delle Relazioni Industriali,* no. 1.

S. Cassese (1993), *Oltre lo Stato: i limiti dei governi nazionali nel controllo dell'economia*, in Galgano F., Cassese S., Tremonti G., and Treu T., *Nazioni senza ricchezza. Ricchezza senza nazione*, il Mulino, Bologna, 35.

P. Craveri (1990), voce *Sindacato (storia),* in *Enc. Dir.,* vol. XLXX, Giuffrè, Milano, 661.

J. Cruet *Le vie du droit et l'impuissance des lois,* Flammarion, Paris, 1908,

G. Ferraro (1998), *Dal lavoro subordinato al lavoro autonomo,* relazione AIDLASS su *Impresa e nuovi modi di organizzare il lavoro,* in corso di pubblicazione.

G. Ghezzi (1995), *Proposte per un Testo Unico in tema di mercato del lavoro,* in *Il Lavoro nella Giurisprudenza,* p. 221 e ss.

G. Giugni (1982), *Il diritto del lavoro negli anni '80*, in *Giornale Dir. Lav. Rel. Ind.*, 375.

M. Jeffery, *The Commission Proposals on 'Atypical Work': Back to the Drawing-Board... Again,* in *Industrial Law Journal,* 1995, 296.

L. Mengoni in G. Giugni, L. Mengoni, B. Veneziani, *Tre commenti alla* Critique du droit du travail *di Supiot.,* in *Giornale Dir. Lav. Rel. Ind.,* 1995, 477.

D. J. B. Mitchell (1999), *E' in atto un processo di convergenza?,* General Report on Forum 5 of the Bologna Meeting of the IIRA, September 1998, in *Dir. Rel. Ind.,* 1999/1, forthcoming.

B. Siau (1996), *Le travail temporaire en droit comparé européen et international,* LGDJ, Paris.

S. Simitis (1997), *Il diritto del lavoro ha ancora un futuro?, in Giornale Dir. Lav. Rel. Ind.*, 609.

M. Tiraboschi (1994), *Temporary Work and Employment agency in Italy,* Università di Modena, Collana del Dipartimento di Economia Aziendale, no. 26.

M. Tiraboschi (1995), *Evoluzione storica e attuale disciplina giuridica delel agenzie di lavoro temporaneo* in *Giappone: un inventario critico e alcuni elementi di riflessione per il caso italiano,* in *Diritto delle Relazioni Industriali,* no. 1.

M. Tiraboschi (1996), *Lavoro atipico e rappresentanza degli interessi,* in Biagi M., Suwa Y. (a cura di), *Il diritto dei disoccupati,* Studi in onore di Koichiro Yamaguchi, Giuffrè, Milano.

M. Tiraboschi (1997), *La legalizzazione del lavoro intermittente tramite agenzia. Prime riflessioni sulla legge* no. *196/1997,* in *Diritto delle Relazioni Industriali,* no. 3.

T. Treu (1990), voce *Diritto del lavoro*, Digesto, Utet, Torino, IV ed., 1990, estratto, 50.

T. Treu (1994), *L'internazionalizzazione dei mercati: problemi di diritto del lavoro e metodo comparato,* in Studi in onore di R. Sacco, Giuffrè, Milano, vol. I, 1117 e ss.

T. Treu (1995), *Le politiche del lavoro del Governo italiano,*in *Diritto delle Relazioni Industriali,* no. 2.

T. Treu (1997), *Politiche del lavoro e strumenti di promozione dell'occupazione: il caso italiano in una prospettiva europea*, in Biagi M. (a cura di), *Mercati e rapporti di lavoro. Commentario alla legge 24 giugno 1997 no. 196*, Giuffrè, Milano, 3 e ss. (e ora in *Scritti in onore di Giuseppe Federico Mancini*, Giuffrè, Milano, vol. I, 597 e ss.).

T. Treu (1998), *Italy,* in Blanpain, *International Encyclopaedia of Labour Law and Industrial Relations,* Kluwer, Deventer, forthcoming.

B. Veneziani (1993), *La flessibilità del lavoro e i suoi antidoti,* in *Giornale di Diritto del Lavoro e delle Relazioni Industriali,* p. 235 e ss.

S. Webb, Webb B. (1926 ma 1897), *Industrial Democracy*, Longmans, Green and Co. Ltd., London.

M. Weber (1961), *Economia e società,* Ed. Comunità, Milano.

5. Deregulation and Labour Law in Japan

Hideyuki Morito

INTRODUCTION

Since the bursting of the bubble economy early in the 1990s, 'deregulation' has been one of the 'hot' topics in Japan. Some adore it as a wonder drug like Viagra to revitalise the Japanese economy, others warn that as a harmful side effect it may turn Japan into an inhumane society where everyone tries to get the competitive edge over the underdogs. I do not intend to give you any good advice about which bandwagon you should jump on; instead, from here on in, I will examine the most direct impact of the current deregulation trend in Japan on industrial relations: deregulation of labour law itself.

This national report deals with the recent developments of Japanese labour law in light of deregulation.

DEREGULATION OF LABOUR LAW

While the current deregulation drives can be traced back to the early 1980s,[1] it was in the 1990s that 'deregulation' became a national slogan. In 1993, two important advisory bodies published their reports one after the other. Both reports, i.e., the Third Administrative Reform Council's final report and the Economic Reform Study Committee's interim report (known as the 'Hiraiwa Report'), advocated the need to deregulate the Japanese economy. At this stage, the main target of deregulation policy was 'economic regulations.' 'Social regulations' such as labour law were not paid much attention.

However, in the midst of the tardy recovery from the business recession after the bubble boom, business circles decided to include labour law as one of the targets of deregulation. The distinction between economic regulations and social regulations was replaced by a new concept, 'deregulation without any exception'.[2] The government

1. T. Araki, Changing Japanese Labor Law in Light of Deregulation Drives: A Comparative Analysis, Japan Labor Bulletin, Vol. 36, No. 5, p. 5 (1997).
2. In 1997, Taichi Sakaiya, then a prominent economist and currently the Minister of State for Economic Planning, commented on a TV program, that 'there should be no distinction between 'economic regulations' and 'social regulations.' The former was still spread here, there, and everywhere under the guise of the latter.' This remark, regardless of its credibility, describes the current atmosphere accurately.

R. Blanpain (ed.), Deregulation and Labour Law, 97–114

could not ignore the trend of the times. In March 1995, the 'Deregulation Promotion Program' ratified by the Cabinet expressly listed employment and labour relations as targets of deregulation. It enumerated thirty subjects relating to employment relations among 1091 subjects in total.

At present, there is a *de facto* consensus that six areas in labour legislation, which were listed in the Fourth Administrative Reform Council's final report of 1997, are considered deregulation targets. These are, fee-charging employment placement services, worker dispatching businesses, working hours-averaging scheme over a one-year period, discretionary work scheme, period of contracts, and protection for women workers.

1. Labour Market Regulations

In December 1995, the Deregulation Sub-Committee of the Administrative Reform Council in the Prime Minister's Office submitted a report reconfirming the need for deregulating labour market regulations, i.e., fee-charging employment placement services and worker dispatching businesses.

1.1. Fee-charging employment placement businesses

The State monopolises employment placement services and people seek jobs free of charge through public employment security offices – this has been one of the important principles in Japanese labour market regulations since the enactment of the Employment Security Law (hereinafter 'ESL') in 1947. The ESL allows fee-charging employment placement businesses only when, by permission of the Labour Minister, they arrange employment for persons engaged in art, music, entertainment, and other occupations requiring special talents (Art. 32, Para. 1, Proviso, ESL).

1.1.1. A shift from the government placement monopoly system to a coexisting system of public and private placement service

Under the regulation until 31 March 1997, 29 occupations were enumerated as qualifying for fee-charging employment placement services: artists, musicians, actors, doctors, dentists, nurses, models, translators, cooks, bartenders, hair dressers, fashion designers, lawyers, accountants, etc. (Art. 24 and Annexed Table No. 2 of the ESL Ordinance). This is the so-called 'positive list system.' Following a proposal in December 1996 from the Central Employment Security Council, a tripartite advisory body in the Ministry of Labour, the government substantially abandoned the placement monopoly system by modifying the Ordinance mentioned above, without revising the ESL itself. The revision went into effect on 1 April 1997. The new Art. 24 of the ESL Ordinance removed general prohibitions and adopted the 'negative list system' listing prohibited occupations individually.

The new regulation lists the following seven occupations which should not be handled by the private fee-charging employment agencies:

(1) clerical occupation by persons within one year after their graduation from school;
(2) sales occupation by persons within one year after their graduation from school;
(3) services except for occupations of housekeepers, barbers, hairdressers, Kimono-dressing helpers, laundering and cleaning technicians, cooks, bartenders, waiters

and waitresses at formal restaurants, models, and demonstrators of goods for retail;

(4) occupation of security guards;

(5) occupation in agriculture, forestry, and fishery;

(6) occupation in transport and communication except for bus tour conductors; and

(7) occupation of technicians, occupation of digging, production and construction, and occupation of labourers except for that of technicians producing fresh confectionery.

The currently permissible occupations cover approximately 60 per cent of total employees, an increase from 18 per cent before the reform. In short, the new regulations liberalised private placement services for white-collar workers, with the exception of services involving employees in their first year of employment after graduating from school. While public employment offices have functioned well for the placement of blue-collar job seekers, the increase in the number of white-collar workers has diminished their importance. It has been pointed out that at most 20 per cent of new recruits come via public employment security offices.[3] The reform is considered an attempt to bridge the gap as well as to create new business opportunities in the area of employment placement service.

1.1.2. Deregulation of placement fees

The ESL stipulates that fee-charging employment placement agencies shall not receive actual expenses or other commissions or compensation under any guise whatsoever, apart from the fee determined by the Ministry of Labour (Art. 32, Para. 6). Under the regulation until 31 March 1997, the maximum fee chargeable to the client company was fixed at 10.1 per cent of the worker's wages up to six months (Art. 24, Par. 14 and Annexed Table 3, ESL Ordinance).

There was a legal question as to whether or not 'headhunting' or scouting activities were regulated by the ESL as 'employment placement.' Many scouting agencies conducted their businesses based on the assumption that scouting activities were different from 'employment placement' in the terminology of the ESL and thus they were able to charge to the client companies more than the ESL's upper limits on fees for placement services.

However, in 1994, the Supreme Court rejected this practice.[4] It held that scouting activities fall under the concept of employment placement in the ESL and the client company did not need to pay fees or remuneration exceeding 10.1 per cent limit (yen 505,000 in this case) in spite of the agreement between the parties to pay yen 2,000,000 in fees for investigation and remuneration. This case fulfilled the need to reconsider whether scouting activities should be regulated in the same way as traditional employment placement activities.[5]

In this light, the 1997 reform[6] introduced a new dual placement fee system. As for basic services for bringing together those seeking workers and those seeking jobs, the approximately 10 per cent[7] upper limit mentioned above still applies. On the

3. T. Araki, *supra* note 1, p. 7.
4. Tokyo Executive Search case, Supreme Court, 22 April 1994, *Minshu*, Vol. 48, No. 3, p. 944.
5. T. Araki, *supra* note 1, p. 7.
6. The reform also contains, as well as the two major revisions explained in detail here, other deregulation measures, such as simplifying the procedures to obtain permission from the Labour Minister.
7. The current rate is fixed at 10.5 per cent (Art. 24, Para. 16 and Annexed Table 3, ESL Ordinance).

other hand, as for consulting, counselling, finding suitable workers, and other similar services conducted upon individual requests, the new regulation allows for extra fees apart from those for basic services on the condition that the amount of the fees is reported to and authorised by the Labour Minister.

1.2. Worker dispatching businesses

Before 1985, worker dispatching (temporary work) businesses were considered illegal as a form of labour supply[8] business prohibited under the ESL. However, many companies conducted their legally questionable dispatching businesses under the guise of 'contract work' which is distinguished from labour supply businesses. In the end the legislator legalised this practice. In 1985, the Worker Dispatching Law (WDL) was enacted to properly regulate these businesses and to provide legal protection of dispatched workers.[9]

The WDL did not liberalise dispatched work completely. It limits the sectors in which worker dispatching may be undertaken (the 'positive list' system). The 1985 law and the Cabinet Order designated only 16 forms of work as qualifying: those requiring professional knowledge (e.g. computer programming, production of broadcast programs, interpretation, translation, shorthand, etc.) and those necessitating special employment management (e.g. conducting tours, cleaning buildings, operation and maintenance of building equipment, etc.).

Since the mid-1990s, worker dispatching has been one of the major targets of deregulation.

1.2.1. Introduction of the 'negative list system' for older workers

The 1994 amendment of the Older Persons' Employment Stabilisation Law partially abandoned the positive list system as one of the principles in the WDL. It allows an employer undertaking worker dispatching to employ persons of 60 years or over as dispatched workers for *any kind of activity* other than port transport services, construction work, security guard services, and manufacturing, provided the dispatcher undertaking is composed *only* of workers of 60 years or over.

1.2.2. Introduction of the 'negative list system' when replacing persons on child or family care leaves

Under the 1996 amendment of the Child Care and Family Care Leave Law, worker dispatching for the positions of those who take child or family care leaves also fell under the negative list system (Art. 40-2, the Child Care and Family Care Leave Law). The new regulation liberalised this type of worker dispatching except for prohibited areas (port transport services, construction work, and security guard services) and on the condition that the period of dispatching was not longer than one year.

1.2.3. Expanding the range of allowable occupations

The Cabinet Order of 10 December 1996, designated 10 new allowable occupations: scientific research and development, business planning, editing of books, advertisement

8. The ESL then defined 'labour supply' as having workers work under the direction and orders of another person based upon a supply contract.
9. T. Araki, *supra* note 1, p. 8.

designing, interior designing, announcing in broadcasting, office automation instructing, telemarketing, sales engineering, and the arrangement of stage setting and properties. Thus, in total, 26 forms of work are allowed under the current WDL.

1.2.4. Lifting the general prohibition?

Apart from the exceptions mentioned above, the current regulation still maintains the positive list system. However, further deregulation of worker dispatching will surely be considered sooner or later. Business circles have insisted that the WDL should adopt the negative list system designating prohibited forms of work only. This argument was basically accepted by the Central Employment Security Council and in October 1998 the government submitted to the Diet the bill amending the WDL, which has not been passed yet but will be discussed again in the next session. The bill proposes shifting to the negative list system under which only three forms of work are prohibited: port transport services, construction work, and security guard services. In return for this deregulation, the bill makes a proposition limiting the period of dispatch to one year at the maximum, except in the case of the 26 forms of work mentioned above which are already allowed under the current regulations.

According to the legislative history, the current WDL restricts allowable forms of work for worker dispatching to professional activities that will not erode the positions of regular employees and established employment practices.[10] In this light, adopting the negative list system would be a drastic change; it would imply the erosion of regular workers' employment by dispatched workers.

2. Individual Labour Relations

In December 1996, the Deregulation Sub-Committee published another report adding four subjects in the area of individual labour relations to the list of deregulation targets: working hours-averaging scheme over a one-year period, discretionary work scheme, period of contracts, and protection for women workers.

2.1. Working hours-averaging scheme over a one-year period

The maximum workweek is 40 h and the maximum workday is 8 hours in Japan. In addition to this 'five-day week' principle, the Labour Standards Law (LSL) provides various working hours-averaging schemes. Most of them were newly introduced or revised in 1987 to make the framework of working hours flexible in response to changes in enterprise activities and work situations in response to the growth of a service economy.[11]

In 1993 the hours-averaging scheme over a one-year period was introduced. If a labour–management agreement[12] stipulates that the average weekly working

10. T. Araki, Characteristics of Regulations on Dispatched Work (Temporary Work) in Japan, Japan Labor Bulletin, Vol. 33, No. 8 (1997) (see http://www.jil.go.jp/bulletin/year/1994 /vol33-08/05.htm).
11. K. Sugeno, Japanese Labor Law (1992), p. 244.
12. Under the LSL, it is 'an agreement with a union organized by a majority of the workers at the workplace concerned, where such a union exists, or with a person representing a majority of the workers where no such union exists.' This agreement is differentiated from a collective agreement. The employer must file it with a Labour Standards Inspection Office.

hours over a fixed period of no more than one year will not exceed 40 h, the employer may have a worker work in excess of the weekly or daily maximum working hours in a specified week or weeks, or in a specified day or days, respectively. With this averaging system, the legislator intended to allow businesses with especially busy or slack periods during the year to distribute working hours and designate rest days more flexibly and effectively (for example, three rest days per week in February and August, one rest day per week in June and December). Yet businesses have insisted that the system's requirements are too strict to make the most of it.

Under the current regulation, if the fixed period mentioned above is set at more than three months, the labour-management agreement must limit the number of weekly working hours to no more than 48, and daily hours to no more than nine. The 1998 LSL reform,[13] which has just passed the Diet and will go into effect on 1 April 1999, relaxed these upper limits up to 52 h per week and 10 h per day.

2.2. Discretionary work scheme

If the hours worked exceed the daily or weekly maximum hours, the employer is required to pay increased wages for the overtime work at a rate of at least 25 per cent over the normal wages per working hour or working day. The 1987 LSL reform introduced the discretionary work scheme as an exception to this principle. Under the scheme, an employer can calculate the number of work hours based on the accepted estimate of work hours agreed upon between the employer and the workers' representative, irrespective of the number of hours actually worked. In other words, it made it possible to compensate workers engaged in specialised and discretionary work on the basis of its quality and results, regardless of its quantity.[14]

It is an accepted analysis that the increase of white-collar workers led to the introduction of the discretionary work scheme.[15] In general, white-collar workers are free from concrete directives from their employers, are given wider discretion in performance of their work, and thus their productivity cannot be appropriately measured by the amount of hours worked. Traditional overtime regulations, which mandate payment of an overtime premium in accordance with performed overtime, could even be unfair, because it would induce more efficient workers to work slowly in order to work overtime and receive the premium.[16]

2.2.1. Current regulation

2.2.1.1. Covered duties. The activities covered by the scheme are 'duties stipulated by Order as duties for which it is difficult for the employer to give concrete directives regarding such decisions as the means of accomplishment and allocation of time and the like, because, due to the nature of the duties, the methods for accomplishment must be largely left to the discretion of the workers engaged in such

---

13. The reform also contains another important revision deregulating the one-year working hours-averaging system. The new regulation allows employers to apply the averaging scheme to employees who are newly hired or resigned during the one-year period, who are excluded from the coverage under the current regulation.
14. K. Sugeno, *supra* note 11, p. 264.
15. T. Araki, Regulation of Working Hours for White-collar Workers Engaging in 'Discretionary Activities,' Japan Labor Bulletin, Vol. 35, No. 7 (1996) (see http://www.jil.go.jp/bulletin/year/1996/vol35-07/05.htm).
16. T. Araki, *supra* note 15.

duties' (Art. 38-2, Para. 4, LSL). The Enforcement Order of the LSL stipulates the following five activities covered under the scheme (Art. 24-2, Para. 6, No. 1–5):

(1) research and development of new products and technology;
(2) planning and analysis of information-management systems;
(3) gathering information and editing in the mass media;
(4) designing; and
(5) producers and directors in TV or movie production.

Besides Article 24-2, Para. 6, No. 6 of the LSL Enforcement Order also provides that the Labour Minister can designate other activities upon deliberation within the Central Labour Standards Council. In April 1997, the following six activities were newly designated: (1) copy writing; (2) public accounting; (3) duties of lawyers; (4) duties of architects; (5) duties of real estate appraisers; and (6) duties of patent agents.[17]

2.2.1.2. The conclusion and filing of the labour–management agreement. To adopt the scheme, the employer must conclude a labour–management agreement with a majority representative[18] at the workplace. It must specify duties covered by the scheme and the number of hours which workers engaged in those duties will be deemed to have spent. The duties must not entail concrete directives from the employer regarding such decisions as the means of accomplishment and allocation of time and the like. The agreement must be filed with the Labour Standards Inspection Office.

2.2.2. Introduction of the 'new discretionary work scheme'

Because the availability of the scheme is strictly limited to the enumerated activities above, very few companies have adopted the scheme.[19] Business circles have strongly contended that the scheme should be made available for most white-collar workers. The Discretionary Work Scheme Study Group's report[20] of 1995 also proposed a drastic revision of the scheme, including further extension of the coverage of the scheme.[21]

---

17. In 1995 the Discretionary Work Scheme Study Group established in the Ministry of Labour recommended that seven more activities should be designated by the Labour Minister as discretionary work activities. The Labour Minister designated six of them, omitting one: research and development of new non-product goods such as financial products. For reference, the group was chaired by Professor Kazuo Sugeno and consisted of six professors including Professors Yasuo Suwa and Takashi Araki.
18. See *supra* note 12.
19. The ratio of companies that use the discretionary work scheme was 0.3 per cent in 1988, 0.6 per cent in 1990, 0.7 per cent in 1991, 0.5 per cent in 1994, and 0.5 per cent in 1996. T. Araki, *supra* note 15; Rodo Sho (Ministry of Labour), Rodo Hakusho 1998 (The 1998 White Paper on Labor), p. 486 (1998).
20. See *supra* note 17.
21. The report proposed, or at least suggested that (1) highly professional or creative duties, such as planning of business administration strategies, legal duties, economic analysis, etc., should be covered by the discretionary work scheme; that (2) the present administrative order designation is so rigid and slow to cope with rapid socio-economic changes that the law should confine itself to a comprehensive definition of discretionary work and should entrust specific designation to the parties at the workplace; and that (3) in addition to the conclusion of the labour-management agreement, the scheme should make individual consent one of the requirements to apply the scheme to the individual.

By contrast, labour has in general opposed expansion of the scheme for fear that it could deprive workers of their rights to overtime pay.[22]

In September 1998, the LSL was amended and the 'new discretionary work scheme' was added to the discretionary work scheme under the current law. The new scheme will take effect on 1 April 2000.

2.2.2.1. Labour-management committee. First of all, to adopt the new scheme, a 'labour-management committee'[23] must be set up at the workplace. Half of the committee members, i.e., labour members, must be designated with a fixed term by a majority union or by a person representing a majority of the workers and win a confidence vote from the majority at the workplace. The establishment of a labour-management committee must be filed with the Labour Standards Inspection Office.

2.2.2.2. Coverage and requirements. The scheme may be adopted at the workplaces where 'important decisions' regarding the operation of the enterprise are made. The activities covered under the scheme are duties of planning, research, and analysis which are performed at the discretion of the workers engaged in such duties and for which the employer does not give any concrete directives. The labour-management committee must specify in its resolution those duties covered by the scheme and the number of hours which workers engaged in those duties will be deemed to have spent.

A worker cannot be covered by the scheme without his or her consent. An employer must not penalise a worker for refusing to be covered by the new discretionary work scheme. This condition was added at the last stage of the deliberation process in the House of Representatives as a compromise with the opposition.

2.3. *Period of contracts*

The LSL prohibits concluding fixed-term contracts longer than one year (Art. 14). The only exception to this restriction, other than labour contracts without a fixed-term, is where an additional period is needed for the completion of a specific undertaking. The purpose of this limitation is to prevent the harmful effects caused by binding a worker for a longer period. However, it has been pointed out that the possibility of such negative effects is the exception and both employers and employees need more diversified contract periods for diversified work patterns.[24]

---

22. Unpaid overtime work is undoubtedly illegal but is not a very rare phenomenon in Japan, particularly among white-collar workers. Many companies regard overtime exceeding a certain number of hours as being done 'voluntarily.' From employers' side, the discretionary work scheme is needed to regulate the reality adequately. From the labour side, extending the coverage of the scheme is legalising illegal unpaid overtime. T. Araki, *supra* note 15.
23. The 1998 LSL reform, under the new regulations from April 2000, provides for two similar mechanisms which may cause confusion: the labour–management 'agreement' and 'committee.' This may indicate that the former has not functioned well under the current regulation. If the new labour-management committee works well, it may be replacing the labour-management agreement.
24. T. Araki, *supra* note 1, p. 8.

The 1998 revision, to go into effect on 1 April 1999, expanded the contract period limitation up to three years from when a contract is concluded with the following three types of workers:

(1) workers with highly professional knowledge, skills, or experience required for development of new products, technology, and services or for scientific research;
(2) workers with professional knowledge required for projects to start, convert, expand, or downsize businesses and expected to be completed within a definite period; and
(3) workers of age 60 or over.

In the cases of (1) and (2), the workers must be newly hired at workplaces short of workers with such professional knowledge, skills, or experience. The three-year contracts are one-time contracts, only renewable for one year only or for an indefinite period.

2.4. *Protection for women workers*

The Equal Employment Opportunity Law (EEOL) was enacted in 1985 to ratify the Treaty on the Elimination of Discrimination against Women. The essential philosophy of the Treaty is that men and women should be treated equally regarding working conditions not related to the protection of motherhood. Nevertheless, according to the government, 'in the light of the heavy burden that was actually borne by women in discharging family responsibilities,' most of the general protective provisions for women workers in the LSL have been maintained with minor modification.

In 1997, a compromise was made. The LSL's provisions on prohibition of night and holiday work and limitation of overtime will be abolished in April 1998 in exchange for intensifying the EEOL.

2.4.1. *The EEOL revision*

The current EEOL imposes on employers a 'duty to endeavour' to treat women equally with men with regard to recruitment, hiring, assignment and promotion. The 'duty to endeavour' is not legally sanctioned, but supposed to be realised by administrative measures.[25] In fact, it is the result of a compromise at the time of the EEOL enactment with business circles that insisted upon the difficulties in modifying the current system of personnel management based on long-term employment practice.

Believe it or not, the 'duty to endeavour' provisions have changed Japanese employers' behaviour, at least to some extent. Enterprises started to hire more women as 'management career track' employees. Job advertisements do not announce 'men only' any more. Yet, it is also true that it is time to advance to more effective provisions to further promote equal employment opportunity for men and women.

The employer side has opposed intensifying the EEOL, insisting that they cannot treat women equally to men without amending the LSL, particularly, the

25. M. Kurokawa, Working Life and Family Life: Policies for Their Harmonization – National Report: Japan, The Japan Institute of Labour Report Series No. 4 on the 1994 JIL Comparative Labour Law Seminar (1995), p. 71.

provisions on limitations on overtime work and the ban on night work. On the other hand, women's advocates have insisted, if anything, upon extending the current protective provisions for women to men to reduce unreasonably long working hours in Japan.

The government gave priority to reinforcing the EEOL. From 1 April 1999, employers shall not discriminate against women workers with regard to recruitment, hiring, assignment, and promotion.

2.4.2. *Abolition of women's protective provisions*

The current LSL provides women workers with the following seven types of protection: limitations on overtime and rest-day work; a ban on night work, underground work, and work harmful to maternal functions; pre-and post-childbirth protections, particularly pre- and post-childbirth leaves; childcare time; and leaves for women for whom work during menstrual periods would be difficult. The first two provisions will be abolished in April 1999.

2.4.2.1. *Limitations on women workers' overtime and rest-day work.* An employer is not permitted to have women engaged in industrial enterprises work more than 6 h of overtime per week or more than 150 h of overtime per year, or work on rest days. In non-industrial enterprises, an employer cannot have women work more than thirty-six hours of overtime in a four-week period or more than 150 h per year, and may have work on only one rest day during a four-week period.

These provisions will be abolished on 1 April 1999. In fact, even under the current regulations, there are two categories of women workers exempted from these limitations: persons with supervisory authority and specialists.

2.4.2.2. The ban on night work. Women workers cannot work between the hours of 10:00 p.m. and 5:00 a.m. This rule does not apply to the following exempted persons:

(1) persons engaged in agriculture and forestry; animal husbandry and fishery; health and hygiene enterprises; hotel, restaurant, and recreational enterprises; and telephone operator jobs.
(2) persons engaged in duties which are not injurious to the health and welfare of women. An ordinance enumerates: (a) flight cabin attendants,[26] pilots, and other workers at airports; (b) a superintendent of a women's boarding house; (c) motion picture camera crew; (d) producers, directors, etc. of broadcast programs; (e) and police officers and fire-fighters.
(3) persons with supervisory authority and specialists.
(4) persons engaged in duties requiring night work because of the nature of the duties, such as the manufacture or processing of foodstuffs which would quickly deteriorate in quality. Typical examples are duties involving the preparation of delicatessen, box lunches, and newspaper delivery. However, this exemption is limited to workers who work 6 h per day or less.

---

26. ... do they seriously believe that working as a flight attendant is not at all injurious to the health and welfare of women?

(5) taxi drivers. In this case, a worker has to show her intention to work at night to the employer. Then the employer applies to the Labour Standards Inspection Office for the approval of night work.

In this light, even under the current regulations, women's night work is already deregulated to a considerable extent. On 1 April 1999, it will be fully deregulated.

THE DRIVING FORCES OF DEREGULATION

While the six areas mentioned above are generically and artificially called 'labour law deregulation,' each of them has a different background which overlaps with the others.

1. The Strongest Drive: The Need for Revitalising the Economy

The answer is simple: the never-ending business recession after the bubble economy is driving the nation to think that everything should be deregulated, including labour law, to revitalise the economy. The slogan of 'deregulation' is all the more appealing to the Japanese because they tend to think that it implies breaking down the 'notorious' bureaucracy. Business circles took this opportunity and succeeded in having their arguments reflected in the government policy. Labour unions have raised objections, as usual. However, my impression is that in fact they did not always mean it.[27] They could have stopped, or at least slowed the current deregulation trend if they had really tried. Probably there is no deep conflict between labour and management as to the need for deregulation to revitalise the economy, though they might differ over what should be deregulated and how much.[28]

Can labour law deregulation revitalise the economy? Maybe, maybe not. At any rate, deregulation of labour market regulations has been put into practice for this very purpose. Fee-charging employment placement services have been deregulated in the hope of creating new business opportunities particularly in the area of placement services for white-collar workers. Deregulation of worker dispatching businesses is now under discussion in expectation of further expansion of the worker dispatching industry.

Recently the unemployment rate in Japan reached the record high of 4.3 per cent. It is still relatively low compared with European countries, but almost at the same level as that in the United States. Nevertheless, proposing 'work-sharing' as a

27. Some labour unions even supported some of the labour law deregulation propositions. Matsushita Electric Labour Union, Yomigaere White-Collar (Revitalizing White-Collar Workers), p. 118 (1994).

28. One of the reasons for this may be that most Japanese unions are organised at company level. As long as the core of the Japanese employment system, i.e., employment security, is untouched, labour unions are basically willing to cooperate with employers. Professor Nishitani, a well-known pro-labour labour law professor of Osaka City University, expressed his irritation with RENGO (JTUC, the Japanese Trade Union Confederation) and ZENROREN (NCTU, the National Confederation of Trade Unions) for not being strong opponents of the government and management position. Satoshi Nishitani, Rodo Ho Kisei Kanwa Ron No Soron Teki Kento (General Examination of the Arguments for Labour Law Deregulation), Kikan Rodo Ho (Quarterly Labor Law), No. 183, p. 8 (1997).

countermeasure against unemployment has so far not been prevalent.[29] Instead, as explained above, deregulation's role in revitalising the economy, and as a result creating new employment opportunities, has been emphasised.

2. The Increase of White-Collar Workers

Due to the growth of the service industry, the number of white-collar workers has been steadily on the increase.[30] Labour law, which was established approximately 50 years ago to protect blue-collar factory workers in feudalistic labour relations, has to adapt itself to today's situation. Public employment security offices did not function well for the placement of white-collar workers. The government gave up reinforcing the public employment placement service and entrusted placement services for white-collar workers to the private sector. The discretionary work and working hours-averaging schemes were introduced and expanded to facilitate employment management of white-collar workers. While protection for women workers under the LSL was established to take into consideration the difference in physical strength of male and female workers, white-collar jobs in general are 'brain work' requiring less physical strength.

3. The Modernisation of Obsolete Labour Laws

The purpose of the State monopoly of employment placement services was to prevent workers from being exploited by 'wicked' labour supply businesses. Today it is no longer fair to regard fee-charging placement or worker dispatching businesses as 'wicked.' The contract period limitation was necessary to keep a worker from being bound to an employer for an 'unreasonably' long period. It implies that workers themselves cannot decide if the contract period is reasonable or not.

The image of workers against the backdrop of the regulations above is one of weak persons who are incapable of making any decisions by themselves, are subject to exploitation by employers, and thus need paternalistic intervention from the government. These feudal customs, obviously obsolete, have not completely disappeared. Today workers are more independent, individualised, and possess various orientations.[31] The discretionary work scheme presupposes these new types of workers. Some warn, to the contrary, that the image of 'independent, new type workers' is overemphasised.[32]

Deregulation has also been used to bridge the gap between reality and the law. While worker dispatching businesses were illegal, or at least legally questionable, they expanded rapidly in the late 1970s and the early 1980s because they met

29. It must be added, however, that on 15 July 1998, The Japan Productivity Center for Socio-Economic Development (JPC-SED) published a report called 'Urgent Propositions on Current Employment Problems.' It includes, among twelve countermeasures, a proposition of creating employment through the concept of the 'work-sharing.'
30. The percentage of white-collar workers, i.e., persons performing professional, technological, clerical, managerial, or sales duties, of the total number of employees reached 54.1 per cent in 1995 from 48.9 in 1975, 49.8 in 1980, 51.7 in 1985, and 53.2 in 1990. The 1998 White Paper on Labor, *supra* note 19, p. 114.
31. T. Araki, *supra* note 1, p. 6.
32. S. Nishitani, *supra* note 28, p. 11.

the needs of both employers and employees, especially for women and older persons.[33] If the government had not enacted the law regulating worker dispatching, inherent problems of dispatched work, such as a lack of employment security and ambiguity of legal responsibilities of both the dispatching agency and the client company, could not have been resolved. In that sense, legalising worker dispatching by the enactment of the WDL was unavoidable in order to give proper protection to those working as dispatched workers. This is almost the same thing that happened to employment placement services. Deregulation of fee-charging employment placement services was in fact giving proper legal protection to white-collar job seekers through the legalisation of scouting businesses.

4. Globalisation and Internationalisation

Business circles insist that deregulation is necessary for the Japanese economy to compete in today's globalised markets, particularly with resurgent American industries and rapidly growing Asian industries. They emphasise that the American economy is in good shape because it is one of the most deregulated economies in the world. Interestingly, they do not mention the fact that the United States regulate some areas more strictly than Japan does. Concerning regulations on industrial relations, they have a comprehensive set of anti-employment discrimination laws (Title VII of the Civil Rights Act, Age Discrimination in Employment Act, and Americans with Disabilities Act), a law protecting workers' pension rights (Employee Retirement Income Security Act, ERISA), etc.

Employers referred to the revision of the ILO Convention No. 96, which was realised in June 1997 as Convention No. 181 and Recommendation No. 188, as one of the international drives for deregulation of fee-charging employment placement businesses. There are plans to consider further deregulation in that area, taking into account the result of the ILO Convention revision. Some criticise business for intentionally interpreting the convention as promoting the liberalisation of private placement services for their own convenience.[34] It should be pointed out that, in order to comply with the new ILO Convention and Recommendation, regulations still need to be strengthened in areas such as the protection of workers' privacy.[35]

5. Modification of the Seniority-Based Wage System

Management is trying to modify the traditional seniority-based wage system into a merit or performance-based system. Since the burst of the bubble, rationalising white-collar management has been a pressing issue for Japanese companies. However, for the moment there seems to exist *de facto* consensus between management and labour that employment security, the core of the so-called 'Japanese

33. See T. Araki, *supra* note 10, for details.
34. Shigeru Wakita, Rodo Sha Haken Jigyo To Yuryo Shokugyo Shokai No Jiyu Ka Hihan (A Critical Study on the Argument for Liberating Worker Dispatching Businesses and Fee-Charging Employment Placement Services), Kikan Rodo Ho (Quarterly Labor Law), No. 183, p. 80 (1997).
35. See Koichi Kamata, Minkan Shokugyo Shokai Jo Ni Kansuru ILO Joyaku No Igi (The Significance of the ILO Convention Revision on Fee-Charging Employment Agencies), Nihon Rodo Ho Gakkai Shi (Journal of Labor law), No. 91, p. 113 (1998).

employment practice,' should be maintained.[36] That is why wage systems have become the main target of rationalisation. The most typical example of such a performance-based scheme is the so-called 'yearly salary system,' which entails yearly individual wage determination based on a worker's performance. According to the 1998 White Paper on Labour, 15.9 per cent of large-sized enterprises with 1000 employees or more have adopted the yearly salary system.[37]

At present, the yearly salary system is widely applied not only to workers in high managerial positions but also to middle-management white-collar workers. However, there is an obstacle to the shift toward more performance-based wage systems: overtime pay regulations. In principle the LSL requires overtime pay in proportion to the amount of overtime. This is not consistent with wage determination based on performance or results. The so-called 'white-collar exemption' under the LSL is strictly limited to 'persons in positions of supervision or management or persons handling confidential matters' (Art. 41, No. 2, LSL).[38] Thus, extending the coverage of the discretionary work scheme was welcomed by employers who have introduced or plan to introduce the yearly salary system for non-managerial white-collar workers.

6. The Need for Mobility

Today, Japanese workers have never been more mobile. Younger workers change jobs often. More and more older workers enter and leave the labour market voluntarily or involuntarily, as a result of early retirement, employment adjustment, etc. Global competition and technological innovation have accelerated the rise-and-fall cycle of industries and thus the flow of workers from declining industries to emerging new businesses needs to function smoothly. However, under the so-called 'long-term (or life-time) employment system',[39] the Japanese external labour market is not

---

36. T. Araki, *supra* note 15. In Japan, restraints on dismissals are not imposed by legislation but by case law. Interestingly there has been no proposal from management to initiate a legislative discussion to modify the case law on dismissals, although employers have emphasised the need for drastic deregulation in other areas. My impression is that the so-called 'life-time employment system' is rooted in Japanese labour relations like a religious belief. The 1998 White Paper reconfirmed that 80 per cent of Japanese employers still express their intention to maintain employment until the mandatory retirement age, and 60 per cent of employers will continue to do so in the future. The 1998 White Paper on Labor, *supra* note 19, p. 319.

37. It was 7.9 per cent in 1994. The 1998 White Paper on Labor, *supra* note 19, p. 220. According to another survey, 78 per cent of the surveyed companies have already introduced or plan to introduce the yearly salary system. Shakai Keizai Seisan Sei Honbu (the Japan Productivity Center for Socio-Economic Development, JPC-SED), Wagakuni Nenpo-Sei No Genjo To Tenbo (Current Situations and Future Prospect of the Yearly Salary System in Japan), p. 6 (1996).

38. The Ministry of Labour and the courts have narrowly interpreted this exemption. It was roughly estimated as of 1995 that the percentage of employees in managerial positions was 4.1–4.4 per cent. T. Araki, *supra* note 15.

39. Traditional employment practice in Japan can be described briefly as follows: a regular employee enters a company immediately after graduation and enjoys secure employment until reaching the mandatory retirement age. He or she receives systematic in-house education and training (OJT) and experiences various types of work under a periodical relocation program. Seniority, or the length of his or her service at a particular company, is the major factor determining promotion and wages. See Takashi Araki, 'Developing Employment Relations Law in Japan (Part 1: Japan's Long-term Employment Practice)', Labor Issues Quarterly, No. 20, pp. 21–24 (1993), at 21.

well developed. One of the purposes of deregulating labour market regulations was to activate the external labour market.

EVALUATION OF CURRENT DEREGULATION AND LABOUR LAW REFORMS

1. Pros and Cons

In general, the current deregulation trend is accepted, if not unanimously, among Japanese people. My impression is that this is because: (1) deregulation is considered the only measure or one of the few measures necessary to revitalise the economy, and (2) most people can tolerate labour law deregulation as long as the core of the long-term employment system, i.e., employment security, is untouched.

In short, objections to deregulation are based on the argument that labour law deregulation only benefits big companies and is detrimental to workers' welfare. As for each target of deregulation, naysayers offer the following concrete reasons for opposing deregulation:

- The government should have reinforced the public employment placement service for white-collar workers through public employment security offices instead of deregulating fee-charging employment placement businesses.[40] Business and government used the new ILO Convention as a pretext for deregulation while purposely ignoring the part of the convention which emphasises the need for increased regulation.[41]
- Dispatched workers are 'non-regular workers' outside the long-term employment practice, who are paid less than regular workers with less employment security. Further deregulation of worker dispatching businesses will only increase precarious employment.
- Modification of the working hours-averaging scheme over a one-year period will only benefit employers in that they can use it to economise overtime pay expenses. In exchange for the adoption of the one-year averaging scheme, the maximum workweek should be reduced from forty to 38 h.[42]
- The new discretionary work scheme covers white-collar workers in non-managerial positions, who in actuality do not have any 'discretion' at the workplace and are being forced to work longer hours. The new regulation only deprives those white-collar workers of their rights to overtime pay.
- Unlike typical European regulations, in Japan no objective reason is required to conclude a fixed-term contract. Its renewal is possible, but case law sets certain restrictions on renewal when the fixed-term contract is renewed repeatedly.[43] Along with the case law, the contract period limitation of one year has in practice contributed to enhancing workers' employment security.[44] Contract period deregulation would be to the detriment of workers' employment protection.

40. S. Nishitani, *supra* note 28, p. 14.
41. S. Wakita, *supra* note 34, p. 80.
42. See *http://www.jtuc-rengo.or.jp/rodofolder/rokihoD.html* (Japanese) or http://www.jtuc-rengo.or.jp/weekly/. week98feb/98feb20.html (English).
43. Toshiba Yanagimachi Factory case, Supreme Court, 22 July 1974, *Minshu,* Vol. 28, No. 5, p. 927.
44. S. Nishitani, *supra* note 28, p. 12.

- Abolishment of the LSL's protective provisions for women was wrong. To reduce unreasonably long working hours in Japan, a general upper limit of overtime, holiday, and night working hours should be set up for both male and female workers.[45]

2. Transitional Stage?

Further deregulation of labour law will surely be considered in the near future. A bill amending the WDL to introduce the negative list system has just been submitted to the Diet. The new discretionary work scheme may lead to extending the current coverage of white-collar work.

From the viewpoint that the main expectation for the discretionary work scheme is to allow employment management based on the result of workers' performance rather than on the amount of hours worked, the current regulation is still insufficient. It only enables an accepted estimate of the number of hours worked and does not override regulations on night work premiums, rest periods, or holiday work. Thus employers must still record how working hours of workers covered by the scheme are allocated.[46] Some evaluate the discretionary work scheme as a transitional stage from direct regulation to exemption.[47]

3. Collective Labour Relations – Already Decentralised

In Japan collective labour relations are already somewhat deregulated. Collective bargaining takes place at a decentralised level, i.e. the company, because over 90 per cent of all Japanese unions are enterprise-based unions. At a workplace where no union is organised, the work rules established by the employer determine working conditions. Under long-term employment practice, the courts have handed down decisions which allow employers, by modifying the work rules, to adjust working conditions flexibly, in accordance with economic fluctuations.

As explained above, the 1998 LSL reform introduced the labour–management committee as a part of the new discretionary work scheme put into effect in 2000. We should keep an eye on whether the committee will play a greater role in determining working conditions in the future.

4. *Quid Pro Quo* for Deregulation?

There are a few areas of labour legislation where regulations have increased. The following is the chronological list of these areas in the 1990s:

- The Child Care Leave Law of 1992 gives workers the right to child care leave if the child is less than one year old. The law was enacted to help workers (especially women) harmonise working life with family life.[48]

---

45. Hajime Wada, Rodo Jikan Ni Kansuru Joshi Hogo Kitei (Women's Protective Provisions regarding Working Hours), Kikan Rodo Ho (Quarterly Labor Law), No. 183, p. 45 (1997); Also see RENGO's web cite, *supra* note 42.
46. T. Araki, *supra* note 15. The situation will be the same even under the regulations of April 2000.
47. Ryuichi Yamakawa, Sairyo Rodo Sei No Shorai (Future of the Discretionary Work Scheme), Jurist, No. 1066, p. 197 (1995).
48. M. Kurokawa, *supra* note 25, p. 73.

- The Older Persons' Employment Stabilisation Law of 1986 was amended in 1994. The amended law provides that a mandatory retirement age fixed by the employer shall not be below 60.
- In 1995, the Child Care Leave Law of 1992 was revised to become the Child Care and Family Care Leave Law. The law gives a worker the right to a family care leave of up to three consecutive months if he or she has a family member in need of care.
- Even the 1998 LSL reform, which introduced the new discretionary work scheme and relaxed the current regulation on contract period limitations, contains several provisions imposing new obligations on employers. For example, from 1 April 1999, an employer must give a newly-hired employee a document indicating his or her wages, working hours, etc., while under the old regulations the worker could be informed orally about all working conditions, other than wages. Likewise, from April 1999, an employee leaving his or her company will be able to have the employer disclose in writing the reason for termination of the employment contract.
- The most important *quid pro quo* for deregulation was the amendment of the EEOL. The 'duty to endeavour' provisions will be reinforced into a legal obligation from 1 April 1999 in return for repealing the LSL's protective provisions for women.

In short, regulations have been strengthened in the areas related to changes in the structure of the workforce. The Japanese labour market is, and will surely be, composed of older workers, more women workers, and fewer younger workers. One could say that these measures intended to encourage women and older persons to enter and remain in the labour market because the expected labour shortage will require a greater utilisation of women and older workers. My impression is that the legislator's intention has been to support women workers who want to, or are forced to, harmonise working life with family life. Or, put more straightforwardly, the government wants women to have more babies!

CONCLUSION: 'INDIVIDUALISATION' AS A KEYWORD FOR THE 21st CENTURY'S LABOUR LAW

Workers have become more and more individualised in various ways. Evidence of this is the decline of the union organisation rate as a world trend. People are irritated at the rigid, inflexible process of collective bargaining. Even in Japan where collective labour relations are relatively decentralised, there are significant numbers of workers who are independent, capable of making their own decisions, and want to negotiate with employers on their own.

The LSL contains several provisions allowing contracting parties to 'contract out' of legal norms set by protective labour legislation through collective agreements or labour–management agreements. The 1998 reform may be considered as allowing contracting-out of working hours regulations for the new discretionary scheme with an individual's consent. It was a minor but significant change since traditional labour law has paternalistically restricted workers' intention and ability to contract out of protective provisions. Some contend that a similar system should have also been introduced for women workers who want to contract out of their protective provisions.[49] Such a contracting-out system may be more widespread in the coming era of individualised workers.

49. H. Wada, *supra* note 45, p. 45

This does not mean that labour law is diminishing. It will likely continue to play two roles in the next century. First, it will offer paternalistic protection for workers as before. Even in the 21st century, individualised workers capable of making their own decisions are not the majority. There will still be much room for traditional protective labour legislation.

Second, for individualised workers, labour law should support them so that they can individually enter into negotiations, conclude transactions, and compete in the labour market on equal terms.[50] In this vein, from the viewpoint of offering equal opportunities for negotiation and competition in the labour market, the introduction of comprehensive anti-discrimination laws should be considered in return for deregulation. The reinforcement of the EEOL in 1999 could be regarded as a breakthrough.

50. Kazuo Sugeno & Yasuo Suwa, Rodo Shijo No Henka To Rodo Ho No Kadai (The Future of Labour Law in the Structurally Changing Labour Market), The Monthly Journal of The Japan Institute of Labour, No. 418, p. 13 (1994).

6. Deregulation and Labour Law: The Swedish Case

Ronnie Eklund

1. INTRODUCTION

Deregulation implies the abolition of rules, but the word is also, misleadingly, used in the context of a change to less interventionist methods and forms.[1] Often the words 'simplification'or 're-regulation' of exiting rules are used. Deregulation, though, is not characteristic of Swedish labour law. It has so far taken place only in the area of the contracting-out of manpower and the lifting of the ban on private employment exchange agencies in 1991 and 1993. There is, however, much talk about 'flexibility', mostly in the area of working time issues. Certainly, for many years re-regulation of labour law as applied to the government sector has been taking place. Maybe it is more correct to say that here re-regulation equals 'privatisation', in the sense that the specific public law framework has been harmonised with that of labour in the private sector.

Note

References to other works in footnotes have not been translated into English. I am responsible for all the translations of the Swedish texts quoted. The following abbreviations have been used:

AD	Labour Court Reports
AMS	Swedish National Labour Market Board
AU	Parliamentary Labour Market Committee Report
Ds	Ministry Reports
EC	European Community
ECR	European Court Reports
EEA	European Economic Area
EU	European Union
HTF	Commercial Employees' Union
ILO	International Labour Organisation
JT	Juridisk tidskrift (law review edited under the auspices of the School of Law, Stockholm University)
LO	Confederation of Trade Unions in Sweden
NJA	Supreme Court Reports
prop.	Government Bill
PTK	Cartel for Privately Employed Employees
SAF	Confederation of Swedish Employers
SOU	Government Official Reports
SPUR	Swedish Association of Temporary Work Businesses and Staffing Services
TfR	Tidsskrift for Retsvitenskap (Nordic Law Review)

1. See A. Ogus, *Regulation. Legal Form and Economic Theory*, 1994, p. 10.

R. Blanpain (ed.), Deregulation and Labour Law, 115–135

2. DEREGULATION OF LABOUR LAW IN SWEDEN

2.1. Labour Market Regulations

2.1.1. Private employment agencies and temporary work agencies

Since long ago these two issues have been dealt with as one in Sweden. It is remarkable that within the group of the Nordic countries only Sweden has adopted such a view.[2]

According to the old Swedish Act of 1935,[3] amended in 1942,[4] contracting out of manpower was deemed to constitute employment exchange and was hence prohibited when the major objective of the arrangement was to procure work for a job-seeking person. It was of no consequence whether the job seeker was employed by an intermediary, or whether the intermediary was employed by the job seeker. The purpose of the 1942 amendment was to bring to an end impresario activities in the entertainment business.[5] The 1942 amendment caused a lot of confusion in legal application as well as practicability.[6] The fine penalties handed down by the courts in the few cases in which the supplier of temporary personnel had violated the law were extremely low. In a 1989 Supreme Court case, the fine penalty was set to some 100 U.S. dollars.[7] The prohibition was less than successful, and the entire scheme subsequently came under fire.[8]

After repeated attempts to work out more effective rules in the 1960s and 1970s, the 1942 amendment was repealed in 1991. Yet, the 1991 Act still contained some slight restrictions on the use of 'temps', and the public employment exchange monopoly was left untouched. It may be worthwhile mentioning that it was the Social Democratic Government which started the deregulation process. The change was controversial. It may be deduced from the legislative history that the changes were seen as an adjustment due to the appearance of new companies

2. For a more comprehensive account I refer to my articles, A Look at Contract Labour in the Nordic Countries, in JT 1995–96 No. 3 pp. 625–654 and Public Employment Exchange and the Use of Temporary Employment Agencies in the Nordic Countries, in Recht der Europa. Festschrift für Hilmar Fenge, 1997, pp. 183–205 and to R. Fahlbeck, Employment Exchange and Hiring out of Employees in Sweden, in TfR 1995 No. 4, pp. 589–622.
3. Prop. 1935:83, ratifying the 1933 ILO Convention No. 34/1933.
4. Prop. 1942:123.
5. Even the exchange of au pair jobs was considered as job placement in violation of the principal ban on private employment exchange, see two Supreme Court cases, NJA 1948 p. 493 (in the disguise of 'language exchange') and NJA 1992 B 1 ('Au Pair Magazine').
6. In court practice, the amendment was also applied to so-called typewriting agencies that had sent their employees to work with principal employers, see Supreme Court cases, NJA 1962 p. 680 and 1989 p. 629. The same treatment in NJA 1973 p. 562 (manpower was contracted out to a dockyard). As time went by, the Swedish Labour Court had to deal with the 1942 amendment with respect to the application of the so-called veto right in Sections 38–40 of the Joint Regulation Act of 1976, see Labour Court judgements AD 1979 No. 31, 1987 No. 154 and 1990 No. 67. The entire issue of the applicability of the 1942 amendment is meticulously discussed in prop. 1970:166 with respect to further amendments of the 1935 Act. At that time the Swedish Government had approached the ILO about the activities of the so-called typewriting agencies, and received the reply that the ILO Convention No. 96/1949, Part II, should apply. See more specifically, a Swedish Report, DsIn 1966:6. Den ambulerande skrivbyråverksamheten.
7. NJA 1989 p. 629.
8. See, e.g., two pamphlets from the Confederation of Swedish Employers (SAF): Nyttiga serviceföretag eller olaga arbetsförmedling, 1988 and Tillåt privat arbetsförmedling, 1990.

offering various kinds of services on the market, and as a corrective measure for the ineffectiveness of the former legislative regime spanning from 1935.[9] The demands of real life and the quest for flexibility had thus defeated this lame-duck legislation.

A further step taken in 1993 by the non-socialist Government implied that the monopoly of employment exchange was over. Aspects of competition were decisive when deregulation was suggested.[10] In the legislative history references to the case law of the European Court of Justice can be found.[11] The supply of manpower falls within the ambit of the freedom to supply services, as provided for by Article 59 *et seq.* of the E.C. Treaty.[12]

It must be mentioned that the ILO Fee-Charging Employment Agencies Convention (Revised) No. 96/1949 (replacing the Fee-Charging Employment Agencies Convention No. 34/1933) was ratified by Sweden in 1950,[13] but was subsequently rescinded in the spring of 1992.[14] The Private Employment Agencies Convention of 1997, revising the 1949 Convention, is now under deliberation in Sweden. In 1949 Sweden also ratified the ILO Employment Service Convention No. 88/1948, requiring that the ratifying members should 'maintain or ensure the maintenance of a free public employment service' (Article 1).[15]

The 1993 Act thus lifted the Swedish ban on private employment exchange with a view to profit.[16] The only restriction left is that in accordance with Section 6 a job seeker may not be charged any fees for registration costs or other services.[17] Violations of this rule will bring penal sanctions (fine or imprisonment). A survey from 1995 indicates that private employment exchange recruiters have not invaded the market; they account for only 0.4% of those who took up new employment. It is much more surprising to find that the public employment exchange accounts for only 12–13% of all those persons who received information about another job that led to new employment.[18]

The 1993 Act on Private Employment Exchange and the Hiring-out of Manpower (as well as the 1991 Act) provides a *definition of contracted-out labour*. Section 2 of the Act states that 'the hiring-out of manpower implies a

9. Prop. 1990/91:124, pp. 13–18.
10. Prop. 1992/93:118, pp. 19–20, see also SOU 1992:116. Privat arbetsförmedling och uthyrning av arbetskraft, pp. 74–75.
11. Case C-41/90 *Höfner and Elser v. Macrotron* 1991 ECR I-1979. In this case the High Court disapproved of parts of the German public employment exchange monopoly under Articles 86 and 90 of the E.C. Treaty. The case concerned the recruitment of a sales manager for a German company. The company had entrusted the assignment to two personnel consultants, but the sales manager was never appointed. The consultants were not paid by the company. Two similar cases relate to the Italian legislation on placement agencies, Case C-55/96 *Job Centre Coop* 1997 ECR I-7119 (intermediary for temporary staff) and Case C-163/96 *Silvano Raso and others* 1998 ECR I-533 (dock work monopoly).
12. Case 279/80 *Alfred John Webb* 1981 ECR 3305.
13. Prop. 1950:188.
14. Prop. 1991/92:89.
15. Prop. 1949:162.
16. An exception has been made for the employment exchange of seamen (Section 3), which is a reflection of the ILO Convention No. 9/1920, ratified by Sweden in 1921, prop. 1921:361.
17. See further SOU 1992:116, pp. 96–98 and prop. 1992/93:218, pp. 27, 29. Once I suggested such a solution in an address held to the Swedish Labour Law Association in Stockholm in 1989, see R. Eklund, Entreprenader – arbetsrättsliga aspekter på en organisationsfråga, JT 1989–90, pp. 271–285, 278.
18. Report from National Labour Market Board, Arbetsförmedlingens marknadsandelar 1995 (Uin 1996:3). AMS, p. 13.

legal relationship between a principal employer and another employer, the purpose of which is that the latter employer places his employees at the principal employer's disposal at an agreed price and in order to let the employees perform work in the principal employer's business'. The stipulated definition has made superfluous any discussion as to who may be regarded as an employer; it is perfectly clear that it is the supplier of personnel who is to be regarded as the employer.

From Section 2 it also follows that the principal employer must direct and allot the work to be performed by the 'temp'. If this is not the case, the supplier of personnel is assumed to be just a job contractor.[19] However, to state without reservation that the right to direct and allot work has been *delegated* to the principal employer might not be a tenable position. The reason for this is that the entire rationale behind short-term employment of this kind is that the supplier of manpower is not supposed to exercise the right to direct and allot work at all – if the practicalities of contracting-out are to be fully considered. *One might say instead that an implied and necessary condition for any contract of employment of this kind is that the 'temp' is placed at the disposal of another principal employer.* However, such a divided employer relationship may create practical legal problems. For example, it seems unclear as to whether it is the user-enterprise or the provider (or both?) that should be legally responsible for the violations of the law, should such violations occur in the user-enterprise while the employees are engaged there.[20] To whom, for example, does an offended employee turn, who was referred to a workplace by a placement agency, in case of harassment by a supervisor of the user-enterprise? The only effective remedy for the provider may be to cancel the commercial contract with the user-enterprise, but what recourse to law has the offended employee? One might argue that the provider would not wish to be held responsible for any violations occurring at the workplace of the user-enterprise. The user-enterprise may want to argue that it cannot be held legally responsible since no employment relationship has been established between the user-enterprise and the employee in question.[21]

The kind of employment contract which is involved in contracting-out is not so easily squared with the fundamentals of the labour law rules which presuppose a strict employer–employee relationship. This is a phenomenon found elsewhere, for example, when the employees of a group of companies are formally employed in one company, but perform work in another company.[22] A great number of aspects may have to be considered in this context, such as, for example, the duty to perform work.[23]

In the Swedish Labour Court case, AD 1990 No. 87, the Court held that the hired-out employees could hold 'their' own employer responsible for the wrongdoings of the user-enterprise. In this case, company A borrowed electricians from

19. Labour Court judgement AD 1980 No. 54.
20. See further, the ILO report Contract Labour. 85th Session of the International Labour Conference 1997, 1996, *passim*.
21. R. Fahlbeck suggests 'that the users have the same obligations as employers'. See his article referred to in note 2, p. 618. This may be a good statement *de lege ferenda*, but – to be frank – no cases supporting the conclusion have been found.
22. See, e.g., R. Eklund, *Bolagisering – ett mode eller ett måste?*, 1992, pp. 156–183. Two and three partite employment relationships are also dealt with in a Norwegian report, H. Torp and S.P. Pettersen, *Markedet for korttidsarbeid*, 1989, pp. 65–77.
23. See, e.g., Labour Court judgement AD 1996 No. 113. The former Swedish Postal Services were incorporated as a State-owned joint-stock company. One of the postmen refused to perform work for the new company. The Court found that he was obliged to do so, since the former employer's major obligations (to pay wages etc.) were still executed by this employer.

company B, both companies acting as units of the same group of companies. The same collective bargaining agreement applied to both companies. The user-employer had violated the wage tariffs of the collective agreement in relation to both groups of employees. The Court found that both employers were in breach of contract and that they were obliged to pay general damages to the trade union that represented the employees. The Court held that company B could not be absolved from liability due to the fact that it had handed over the right to direct work to company A. The Court did not voice an opinion, however, on the matter of whether the user-employer could be held responsible for the violation of the collective agreement in relation to the electricians borrowed from company B.

The 1993 Act also abolished some restrictions laid down by the 1991 Act. Section 4(1) of the 1993 Act provides that the hired-out employee is guaranteed the right to take up employment with the principal employer after having fulfilled the assignment. So-called competition clauses set up by the temporary work agency in order to discourage the employee from taking up such employment have thus been outlawed. Section 4(2) also provides that an employee who has left the principal employer in order to take up employment with a temporary employment agency cannot be hired out to his former employer earlier than six months after the expiry of his former employment. This restriction is motivated by the fact that employees must not be subjected to unfair recruitment procedures by temporary employment agencies.[24] It is an open question, however, whether this restriction applies to cases in which the employee has been made redundant, and subsequently takes up employment with a temporary employment agency. It is obvious that the restriction cannot apply, if, for example, a temporary employment agency has taken over certain functions of the principal employer, including the employees of the principal employer. This is job-contracting proper and must hence be distinguished from labour-only contracting. A case of this kind may also be deemed to be a legal transfer of a part of an undertaking or business under the E.C. Directive 77/187 concerning the safeguarding of the employees' rights in relation to transfers of undertakings and parts thereof, as well as the applicable provisions of the Swedish Employment Protection Act and Joint-Regulation Act, as amended in 1994.[25]

The 1993 Act was evaluated in 1997.[26] The report found, among other things, that very few private employment exchange agencies had been set up and that no negative experiences had been noted with the exception of artist exchange agencies which started to exact fees from job applicants.[27] There was no evidence that the frequency of regular jobs was affected by the fact that manpower was contracted-out. The frequency of contract manpower had increased, however. Still, it related to only 0.2% of the total labour force.[28] In May 1998 the same figure was estimated to be 0.44% (approx. 18,500 persons).[29] The three largest companies had each more than 1500 employees.[30] The largest companies belong to the branch organisation SPUR.

24. Prop. 1990/91:124, p. 55, prop. 1992/93:218, p. 32.
25. Prop. 1994/95:102.
26. SOU 1997 : 58. Personaluthyrning.
27. Op.cit., pp. 34–36.
28. Op.cit., pp. 40–41 (9400 persons in late 1996).
29. Source: Branschens utveckling och omfattning. Personaluthyrning, entreprenader, rekrytering. SPUR, 1998, p. 9.
30. The three largest companies were: Manpower Teamwork (3000 employees), Proffice (1800 employees) and Olsten Personalkraft (1500 employees). Source: the daily *Dagens Nyheter*, 29 May 1998.

The branch includes not only companies that are involved in the contracting-out of manpower, but also companies doing business in recruitment, consultant services and job-contracting (usually 'out-sourced' activities). The 1997 report suggests that a statute should regulate the institutionalisation of a board, and the monitoring of the service agencies, and that they should be registered if certain basic conditions are fulfilled. The Government has, however, declared lately that it has no intention to intervene.[31]

2.1.2. *Fixed-term contracts*

The number of fixed-term contracts has been steadily growing. Recent statistics indicate that such contracts amounted to 644,000 in August 1998. The number of self-employed persons, including those helping family members, was 416,000 in 1998.[32] The entire labour force on the Swedish labour market amounted to 4,046,000 persons in the August of 1998. This means that approx. 1/4 of the working force do not have regular employment. The group of fixed-term contracts included in the statistics is made up of: substitute employment, trial employment, holiday work, employment for a special job or project, employment 'out of necessity' (labour on call), probationary and seasonal work. This catalogue does not coincide with the list of fixed-term contracts stipulated by the Employment Protection Act (see below). A survey from 1996 shows that substitute employment is the most frequent type of fixed-term contract.[33] Some 180,000 employees work as substitutes (40%). The growth of labour-on-call employment has been considerable, amounting to some 100,000 persons (18%). The latter type of employment is not employment in the legal sense of the word, requiring classification in other legal terms.[34] Likewise, employment for a special job or project is on the increase (90,000).[35]

The increase in the various types of fixed-term employment expresses the need for increased flexibility in the labour market.[36] It is noteworthy that the call for flexibility seems to have appeared without any changes in the legal framework,[37] implying that the employers have extended the use of the options already available by means of the statutes. No deregulation of the legal framework, giving the employers a total or more extensive freedom to act, has taken place. It is also necessary to say that many concessions have been made in the respective collective bargaining agreements covering the various sectors of the Swedish labour market entitling employers to opt for fixed-term contracts on terms less stiff than the ones provided by the statute. It is a peculiarity in Swedish labour law that some statutory provisions may be derogated from by means of a collective bargaining agreement (see below).

A short description follows detailing the ways in which employers may conclude fixed-term employment contracts. It should be emphasised that the basic

---

31. Prop. 1997/98:150, p. 105.
32. Arbetskraftsundersökningen i augusti 1998 (Labour Force Survey, August, 1998). SCB, p. 8.
33. Report from the National Labour Market Board, Anställningsformer. Ura 1997:4, p. 6.
34. It is a form of employment in which an employment contract usually exists, but where the employee performs gainful work occasionally and only when the employer has such work to offer. See, A. Henning, *Tidsbegränsad anställning. En studie av anställningsformsregleringen och dess funktioner*, 1984, pp. 212 *et seq.*
35. Report from the National Labour Market Board, Anställningsformer. Ura 1997:4, p. 6.
36. SOU 1997:58, p. 24.
37. The same conclusion in Arbetsmarknad utan AMS. SAF 1997, p. 32.

rule of the 1982 Employment Protection Act gives preference to regular employment (Section 4). Exceptions to this rule are found in Sections 5, 5a and 6 of the Act. Section 5 originates from the 1974 and the 1982 Employment Protection Acts.[38] Section 5 provides, *inter alia*, that short-term employment for a limited time, season or job may be entered into 'if the work is of a specific nature', in case of 'substitute employment, probationary or holiday work', or when there is 'a temporary work load' lasting for not more than six months during a period of two years. Section 6 provides for 'trial employment' up to six months. Trial employment may be discontinued at any time.

Section 5a is an innovation and the result of an amendment in 1996/1997 introduced by the Social Democratic Government after heated debate. It provides for so-called 'consensual fixed-term employment'. It entitles the employer to enter into this form of employment, for whatever reason, limiting it, however, to 12 months (18 months in special cases) during a period of three years. Only five employees may be so employed simultaneously. The basic objective of the introduction of such a provision has been to make it easier for small enterprises to hire.[39]

The above-mentioned 1996/1997 amendment of the Employment Protection Act did not come as a bolt from the blue. The history of the amendment reveals all the frustrations and difficulties in introducing an even more innocuous labour law provision. It all started in 1993 when the non-socialist Government proposed an amendment to the Employment Protection Act in the situation of high unemployment. Many more far-reaching proposals were suggested at the time,[40] but the Government was satisfied to submit only a few of them to the Parliament.[41] The amendment went into force on 1 January 1994. It included, *inter alia*, a provision which entitled the employer to extend trial employment from six months to 12 months and which gave the employer the right to exempt two 'key-persons' from the seniority list in case of redundancies. The reform package was heavily contested by the trade unions and the Social Democrats. In the national elections in the autumn of 1994 the Social Democrats promised to 'restore' the labour law. The Social Democrats won the elections and the new Government submitted a 'restoration bill' at the end of 1994.[42]

So, the state of law in the discussed area was back to square one on 1 January 1995. Soon thereafter, in March 1995, the Government appointed a commission headed by an independent chairman and composed of representatives of the labour market parties. The task of the commission was to prepare a 'social contract' concerning the controversial labour law issues against the background of high unemployment. The Minister of Labour stated that the main objective of the commission was to 'find ways and means of designing the future labour law, preferably by means of collective bargaining agreements'.[43] The commission could not reach a joint conclusion. The debate culminated in May 1996 when the commission's (i.e. the chairman's) proposals, which were designed as a collective bargaining agreement and which was meant to be in effect for five years, were rejected by both SAF and LO, the two major employer and employee organisations, respectively, on the

38. Prop. 1973:129 and prop. 1981/82:71.
39. Prop. 1996/97:16, p. 32.
40. SOU 1993:32. Ny anställningsskyddslag.
41. Prop. 1993/94:67.
42. Prop. 1994/95:76.
43. L. Blomberg, Anställda ska få inflytande, in the daily *Dagens Nyheter*, 17 March 1995.

Swedish labour market. The proposal contained, among other things, the introduction of rules on 'consensual fixed-term employment' (very similar to the rules of Section 5a of the Employment Protection Act described above), variations in the periods of notice, new provisions on part-time employment, the introduction of manpower competence funds and the lifting of some of the restrictions relating to the seniority rules in connection with redundancies.[44]

At face value the package looked attractive, but the differences between the two major combatants (SAF and LO) regarding particularly the seniority issue were irreconcilable. There was a lack of trust between the labour market parties, said the commission's chairman, and continued: 'The political pressure to make the labour market parties reach a joint conclusion on labour law in the promised land of collective bargaining agreements is strong. Why doesn't it happen? The answer is very simple. They do not have to agree upon anything since the Employment Protection Act is to a large extent an alternative to collective bargaining agreements. There is no economic pressure exerted on them to come to an agreement.'[45] So, the Government's attempt to find a solution by means of a tripartite experiment failed. The trade union representatives hoped for continued discussions, but the employer representatives refused. However, on 28 May 1996 the labour market parties agreed to continue the discussions at the request of the Government. Another round of conciliation talks should have ensued, with experienced conciliators taking part, but the talks never came about.[46]

Again the Government was cornered. In the meantime, the SAF had won over public opinion after leading an intensive campaign law since the beginning of the 1990s whose essence was to reform labour law. On 23 August 1996 the Government declared that it intended to present a modernised labour law proposal before the Parliament. A limited package, including the above-mentioned 'consensual fixed-term employment', was presented together with the Centre Party. The co-operation of the Centre Party was necessary because the Government had no parliamentary majority. The package also included amendments related to the Act's recall right, period of notice, part-time and substitute employment and the conclusion of local collective agreements.

The reform agenda was highly moderate. No proposal other than the 'consensual fixed-term employment' offered more flexibility. The contrary could be said of the other proposals.[47] The package came immediately under fire from one of the leading trade unionists, the negotiations secretary of the LO, who said that the Social Democratic Government had to face 'a historical cross-roads', if it opted for the suggested 'neoliberal deregulation'.[48] The Government's proposal was untimely as in 1996 the LO Congress was holding its convention at the same time. Vehement protests were launched from the rostrum by the trade union delegates. The delegates even demonstrated openly on the streets of Stockholm on 9 September 1996. A leading industrial relations expert said that the controversy between the Social

44. Samarbetsavtal? 10 May 1996 (mimeographed).
45. T. Hagström, Undantagslag får ersätta las, in the daily *Dagens Nyheter*, 26 May 1996.
46. However, a preliminary agreement was concluded between the Swedish Agency for Government Employers, on one hand, and two of the public sector trade unions, on the other, on 23 August 1996. The agreement never came into force.
47. Same observation in R. Fahlbeck, *Flexibility. Potentials and Pitfalls for Labour Law*, 1998, p. 32.
48. See, e.g., H. Karlsson, Ovärdigt en arbetarregering, in the daily *Dagens Nyheter*, 5 September 1996.

Democratic Government and the LO was unprecedented in the history of the consolidated labour movement in Sweden.[49] The Government did not yield. A bill was submitted to the Parliament on 24 October 1996.[50] The bill struck a 'reasonable balance' between the employees' needs for employment security and the employers' needs for adjustment to the market situation. It was meant to facilitate employment of new staff for employers.[51] The proposals went into force on 1 January 1997. It was a setback for the employers soon thereafter to find, however, that the new provision on 'consensual fixed-term contracts' did not automatically supersede the corresponding less generous provision on fixed-term contracts as set forth in the forestry collective bargaining agreement when the first case was handed down on 1 April 1998.[52]

2.1.3. Labour law as applied to the government sector

The deregulation of various specific rules applicable to the government sector has been taking place during a time-span of more than 30 years. The point of departure was the year 1965 when the public sector trade unions were accorded the right to strike and to conclude legally binding collective bargaining agreements.[53] The prior administrative legal framework of public employment was done away with. The basis of the employment contract was henceforth the private contract. The second step was taken in 1976, when an attempt was made to harmonise the government sector's labour law with that in the private sector, as part of the major revision of collective labour law which resulted in the 1976 Act on Joint Regulation.[54] The Act on Official Employment came into force on 1 January 1977. The Act applied mostly to the state sector. Further refinements of the state sector labour law were made in the 1980s.[55] A third major step to harmonise the state sector's labour law with that of the private sector's labour law was taken in 1994. A new Act on Official Employment came into force. Another wave of deregulation measures swept over the existing rules and many of them were abolished. The reform was dictated by two objectives: to increase the efficiency of the public sector and to facilitate and improve the handling of personnel issues.[56] Some of the special provisions applicable to

49. Comment by N. Elvander, professor of industrial relations in Uppsala, in the daily *Dagens Nyheter*, 7 September 1996.
50. Prop. 1996/97:16.
51. Op.cit., pp. 19–20, 23.
52. Labour Court judgement AD 1998 No. 36.
53. Prop. 1965:60.
54. Prop. 1975/76:105. App. 2.
55. So, for example, efficiency aspects dictated that the skills factor should be paramount in connection with the appointment of civil servants in 1985 and 1986, see prop. 1985/86:116, DsC 1983:16. Meritvärderingen vid statliga tjänstetillsättningar m.m. The right to appeal the (state) employer's decision on certain issues was curtailed in 1986, see, *inter alia*, prop. 1986/87:84, DsC 1985:20. Överprövning av beslut i personalfrågor. Recently, the collective bargaining parties in the state sector have also asked the Government to limit the right to appeal certain decisions related to time-off for civil servants; see Ramavtal 1998–2001, 8 May 1998. App. 11. In fact, very few decisions taken by the (state) employer are nowadays subject to the exercise of state authority. Appointment of a person to a post is one such decision, subject to a right of appeal; see the 1974 Labour Disputes Act, Chapter 1, Section 2.
56. Prop. 1993/94:65, pp. 29–30.

public employees, especially state employees, have survived, but their volume has been dramatically reduced.[57]

These developments can hardly be described in terms of deregulation; it is rather an example of re-regulation. The objective of the legislative efforts described above has been to harmonise the rules applied in the various sectors of the labour market. This meant doing away with a huge number of specific rules which applied solely to government employees. In common Swedish parlance, one often talks about the 'privatisation' of the public employment labour law.

2.1.4. Company health services

Company health services once benefited from a state subsidy covering just about 1/3 of the total costs. The subsidy was abolished on 1 January 1993[58] since one could no longer discern any incentive effect of the subsidy in the promotion of health services among smaller enterprises with less than 20 employees. It was found that some 80% of all the employees benefited from health services, while the goal had once been set at 75%. One could say that the goal had been reached. The abolition of the subsidy system is no doubt a form of deregulation, since from 1993 employers may provide for health services either with in-house facilities or by procuring the services from external service providers.

2.2. Individual Labour Relations

2.2.1. Working time issues

Sweden applies a 40-h working week.[59] The 'flexibility' debate has been lively with regard to this matter. A special type of flexibility would be to give the employer a *right to vary the working time* over a longer period of time. Such a solution is dictated by the employer's efficiency interests, so that he could allocate work to periods when the work-load is high.[60] The legal point of departure is, however, different. The employer is the sole decision-maker as regards the daily allocation of working hours, unless a collective bargaining agreement stipulates otherwise, which is usually, however, the case. If an agreement stipulates a 40-h working week, working time is also considered fixed under the agreement week after week, and cannot be varied from one week to another. If the 40-h working week is not part of the agreement, the 1982 Act applies instead.[61]

---

57. So, for example, the rules applicable to dismissals and summary dismissals, as designed by the 1982 Employment Protection Act, apply to all employees in Sweden since 1994, though special rules apply to judges (Swedish Constitution, Chapter 11, Section 5) and other long-tenured employees, such as prosecutors, previously appointed professors and military personnel (1994 Act on Life-Long Tenured Employment).
58. Prop. 1991/92:100. App. 11, pp. 28–29.
59. In fact, the average work-week for all employees (both full and part-time) is shorter, as low as 31.3 h if all absence from work is accounted for, SOU 1996:145. Arbetstid – längd, förläggning och inflytande, p. 84.
60. See D. Johnsson and J. Malmberg, *Avtalsutveckling på arbetstidsområdet*, 1998, pp. 22–26.
61. Labour Court judgement AD 1984 nr 108.

A hotly debated issue in Sweden is the demand for a shorter working week of 35 (or even 30) h under the law.[62] The objective of this proposal is to create new jobs. In a recent Government report the problem has been referred to the labour market parties.[63] It is not surprising therefore that as a response to the Government report the major labour market parties were unanimous in their public remarks, rejecting legislation.[64] Early in 1998 the Deputy Minister of Labour declared that she had no intention of submitting a new working time act to the Parliament since the working time issues had been on the agenda during the 1997–1998 wage negotiations.[65]

This brings me to the issue of the 1997–1998 wage negotiations. Many trade unions had asked for a shorter working week in their opening proposals. The employers rejected the bids. One of the most influential trade unions, the Paper and Paper Pulp Workers' Union was the first one to act. After protracted negotiations, the Paper and Paper pulp Industry Collective Bargaining Agreement was ready during the first days in January 1998 following the active intervention of impartial arbitrators under the 1997 industrial peace agreement. It was otherwise a meagre agreement, said the President of the union, but held also that 'it was a breakthrough as regards the matter of a shorter working week'.[66] The essence of the agreement is that working time was reduced by 1.5% of the total number of hours worked per year. Technically, and this is the innovation introduced by the impartial arbitrators, it has been achieved by the institutionalisation of *individual working time accounts* to which a fixed percent of the yearly wage is allocated. The account may be used in a three-fold way: paid non-working time, pension bonus or cash money. This opens up a plethora of alternatives and increases the individual's freedom of choice. It is also one of many examples that flexibilisation is not the same as deregulation. The Paper and Paper Pulp Agreement also gives the employer the right to vary the working time of an individual worker by up to 40 h per year for daytime work (not shift-work). The employers had been clamouring for flexible working hours for a long time.[67] The union yielded this time. Usually, the trade unions strongly resist ideas of this kind; working time issues are looked upon strictly as a matter of collective labour law.[68] The paper and pulp agreement paved the way for similar designs in other collective bargaining agreements entered into at the beginning of 1998.

In the above-mentioned Government Report the appointed commission is asked to investigate the need for flexibility on working time issues. The Swedish 1982 Working Time Act is only semi-mandatory (Section 3), which means that the Act gives the social partners an option to deviate from the statute and, being thus able

62. See SOU 1996:145, pp. 270–312 (relating to the politicl parties' views on the 35-h working week; this is the view advocated by the Left Party and the Green Party, while the Social Democrats and non-socialist parties – the Conservatives, Liberals, Christian Democrats and the Centre Party – are against it). The Parliamentary Labour Market Committee has lately rejected bills from members of the Parliament on the reduction of the working week to 35 h; see 1997/98: AUI, p. 20 and 1997/98: AU8, p. 11.
63. SOU 1996:145, pp. 148, 229–234.
64. Summary in Lag & Avtal No. 4/1997.
65. Riksdagens protokoll 1997/98:54, 22 January 1998. As a result of the outcome of the national elections in 1998 the Social Democratic Government has come to an agreement with the Left Party and the Green Party to refer the issue of a shorter working week to a joint working committee. Source: the daily *Dagens Nyheter*, 7 October 1998.
66. Comment in the daily, *Dagens Nyheter*, 5 January 1998.
67. See, Arbetsmarknad utan AMS. SAF, 1997, pp. 37–39.
68. 'This is an important power issue', says a trade union lawyer, K. Junesjö, *Strejk – en demokratisk rättighet för bättre arbetsförhållanden*, 1998, p. 25.

to sidestep the supervision of governmental agencies, makes them masters of the Act. This is also the rule on the Swedish labour market. But such derogations must as a basic rule take place at branch level. It is now argued in the Government Report that flexibility considerations require that derogations should take place in the normal course of events at entrepreneurial level; this would give 'a signal from the legislator that flexibility at the workplace level should be accorded more weight'.[69] Looked upon from this point of view it is no wonder that the trade unions have publicly rejected the proposal, while the employers have embraced it.[70] Other flexibility aspects discussed in the Report relate, *inter alia*, to the employee's individual working time,[71] and the option to use vacation days exceeding four weeks to shorten the working day.[72] Another special flexibility aspect concerns the calculation period for the average 40 h working week which is now limited to a four-week period. The commission suggests that the calculation period should be extended to ten weeks.[73] This is, it is held, 'a signal that the regular working time should be used to a larger extent than at present to meet the variations in the need for manpower'.[74]

It may be of interest to highlight the views advanced by the representatives of the labour market parties in the above-mentioned Government Report.[75] The employer side (both private and public sector employers) argues that the commission has failed to introduce sufficiently flexible rules. For example, employer representatives insist that the individual employee should be the sole decision-maker as regards issues such as whether the employee should have breaks, daily and weekly periods of rest, and even whether the stipulated 40-h working week should be calculated on a yearly basis instead of on a 10-week basis. The present overtime standard (200 h calculated on a yearly basis) should be maintained. On the trade union side, the LO representative held, *inter alia*, that the flexibility aspects have not been sufficiently well analysed. She stated that flexibility was already provided for in the present Act. She rejected the idea that the power to derogate from the Act should be passed down to the enterprise level because it would lead to opportunistic behaviour on the employer side, who could take advantage of, e.g., retrenchments in order to ask for concessions with regard to sensitive working time issues. Criticism was also launched against the calculation period of 10 weeks as the basis of the average 40-h working week. She argued that the employer's unilateral right to vary the working time within a longer period of time would weaken the employees' position.

2.2.2. *Derogation from statutory norms*

Derogations from some of the Swedish statutory norms is a device which has been used for a long time by the labour market parties. This technique has been used in the areas of employment protection, vacation, time-off legislation, joint regulation, etc. It creates flexibility in the application of the statutes. When the seniority rules were introduced into the 1974 Employment Protection Act, it was held that 'the conditions of the working life and the organisation of the undertakings were so

69. SOU 1996:145, p. 196.
70. Lag & Avtal No. 4/1997.
71. This issue is discussed in SOU 1996:145, pp. 188–192.
72. This issue is discussed in op.cit., pp. 192–193.
73. This issue is discussed in op.cit., pp. 218–221.
74. Op.cit., p. 220.
75. See the following, op.cit., pp. 313–329, 333.

varied that it was impossible to design a universal seniority rule, because there will always be cases when it will not work well'.[76] Hence, the seniority rules were made semi-mandatory. No doubt, the power to derogate from the Act gives the said parties a good chance of adjusting the statute to their special needs or the modalities of the specific case. It gives the parties a procedural flexibility.[77] The legislative technique must be looked upon as one of characteristics of the Swedish model; it is, again, an example of the interplay between statutory law and industrial common law fostered by collective agreements and prevalent in Swedish working life. In the 1996 report on working-time issues it was held that this technique created both flexibility and stability.[78]

In some cases, derogations may be due to the result of an agreement between the employer and an individual employee. This is the case, for example, as regards a longer period of notice than the one provided for in Section 11 of the Employment Protection Act. Similar provisions are found in the Vacation Pay Act.

As a rule, the said statutes prescribe that the derogation must be approved by the central labour organisation. In other words, the local union is not permitted to derogate from the provisions of the statute unless it is given powers to do so by means of, for example, a delegation clause in the branch collective bargaining agreement, or by means of the fact that the trade union internally delegates such power to the local union. The employers prefer to insert the delegation clause into the collective bargaining agreement. The clause cannot thus be unilaterally withdrawn. The reason for placing the derogatory power at the level of the central labour organisation is that the legislator wanted to be convinced that the employees were represented by a strong counterpart. However, it must be added that the major provisions of the 1976 Joint Regulation Act are semi-mandatory and that the legislator assumes in this respect that derogations will be made at the entrepreneurial level.

One interesting point emerged in the context of the 1996/1997 amendment of the Employment Protection Act (see above). The provisions for fixed-term contracts in the Employment Protection Act, Sections 5, 5a and 6, are semi-mandatory, which means that they can be derogated from. One may also find plenty of such possibilities in the respective branch collective bargaining agreements. When the 1996/1997 amendments were presented, Section 2 of the statute no longer required that derogations from the fixed-term employment and seniority provisions had to be sanctioned by a collective bargaining agreement concluded at the national/branch level. It was held that the basis for this change was that the statute should be 'neutral' and not specifically designate a specific level.[79] Some of the LO trade unions immediately intervened in order to prevent their local unions from derogating from the statute in these matters. The unions claimed that they could do so, referring to the Charter of the LO which accorded to the Board of the Union the right to conclude a collective bargaining agreement (which is indisputable).[80] From the legal point of view such a standpoint is questionable since the legal power to derogate from norms such as those found in the actual provisions of the Employment Protection Act emanates from the statute and not from the union's charter.

76. Prop. 1973:129, p. 160.
77. The concept is also used by A. Numhauser-Henning, Arbetets flexibilisering, in *Studier i arbetsrätt* tillägnade Tore Sigeman, ed. by Arbetsrättsliga föreningen, 1993, p. 262.
78. SOU 1996:145, pp. 229–230.
79. The issue is discussed in prop. 1996/97:16, pp. 27–28.
80. The daily *Svenska Dagbladet*, 10 September 1996, *Dagens Nyheter*, 28 November 1996, *LO-tidningen* No. 37, 29 November 1996.

2.3. Collective Labour Relations

2.3.1. Wage process is being decentralised

Decentralisation of wage setting in terms of both the process and the actors involved has been going on for a long period of time, the critical year being 1980. Until then wage agreements were entered into at a high central level between SAF and LO – the model wage setters on the labour market in Sweden. Since the re-regulation of the public sector labour law in 1965 other actors have made wage negotiations more multi-faceted. For a long period of time Sweden applied probably one of the most centralised collective bargaining wage systems in the world.[81] In 1980, in the aftermath of a devastating conflict involving the largest number of employees ever affected by industrial action on the Swedish labour market, the central employers' organisation (SAF) decided to no longer engage in centralised wage bargaining.[82] The centralised wage bargaining system was considered to have fallen into disrepute.[83] As a result of this, with the exception of the wage negotiations in 1990 when a stabilisation agreement under the aegis of a Government appointed commission made SAF change its mind in order to de-escalate the rate of the galloping wages, the wage-setting process was transferred to the branch level.

Simultaneously, the earlier rigid tariff-wage systems have been abandoned. These systems were frequent in the public sector, but they never applied to, for example, the engineering and building industries, where the minimum wage systems prevailed. The tariff-systems related the individual wage to the post occupied by the employee. Factors such as efficiency played no role in those systems – hardly a good incentive for work! Today, wages are set individually and differ according to the criteria found in the various collective bargaining agreements. This means a move downwards in the negotiation systems, often to the level of a given enterprise or authority.[84]

3. THE DRIVING FORCES BEHIND THE DEREGULATION

A few aspects related to the more frequent use of *contract labour* must be highlighted, since this group of employees is a paramount example of the deregulation process in Sweden. In brief, the practice of hiring temporary manpower from an external provider of personnel is a reflection of the need for a temporary substitute, which is often due to the simple fact that some of the regular employees are ill or on leave, or else in cases when there is a sudden increase in the work load, or in periods when business reaches a peak. In some instances, the use of temporary manpower may be dictated by the need for specialised workforce. It is also apparent that employers occasionally use temporary employment agencies as a recruitment tool, sometimes referred to as '*try-and-hire*'.[85]

---

81. See A. Victorin, The implementation of a wage-policy: centralized collective bargaining in Sweden, in Scandinavian Studies in Law 1975, pp. 295–315.
82. See H. De Geer, *Arbetsgivarna. SAF i tio decennier*, 1992, pp. 143, 158–175.
83. See A. Victorin, Niedergang und Ende des zentralisierten Tarifsystems in Schweden, in Zeitschrift für Arbeitsrecht 1985, pp. 423–445.
84. The private employers' view is that the individual wages should always be set at the entrepreneurial level, Arbetsmarknad utan AMS. SAF, 1997, p. 35.
85. See H. Jakhelln, Try and Hire – Arbeidsformidling eller vikarbyråvirksomhet?, in Lov, dom og bok. Festskrift til Sjur Brækhus, 1988, pp. 241–251.

Restrictions in the statutory framework related to the conclusion of short-term employment contracts may be the cause of the emergence of this form of employment. Data indicate that the majority of 'temps' seem to get permanent employment after some time.[86] The practice of contracting-out manpower also reflects the shortcomings of the *public employment exchange* and its inability to provide employers with short-term employment forms. It remains an open question whether the contracting-out of manpower really reduces manpower costs. The cost of buying external manpower may be actually higher than that of paying wages to the personnel if they were employed, taking into consideration all the marginal costs connected with the former.[87]

Parallel to the growth of temporary staff, another trend is becoming more prominent in all sectors of the labour market, including the public sector: the principal employer reduces, or cuts down on the so-called *satellite activities or peripheral functions*. This feature has far-reaching repercussions on the way in which the work is organised in the auxiliary activities. The employer concentrates on the core-activities.[88] Auxiliary activities are 'out-sourced'.[89] It has been held that this method ensures flexibility and reinforces the marketing contacts on both sides of the process: customers and suppliers.[90] Hence, the borderline between the use of temporary employment agencies as a reserve to manpower, on the one hand, and the more extensive use of job contracting, on the other, is blurred. The trend is that part of the employer's labour force becomes *externalised*. Classical industrialism meant that the entire production chain was *internalised*. This phenomenon is now quickly disappearing.

This also means that the borderline between the organisation (hierarchy), on the one hand, and the market, on the other, is becoming less clear.[91] From the scientific point of view, this is only another variant of the old theme discussed in Ronald Coase's classical article, '*The Nature of the Firm*', that appeared in ECONOMICA in 1937. According to Coase, it was *transaction costs* that determined whether work was to be performed inside or outside a firm. Coase writes on p. 395: 'A firm will tend to expand until the costs of organising an extra transaction within the firm become equal to the costs of carrying out the same transaction by means of an exchange on the open market or to the costs of organising another firm.' Hence, transactions will be performed within a firm ('in-house') as long as this is the most profitable arrangement. When this no longer applies, they will be externalised and passed along onto the market. Additionally, modern companies or self-employed persons tend to organise production and services along the lines of networks.[92]

---

86. SOU 1997:58, p. 48.
87. See also SOU 1997:58, p. 56.
88. See, e.g., Branschens utveckling och omfattning. Personaluthyrning, entreprenader, rekrytering. SPUR, 1998, p. 3.
89. E.g., Arbete utan anställning. Om de förändrade relationerna på arbetsmarknaden. SAF, 1996, pp. 15–16.
90. H. Lundgren, *Bortom de mentala murarna. Bilder av morgondagens arbetsliv och arbetsmarknad*, 1997, p. 32.
91. This is an area which has been extensively analysed in economic research. The major work in institutional economics, often cited, is O. Williamson, *Markets and Hierarchies: Analysis and Antitrust Implications. A Study in the Economics of Internal Organization*, 1975. See also a field study, R. Eklund, *Bolagisering – ett mode eller ett måste?*, 1992, concerning the impact upon labour law when large and medium-large companies reorganise in order to set up subsidiaries instead of conducting the same business within the former divisions or departments of the parent company.
92. See B. Hedberg *et al. Imaginära organisationer*, 1994, Arbete utan anställning. Om de förändrade relationerna på arbetsmarknaden. SAF, 1996, p. 5 and H. Lundgren, *Bortom de mentala murarna. Bilder av morgondagens arbetsliv och arbetsmarknad*, 1997, pp. 25–30.

Furthermore, caution exercised by the law in the area of employment protection indicates that the major motive to make the legal framework less stiff in the most recent legislative schemes has been to *curb the high unemployment*, and to make it easier for smaller enterprises to employ new personnel. It is feared, however, that these amendments have not changed the minds of the employers; they want more of the cake. Certainly, the rate of employed persons has recently increased.[93] Yet, the growth in fixed-term contracts seems to have come about without the recourse to the 1996/97 amendment of the Employment Protection Act (see above). One is tempted to say, when thinking about the turbulence surrounding the 1996/97 package, that it was 'much ado about nothing'.

Aspects of '*flexibilisation*' and '*decentralisation*' apply to both the discussion on the future working time act, and the wage-setting procedures. Generally, it can be said that the private employers' organisation (SAF) has been successful with respect to the wage-setting structures. Individualised and differentiated wages are now the rule. The pattern has spread to other sectors of the labour market. The employer organisations have also been rather successful in achieving more lenient provisions on fixed-term contracts inserted into the respective collective bargaining agreements. SAF or its member organisations have also successfully convinced their counterparts to accept new rules on industrial action, which will curb the frequency of labour conflicts. It is generally perceived that the above-mentioned 1997 industrial peace agreement signed 17 March 1997, is a 'success'.[94] This agreement was an innovation to foster peaceful wage negotiations among the major social partners in private industry. The agreement lays down a special procedure whose aim is to prevent the parties from resorting to industrial action too quickly and gives unique powers to the appointed impartial arbitrators to enforce the good intentions of the agreement. The 1997–1998 wage round could be concluded without resort to industrial action.

4. EVALUATION OF CURRENT DEREGULATION AND LABOUR LAW REFORMS

Even if flexibilisation of ideas has had its breakthrough on the Swedish labour market, the countervailing forces have been stronger.[95] Two features are instead more conspicuous, namely the re-regulation of existing norms or the introduction of new norms, in response to the *current flow of E.C. regulations*, and the introduction of entirely *new domestic statutes*, quite apart from the impact of the E.C. development.

The list of cases of re-regulation of Swedish labour law according to E.C. law is quite long. Did not someone say once that the E.C. was only a peace project? Isn't it instead Fortress Europe that is emerging? Suffice to say that the Swedish labour law was amended in response to the following E.C. Directives, partly due to the E.E.A. Agreement, which came into force on 1 January 1994, and Sweden's entry into the E.U. on 1 January 1995: equal pay, E.C. Directive 75/117,[96] transfers of

93. Arbetskraftsundersökningen i augusti 1998 (Labour Force Survey, August, 1998). SCB, p. 1.
94. See the evaluation made by the two impartial arbitrators in their report to the industrial committee set up by the contracting collective parties, see Industriavtalet i 1998 års förhandlingar, September 1998, p. 64 (mimeographed).
95. The same observation in R. Fahlbeck, *Flexibility. Potentials and Pitfalls for Labour Law*, 1998, pp. 12, 14.
96. Prop. 1990/91:113 (indirect discrimination and job evaluation were affected).

undertakings and collective dismissals, E.C. Directives 77/187, 75/129 and 92/56,[97] insolvency, E.C. Directive 80/987,[98] health and safety of atypical workers, E.C. Directive 91/383,[99] information about the essentials of the terms and conditions of the employment relationship, E.C. Directive 91/533,[100] pregnant workers, E.C. Directive 92/85,[101] working time, E.C. Directive 93/104,[102] European works councils, E.C. Directive 94/45[103] and parental leave, E.C. Directive 96/34.[104] There are more E.C. Directives in the pipeline to take account of: posting of workers (96/71),[105] burden of proof in sex discrimination disputes (97/80), part-time work (97/81) and the amendment to Directive 77/187 on transfers of undertakings (98/50). Mention must also be made of the 'four freedoms' – the free movement of workers as set forth in Article 48 of the Treaty of Rome, and Regulations 1612/68 on equal treatment of migrant workers and 1408/71 on the social security rights of migrant workers, which were replicated into Swedish law already in the context of the E.E.A. Agreement.

New domestic acts relate to the right to take time-off to investigate possibilities of self-employment,[106] amendments to the Sex Discrimination Act on sexual harassment,[107] and a three-fold non-discrimination legislation coming up: on sexual orientation,[108] on disabled persons in working life[109] and (a revised statute) on ethnic discrimination.[110]

A discussion on the evaluation of current deregulation and labour law reforms would not be complete if the private employers' organisation's (SAF) campaign during the entire 1990s, almost akin to waging a 'war' against labour law, were left out.[111] SAF's activism is *unprecedented*, causing their counterparts on the labour market to retreat to defensive positions. A special concern of SAF has been

97. Prop. 1994/95:102. The two issues were treated together. The legislative scheme on transfers of undertakings was entirely amended. The amendments on collective dismissals were less dramatic.
98. Prop. 1996/97:102 (qualifying period to be entitled to wage guarantee abolished). See also EFTA Court opinion, E-1/95 wherein the Swedish rule was disapproved.
99. Prop. 1993/94:186 (related to the status of contract labour at the actual workplace).
100. Prop. 1993/94:67 (no such provisions were formerly found in Swedish labour law).
101. Prop. 1994/95:207 (only minor adjustments).
102. SOU 1995:92, prop. 1995/96:162 (implementation probably unsatisfactory).
103. Prop. 1995/96:163 (an entirely new statute was enacted, but the domestic precursor was partly found in the 1982 Development Agreement between the SAF, LO and PTK related to the 1976 Joint Regulation Act).
104. Prop. 1997/97:81 (a separate statute was enacted related to time-off for urgent family reasons).
105. Implementation suggested in SOU 1998:52. Utstationering av arbetstagare.
106. Prop. 1997/98:27.
107. Prop. 1997/98:55, partly inspired by E.C. Resolution 29 May 1990 on the protection of the dignity of women and men at work and E.C. Recommendation 27 November 1991 on the protection and dignity of women and men at work.
108. SOU 1997:175, prop. 1997/98:180 (not yet law).
109. SOU 1997:176, prop. 1997/98:179 (not yet law).
110. SOU 1997:174, prop. 1997/98:177 (not yet law).
111. It may be added here that a closer scrutiny of the political party bills introduced before the national elections which took place in September 1998 shows a variety of demands, partly based on the ideas of 'deregulation' or 'flexibility' of the labour law rules; see Conservative Party bill 1997/98:Fi205, Liberal Party bills 1997/98:Fi212, 1997/98:A259, Christian Democratic Party bill 1997/98:A269, Centre Party bill 1997/98:A272, Green Party bills 1997/98:A256, 1997/98:A309 and Left Party (former Communists) bill 1997/98:A710. The bills were dismissed in the deliberations by the Parliamentary Labour Market Committee, see 1997/98:AU1, pp. 19–20.

smaller enterprises and the vexing volume of rules. In sum, SAF has argued that the amount of regulation which companies have to assimilate acts as a brake on enterprise and the job creating process.[112] It is also indicative that a catalogue of proposals to reform labour law, submitted by SAF in 1997, was bluntly rejected by LO.[113] A citation, taken from one of the many pamphlets issued by SAF, will summarise quite neatly the view of the employers:

> 'Instead of allocating billions of crowns to labour market policy, we need active support for creating new jobs. A decentralized wage formation process, balanced rules applied to industrial action, a reform of the unemployment insurance system and labour law, more flexible working time, lower taxes and forceful deregulation – such are the measures which create growth and new jobs.'[114]

SAF's reform proposals concerning labour law calls for, *inter alia:*[115] non-mandatory application of the employee concept, freedom of the employer to contract for regular, job or fixed-term employment, a more lenient 'objective cause' standard should apply to dismissals, abolition of the seniority rules and the recall right in connection with redundancies, abolition of the trade union veto right when job contractors are engaged, more balanced rules in industrial conflicts, e.g., members' voting, prohibition of sympathetic industrial action (secondary boycotts) and – finally – a modification of the binding force of the collective bargaining agreement (members should give proxy to the union, or voluntarily accede to the agreement).

One comment regarding the last proposal. The weakening of the most central regulatory instrument used in Swedish industrial life, i.e. the collective bargaining agreement, seems to be tainted by ideas borrowed from the general principles of contract law. It is questionable whether such a proposal is an adequate tool in the 'flexibilisation' context. It is widely known that the collective bargaining agreement is a landmark invention in contractual theory with respect to its legal effects.

112. The Social Democratic Government appointed a 'small enterprise delegation' in 1996 to cope with issues related to obstacles to the establishment and growth of smaller enterprises. Several reports have been issued, see SOU 1997:186. Bättre och enklare regler, SOU 1998:64. Bättre och mer tillgänglig information, SOU 1998:77. Kompetens i småföretag, SOU 1998:78. Regelförenkling för framtiden, SOU 1998:92. Goda idéer om småföretag och samverkan, SOU 1998:93. Kapitalförsörjning till småföretag and SOU 1998:94. Förslagskatalog. The dismal lesson seems to be that the volume of rules has steadily increased in spite of the fact that various governments have long before attempted to limit the flow of regulation, see SOU 1998:78, p. 20.

113. SOU 1997: 186, pp. 69–74. See SAF: s svar på Småföretagsdelegationens upprop, dated 1997-08-14, p. 6 (mimeographed). In the final report, the 'small enterprise delegation' concludes that it has chosen not to dig deep into the areas of labour law since 'the area is complex, controversial and has been subjected to comprehensive investigations', see SOU 1998:94, pp. 17–18, 29–30 (two innocuous suggestions relate to the simplification of the Vacation Pay Act and the Labour Inspectorates' services).

114. 'En arbetsmarknad utan AMS. SAF, 1997, p. 63.

115. See the following pamphlets: Arbete utan anställning. Om de förändrade relationerna på arbetsmarknaden. SAF, 1996, pp. 22–27, En arbetsmarknad utan AMS. SAF, 1997, p. 36, Från krig till fred på arbetsmarknaden – Balansera konfliktreglerna! SAF, 1997. Most of the suggestions date back to the beginning of the 1990s, e.g., SAF: s uppfattning om den framtida arbetsrätten, SAF, 1991. A critical appraisal of the SAF proposals is found in two books written by trade union lawyer, K. Junesjö, *En ny arbetsrätt. Tankar och förslag,* 1995 and *Strejk – en demokratisk rättighet för bättre arbetsförhållanden*, 1998.

The ingenuity of such agreements is that they reduce the *transaction costs* of passing on their content to the employment contracts (cf. the idea of standard contracts). The alternative would imply that every single employee would have to contract individually for the same terms and conditions of work. This would not only be burdensome, but it would also involve astronomical costs, if tens of thousands of employees were affected.[116] Which employer is prepared to engage in such fruitless endeavours?

The discussion on deregulation would also be incomplete if the *seniority issue* were left out. No other issue has haunted the labour market parties so much and caused so many political stalemates as the seniority rules laid down in the Employment Protection Act. The status of the law is quite clear. The 'last-in-first-out' principle applies in redundancy situations (Section 22 of the Act). The length of employment thus prevails. However, seniority is not strict; attention must be paid to the fact that the employee must have sufficient qualifications to be transferred to another job, already occupied by another employee. The essence of this is that even if the other employee is more qualified he must yield. In the case when two employees have the same seniority, the older employee has priority. The seniority principle also applies to recall situations, when the employer is about to take in new personnel. The recall right applies only after the employee has been dismissed due to redundancy and during nine months after the employment has ceased to have effect.

The seniority rules were introduced in the 1974 Employment Protection Act. There was a break from the earlier, 'softer' seniority rules as provided in the master agreement between LO and SAF, which gave priority to the 'efficiency' principle.[117] No amendments were made in the 1982 Employment Protection Act, though the issue was widely discussed.[118] As a result of the non-socialist Government bill in 1993/94 the employers were entitled to exempt two employees ('key persons') from the seniority list.[119] These exemptions were abolished with the change of Government after the national elections in 1994.[120] The seniority rules are semi-mandatory and may thus be derogated from by a collective bargaining agreement. Derogations are frequent, but, in the employers' view, too costly.[121] The trade unions have fought for the maintenance of the statutory rules since they were introduced in the 1974 Act, while the employers, likewise, have fought the law, but failed to attain a sustainable amendment. One reason for the stalemate is that during the 1970s the bulk of the new labour regulation was introduced through the intervention of the legislator. The labour market parties never had to act as 'godfathers' nor 'sweat' in order to reach an agreement. The shadow of the labour-statute-prone legislator of the 1970s is therefore unquestionably a major cause of the

116. Cf. J. Malmberg, *Anställningsavtalet*, 1997, pp. 374–375. The employers' sought-for flexibilisation may very well end up in rigidity, argues Malmberg. 'To some extent, the legal system can assist in making available devices which serve to reduce the transaction costs', says A. Ogus, *Regulation*, 1994, p. 17.

117. Prop. 1973:129, pp. 154–155.

118. Prop. 1981/82:71, pp. 54–64.

119. Prop. 1993/94:67.

120. Prop. 1994/95:76.

121. The seniority rules no doubt give the union leverage in such negotiations, see R. Eklund, *Bolagisering – ett mode eller ett måste?*, 1992, p. 226.

controversy among the parties today, when modified and simplified rules are on the agenda.[122]

5. THE ROLE OF LABOUR LAW IN THE 21st CENTURY: DO WE NEED A NEW CONCEPT OF LABOUR LAW?

In my humble view it is not realistic to expect that future labour law will change dramatically. Nothing like 'the fall of the Berlin wall' is going to come about. The inertia of the present legal framework and among the major actors must not be underestimated. The E.C. will continue to produce legal acts. Even if the externalisation of the labour force probably will continue, it requires that all persons become self-employed in order to dissolve the labour law from within. Not even the age of the information society/revolution will make the basic rules of labour law obsolete.[123] It is another matter that management style may have to change.

Even though we haven't yet seen the latest drafts of the individualised labour law norms or felt the effects of the flow of E.C. legal acts, *individualisation* of the collective labour law as suggested by the Swedish employer organization (SAF) must be rejected – for economic and efficiency reasons. The transaction costs for concluding, for example, wage contracts will only increase if the effects of a collective bargaining agreement are made conditional upon the contractual approval of the affected employees. This does not exclude the possibility that the agreement is subject to trade union members' voting, though this is not practised in Sweden. It is conspicuous that the 'war' against labour law propounded by SAF has met with failure if one looks upon the results achieved; on the other hand, SAF and its member employer organisations have been more successful in achieving concessions within the general framework of the various collective bargaining agreements, though the SAF campaign was pointedly directed towards the reform of the statutory law.

The *non-discrimination principle*, in its broadest sense, will no doubt call for solutions where the social/moral dimension will have a definite impact upon labour law norms in the near future. The impact of the E.C. law is discernible here. It is also my view that much legal work should be devoted to the *simplification* of the labour law rules in order to avoid complex techniques in areas which could be regulated in a uniform way. A small enterprise should not be required to employ a full-fledged personnel director or a legal counsel to master daily operative challenges. From the Swedish point of view one is inclined to question, for example, the extent to which the various types of short-term employment forms found in the Employment Protection Act offers guidance to employers in their choice of schemes when one type of employment overlaps with another. The same can probably be said with

122. A comparison can be made here with the 1982 Development Agreement between SAF, LO and PTK – a joint regulation scheme which provides basic rules for daily operations of the employer's business in his relations with both the employees and the trade unions. It is an agreement with only a minimum of details, but contains more of a joint spirit of co-operation. The agreement is an application of the 1976 Act on Joint Regulation. It took the parties six years to prepare the 1982 Agreement. This agreement has a greater legitimacy than any other statutory solution on the same issues would have had. In the agreement the parties have, e.g., paved the way for far-sighted solutions related to the many facets of groups found in companies, see R. Eklund, *Bolagisering – ett mode eller ett måste?*, 1992, pp. 294–296.

123. Cf. R. Fahlbeck, Ett revolutionerat arbetsliv? Informationssamhället och arbetslivets omvandling, in JT 1997–1998 No. 4, pp. 1016–1033.

regard to many other issues, such as those found in the non-discrimination and the leave-of-absence legislation. To succeed in the simplification efforts the legislator must be prepared, however, to give up something in one area of law, in order to attain something in another. This may, in fact, turn out to be more difficult than first thought, since it may mean providing a platform for lobbyists from which to trumpet calls for the preservation of the status quo in the respective areas of law.

7. Deregulation and Labour Law in The Netherlands

Gustaaf Heerma van Voss

1. INTRODUCTION

This article describes recent developments of labour legislation and practice in the Netherlands as a result of the trend to flexibilise the Dutch economy and labour markets.

1.1. Political Drive for Deregulation in Labour Law

'Deregulation' was officially declared Government policy in the Netherlands in 1982 when a centre-right cabinet took office under Prime Minister Lubbers. The appointment of this new cabinet came at a time when the budget deficit of the Dutch government had reached its all-time high and unemployment was also increasing rapidly. Reducing the national budget deficit was the most important objective of this cabinet. The goal of 'deregulation' was partly an ideological phrase, following the then newly elected conservative governments in the United Kingdom and the United States. Government wanted to reduce costs, possibly to build confidence in business circles. In practice, the influence of traditional thinking in social policy remained. The influence of deregulation on Labour Law was relatively small. Most of the Labour Legislation was left unchanged, except for some details. On the other hand not much new labour legislation was enacted during this period. More important were cuts in Social Security benefits schemes to reduce Government expenses.

In 1989 a centre-left cabinet under Lubbers took over, but made no important changes in this policy. Since 1994 a left-right coalition under Prime Minister Kok is in power. The term 'deregulation' is not very prominent anymore. 'Deregulation' was relegated to a project, led by the Minister of Economic Affairs, on 'Market Working, Deregulation and Quality of Legislation' but focused on aspects such as closing hours of shops and, with regard to Labour Law, on the competition clause in employment contracts. The policies of this cabinet were a mixture of liberalisation of the Labour markets, with respect for certain guarantees of social protection. Most important in this respect was the introduction of the law on 'Flexibility and Security' by 1 January, 1999. The coalition has continued since 1998 in the Cabinet Kok-II.

R. Blanpain (ed.), Deregulation and Labour Law, 137–146

1.2. Structural Changes in Employment Relations

In the early eighties the Dutch economy was not doing well. There was high unemployment and as a result high consumption of social security benefits. The sickness and disabled benefits schemes were often used to solve problems in labour relations. Employers were reluctant to hire new personnel in economically uncertain times. The tight dismissal restrictions were felt to be a handicap. Discussions on deregulation of the dismissal legislation ended in a stalemate between unions and employers. In practice, employers found a solution in the use of so called 'flexible labour relations':[1] fixed-term contracts, on-call contracts and dispatched workers. The courts accepted these new forms of labour, but also provided for a certain protection of employees working under these conditions. Another element was the introduction of part-time labour on a large scale. For women with children this became a popular form of work, facilitating the combination of work with family responsibilities.

Under the first Kok-Cabinet the budget deficit was finally brought down to an acceptable level to enter the European Economic and Monetary Union and the unemployment was brought down, partly thanks to the new forms of labour. The Act on Flexibility and Security introduced flexibilisation of dismissal protection (especially for fixed-term contracts) and regulated the new forms of labour by more or less codifying the case law of the courts.

As a result, Dutch labour markets appear drastically changed since the early eighties. The concept of the full-time worker with stable and long-term employment contract is no longer dominant. There is a wide range of contracts with different forms of flexibility to serve the different needs of the employer and worker. Sometimes this is a disadvantage for the workers (like being dependent on the available amount of work), sometimes, however, their position is improved (like making decisions about working hours). Labour Law managed to incorporate the new forms of work within its system, equalising the positions of both parties in this new field.

2. DEREGULATION OF LABOUR LAW

2.1. Labour Market Regulations

Employment services

Since 1982 the role of the state in Employment Services has been gradually weakened. The State has no monopoly in this field. In the new Acts on Employment Services of 1990 and 1997 this development was legally recognised. In practice, three types of organisations are active:

a. *The public Employment Offices.* In 1990 the public Employment Organisation became legally independent of the government. Although still largely financed by government, the administration of this organisation was removed from the

1. Wet Flexibiliteit en zekerheid, Staatsblad (Bulletin on Acts and Orders) 1998, 300.

Ministry of Social Affairs and Employment. Organised Labour and Management got positions in the Boards of the Organisation at the central as well as the regional level. Unemployed workers have to register their unemployment with the public Employment Office but cannot often be provided with a new job there. In spite of attempts to compete with other organisations, for instance by starting its own worker dispatching service, the public Employment Office is not very effective in providing jobs.

b. The second group is formed by *private employment services*. These work for either the employer or the worker in order to help them find a worker or a job. Examples are 'head hunters' or specialised agents for artists, professional soccer players, etc. These organisations need a government permit for their activities. A recent phenomenon is the so-called 'outplacement offices' that help workers to find another job with another company, a service often paid for by the former employer.

c. The third group are the *dispatching (temporary work) agencies*. They have become very important because they often provided the best job opportunities for unemployed workers. Formally, they are not seen as employment services because they act as employers themselves. Since today these agencies no longer provide exclusively for temporary work, but also for long-term arrangements as well, the term 'dispatching agencies' seems more accurate than the formerly used term 'temporary work agencies'. In this category one can also identify the 'detachment offices' that maintain long-term contracts with employees who are dispatched to other employers, like in the high-tech industry.

Worker dispatching services

Since 1975 the restrictions on Worker dispatching services have been drastically reduced step by step until they are finally almost abolished. In that year the official ban on these services was replaced by a system of licenses. A worker dispatching service needed a permit from the government for its operations. The government wanted to monitor whether the service was following good practices. It demanded that social security premiums be paid by the agencies, that the administration was run properly and that workers earned wages that were equal to those of ordinary workers in the same company who performed the same job. In some areas (like the construction sector) these services were still banned because of previous bad experiences with uncontrollable 'black work'. In other branches it was eventually permitted to dispatch temporary workers for three months at most. Later this period was prolonged to six months and in the end one year was tolerated.

Over the years this type of work became very popular in the Netherlands. Employers used it to avoid the strict regulation of dismissal law. With the high unemployment during the eighties, this type of work offered for many unemployed the best opportunity to find employment. It was also often the best way to find a permanent job in a company if the worker performed well. Temporary work became a form of 'employee recruiting'. On the other hand, the legal position of temporary workers was uncertain. The temporary work offices denied that they concluded employment contracts with their workers. But the expansion of this type of work and the need by the temporary work business for recognition of its existence led gradually to a change. During the eighties the general trade unions managed to reach a nation-wide collective agreement for temporary workers with the Organisation of

Temporary Work Agencies (ABU). And more and more courts considered that a temporary worker, after starting a job, was working on the legal basis of an employment contract. Finally, the Advocate-General concluded before the Hoge Raad (Supreme Court of the Netherlands) that this was the leading legal opinion.[2] At this point, the ABU left its previous position and in a 1996 Agreement with the unions accepted the principle that temporary workers work on the basis of an employment contract.

In 1999 this was formalised in the Civil Code by the introduction of the articles 690 and 691 of Book 7 as a result of the Act on Flexibility and Security. Article 7: 690 defines the 'Dispatching work contract' as a special type of employment contract. Its flexibility is guaranteed by the exclusion of restrictions on dismissals of prolonged temporary contracts during the first 26 weeks and the possibility to agree on a clause that terminates the contract immediately in case the hiring company ends its assignment during this period. In the case of such a clause, the dispatched worker is also allowed to terminate his work at any time. It is possible to extend these periods of 26 weeks by collective agreement. In the New Collective Agreement for Temporary Workers (1999–2001), this was done: these exceptions are extended to one full year. In return the unions stipulated for the temporary workers the right to training and access to a pension scheme when they work longer than 26 weeks for a Workers Dispatching Agency. It is expected that the larger temporary work offices will hire temporary workers for longer periods in the future.

Since these offices are generally accepted today, the system of permits was abolished on 1 July 1998 under the new 'Act on Allocation of Workers by Intermediaries.'[3]

Temporary work offices are now free to work like any other company. Only two principles were maintained in the new Act: dispatched workers may not be used to undermine a strike, and the wage of the dispatched worker should be the same as that of the worker who does the same work as an employee of the company where the work is done. However, the latter rule may be set aside by collective agreement (either that of the hiring company of that of the workers dispatching agency). The Workers Dispatching Agencies are in favour of such an independent wage policy with the following argument. They see themselves as employers with their own employment policies: sometimes they will hire workers for several years and send them to different companies in consecutive periods. Therefore, they want to give workers with a higher seniority or a better performance a higher salary in order to bind them to their company.

Fixed-term contracts

Fixed-term contracts can be freely concluded in the Netherlands, for whatever purpose and whatever period. In principal, their use is not legally restricted. However, the Civil Code stipulated until 1999 that a second consecutive fixed-term contract could not be ended without notification. This implied the requirement of previous permission of the Regional Director of the Employment Service Organisation (who checks the validity of the reason for dismissal) and the observance of a notice period.

2. Conclusion Advocate-General T. Koopmans 7 April 1996, Jurisprudentie Arbeidsrecht (Caselaw Labor Law) 1996/168. The Hoge Raad did not render a judgment in the case because it was withdrawn.
3. Wet Allocatie van arbeidskrachten door intermediairs (Waadi), Staatsblad (Bulletin of Acts and Orders) 1998, 306.

Since these restrictions are not different from those of a contract for an indefinite period, this legislation was felt to be very restrictive by employers.

There were in principle two ways to evade the restrictions:

a. To observe a period of at least 31 days between two contracts. After this period, the second contract was not seen as a consecutive contract. In practice, they often hired the same worker in the interim for the same job through a Worker Dispatching Agency (so-called 'revolving door construction' – draaideurconstructie). The Hoge Raad (Supreme Court) decided in the 1991 Campina-case that when an employer uses this strategy for several years, a reasonable application of the law implies that the fixed term-contract should be considered a consecutive fixed-term contract in the sense of the Civil Code.[4] If the worker was hired in the first instance through a Workers Dispatching Office and then got a employment contract with the hiring company, the time worked for the Workers Dispatching Office was included in the calculation of the maximum probation period of two months as provided in the Civil Code.[5]
b. To make use of the possibility in the Civil Code to deviate from this rule by collective agreement. Due to the high unemployment during the eighties the unions often accepted exceptions to this rule in collective agreements. In several collective agreements on branch and company level it was agreed that the duty to give notification was only applicable after the worker had worked a certain period (often two years) for the same employer.

Since the first possibility was restricted by the courts, as indicated, the latter option grew in importance. As a result of an agreement between the national organisations of employers and trade unions, the government introduced such a rule in the 1999 Act on Flexibility and Security. This constituted the most important form of deregulation in the Act.

Under the present rule (article 7: 668a Civil Code), it is possible to have three successive contracts that may be ended without having to give notice, as long as they fall within a period of 3 years. The fourth contract or the contract that exceeds a period of 36 months will change automatically into a contract for an indefinite term, which gives the worker the before-mentioned protection against dismissal.

This change is an important form of deregulation that will make the fixed-term contract more attractive for employers.

Dismissal regulations

The Netherlands has quite a unique system of protection against dismissals. In principle notice of termination of an employment contract is not possible without the previous permission of the Regional Director of the Labour Service Organisation. Despite the criticism of the large companies this system will be extended.

The labour unions and the small enterprises are in favour of the system, the unions because of its preventive effect: employers can only dismiss a worker with

4. Hoge Raad (Supreme Court) 22 November 1992, Nederlandse Jurisprudentie (Dutch Case Law) 1992, 707 (Bootsma a.o./Campina).
5. Hoge Raad (Supreme Court) 13 September 1991, Nederlandse Jurisprudentie (Dutch Case Law) 1992, 130.

cause. The small enterprises see the system as a guarantee against lawsuits from employees for wrongful dismissals.

Several measures in the Act on Flexibility and Security are meant to make the dismissal procedure faster. These measures include shortening of notice periods, easier access to unemployment benefits in case of dismissals on economic grounds, and a procedure of 'no objection' in case the worker accepts his dismissal and only claims an unemployment benefit. In order to prevent abuse of rights, the ban on dismissal of sick workers is lifted if the sickness came up after the Regional Director of the Labour Service Organisation received the request for permission to dismiss.

In addition, in practice some deregulation has occurred because many employers avoided the 'permission procedure' by asking the court for dissolution of the employment contract. Although this is only possible on 'serious grounds', for practical reasons the courts made this into a normal dismissal procedure which became very popular. Today, half of the dismissals follow this procedure. The only disadvantage for the employer is that the court can oblige him to make a payment to the worker, which is usually done. In 1997 the 'circle' of competent judges published a recommendation that contained a formula to calculate these payments. The formula is $A \times B \times C$, which stands for seniority times monthly wage times correction factor. In practice this introduces more or less a right to severance payment for dismissed workers at least when this procedure is followed.

In the forthcoming years it seems likely that the dismissal procedures will be continuously under discussion. The Minister of Social Affairs and Employment already promised Parliament to do more research and to install an Evaluation Committee.

2.2. Individual Labour Relations

Flexibilisation of working-hours regulations

In 1994 the new Act on Working Hours (Arbeidstijdenwet) was introduced, replacing the former Labour Act (Arbeidswet) of 1919. In conformity with the 1993 EC-Directive on working time,[6] this Act introduced several aspects of flexibilisation of working hours. The protection of the worker often refers to an average working time during a reference period rather than to identical daily or weekly working time. Most interesting is that the new system distinguishes between legislative and negotiated standards. For instance, the maximum working hours per day under the Act are nine, but it is possible to negotiate in a collective agreement that it be 10 h daily. With this system the Act aims to promote consultation of the unions and works councils with regard to working hours. The role of the labour inspector is reduced, since it no longer has to give permission for overtime.

Lifting of ban on women's night work

The Netherlands had a ban on women's night work in heavy industry. This ban was lifted in 1989 as a result of the 1976 EC-Directive on equal treatment for men and

6. Council Directive of 23 November 1993 concerning certain aspects of the organization of working time, 93/104/EC, OJ 1993, No. L 307/18.

women.[7] This was seen as too restrictive for job opportunities for women in industry. Only the ban on night work for pregnant women was upheld since this offers protection on medical grounds.[8]

Derogation from legal norms

It was already described above that the new Working Hours Act (Arbeidstijdenwet) of 1994 made it possible to derogate from the legislative working hour regulations through collective agreements.

Although it was already possible to derogate from certain legal norms in the Civil Code through collective bargaining agreements, these possibilities were extended in The Act on Flexibility and Security of 1999. For instance, in the new regulations for worker dispatching services, collective agreements weakened certain forms of protection of the workers concerned. In return, the unions realised the introduction of training and pension rights for the dispatched workers who serve during an extended period.

Change clause

The Supreme Court accepted in the IBM case of 1988 the possibility that in the employment contract an employer reserves the right to change this contract unilaterally, as long as he acts in good faith.[9] Following this decision, many employers introduced such a clause in their standard employment contracts. The decision was heavily criticised in the literature because of the danger that it gave the employer too wide a margin of appreciation. As a result of this discussion the rule was codified in the Civil Code in 1998, but in a more restricted form. According to the new article 7: 613 Civil Code, the use of such a clause is only permitted if the employer has such 'serious grounds' to do so that the interest of the employee hurt by the change in the contract should be put aside on the basis of fairness and reason. In principle, this possibility opens room for more internal flexibility in companies. It is up to the courts now to determine how far the discretion of the employer will go in practice.

The outdated articles on work rules in the Civil Code were repealed on the same occasion.

2.3. Collective Labour Relations

Decentralisation of collective bargaining

There is a tendency towards decentralisation of collective bargaining in the Netherlands. During the fifties and sixties wage raises were to a large extent determined on the

7. Council Directive of 9 February 1976 on the implementation of the principle of equal treatment for men and women as regards access to employment, vocational training and promotion, and working conditions, 76/207/EEC, OJ 1976, No. L 39/40.
8. See also article 7 of the EC-Council Directive of 19 October 1992 on the introduction of measures to encourage improvements in the safety and health at work of pregnant workers and workers who have recently given birth or are breastfeeding, 92/85/EC, OJ 1992, No. L 348/1.
9. Supreme Court (Hoge Raad) 7 October 1988, Nederlandse Jurisprudentie (Dutch case law) 1989, no. 335 (IBM). This case may be compared with the case of the Japanese Supreme Court of 25 December 1968, *Minshu*, Vol. 22, p. 3459 (Shuhoko Buscase).

national level in negotiations between the national associations of unions, employers and government. Although there is still an important national discussion and co-ordination on the topic, the wages are in practice negotiated on the branch level, or in some cases on company level.

Today, the discussion is to what extent a further decentralisation to the company level should be promoted and, in that case, who should be the negotiating party on behalf of the employees, the unions or the works councils. Although the opinion is still dominant that wage negotiations should be the prerogative of the unions, more voices are now heard that the works council should be involved too. In some companies where workers are not well organised in unions (like newly emerged, high-tech industries), there are in practice negotiations with works councils.

Formally, the agreements reached with works councils are not legally recognised collective agreements and therefore not binding for individual workers. However, it is possible to imply a clause in the employment contract that binds the worker to such agreements. In the 1998 revision of the Works Council Act (Wet op de Ondernemingsraden) the notion of 'company agreements' between company and works council was formally recognised. Nevertheless these company agreements continue to have no binding effect for individual workers.

Interesting is also the new collective agreement of 1997 between the association of employers in the printing (graphic) industry and the unions. This collective agreement allows individual employers to negotiate with trade unions on the plant level on specific issues indicated in the collective agreement. The agreements resulting from this process are also binding on plant level. It is not yet certain that this binding effect will be accepted by the courts.

Relation between trade unions and individuals

There has been no formal re-examination of the relation between trade unions and individual workers or their respective bargaining position. However, it seems clear that there is a tendency towards 'individualisation' of relations. Workers are generally better educated than before and demand more room for their individual wishes to be heard in labour relations. For instance, a scheme has been introduced whereby workers can choose either to have a pension scheme for widows/widowers or to have a better old age-benefit scheme. This scheme will be preferred by those workers who are not married, or if both partners work and/or they have no children. This seems to be the first step in the direction of more individual freedom in labour relations.

3. THE DRIVING FORCES OF DEREGULATION

The driving forces of deregulation in the Netherlands include of course several factors. The high unemployment during the eighties was reduced during the nineties. This was partly a result of the growth of part-time work. Many women re-entered the labour market or wanted to reduce their working hours after having children in order to combine working life and family responsibilities. Part-time jobs made this possible and at the same time introduced some flexibility for employers. Other elements that promoted employment were tax reductions and cuts in social security schemes which reduced labour costs. An important factor was the willingness of unions (and their members) to accept moderate wage increases in order to promote economic recovery. The success of this process (the unemployment rate was reduced to 4% at the end of the nineties) earned the admiration of some foreign governments and it was called the 'Polder model'. This term refers to the Dutch term 'Polder', which stands for land that is regained from the water by building dikes around it and pumping the water away. This romantic idea is that the Dutch culture is formed in the everlasting struggle against the water, which forces the Dutch to cooperate and accept compromises. Today, the 'Polder model' stands for co-operation of employers and unions to serve mutual interests.

The pressure of global competition was of course important as well. As a trading and transport nation, the Netherlands are very dependent on international trade and the ups and downs of world markets. Therefore, the need for a flexible response to global competitors is often stressed. In particular, the influence of the internal EC-market is felt more and more. The Netherlands were not able to maintain a relatively high level of social security benefits for disabled workers, partly as a result of the fact that the level was unique in Europe. Employers stress that with regard to health and safety legislation, for instance, the Dutch legislation should not exceed the European minimum standards. During the implementation of the EC-Directive on European Works Councils[10] there was an agitated discussion in Parliament on how few and minor the issues were where the government proposed to go further than the European Directive required. Even the American and Japanese Chambers of Commerce intervened in this discussion.

Structural changes in industries are important too. There is a tendency towards a service-oriented society. Traditional industries with mass fabrication and low-skilled workers are declining. Workers are supposed to be better trained. Industries are diversifying and rapidly changing to respond to the changing wishes of customers. It is more difficult to set general rules in legislation or even in branch-wide collective agreements. There seems to be a tendency towards procedural rather than substantive rules in legislation. An example is the growing influence of general rules in case law, like human rights and general principles like equal treatment. The Dutch Civil Code contains an article that requires employer and employee to behave like a 'good employer' and a 'good employee'. The 'good employer'-clause was used more and more to deal with problems that were not settled by the legislation or came up for the first time. For instance, the principle of equal pay for equal work was accepted by the Dutch Supreme Court, not only for men and women, but in general. This decision was based on the principle of 'good employership'.[11]

On the other hand, in the recent Taxi Hofman case, the Supreme Court based on the standard of 'good employeeship' its decision that the worker should in general accept reasonable proposals of the employer related to changed circumstances on the job site, and may reject such proposals only when acceptance could not reasonably be asked of him.[12] The decision does not make completely clear whether this is a general rule or a special rule applying to handicapped workers. But it could imply that the employer could ask for a high degree of internal flexibility from the worker.

---

10. Council Directive of 22 September 1994 on the establishment of a European Works Council or a procedure in Community-scale undertakings and Community-scale groups of undertakings for the purposes of informing and consulting employees, 94/45/EC, OJ 1994, No. L 254/64.
11. Supreme Court (Hoge Raad) 8 April 1994, Nederlandse Jurisprudentie (Dutch case law) 1994, no. 704.
12. Supreme Court (Hoge Raad) 26 June 1998, Jurisprudentie Arbeidsrecht (Case-law Labor Law) 1998, no. 199 (Taxi Hofman).

4. EVALUATION OF CURRENT DEREGULATION

Although deregulation is no universal phenomenon in the Labour Law of the Netherlands, the influence of flexibilisation is important. Nevertheless in some areas regulations have increased, for instance by the introduction of a General Act on Equal Treatment which protects workers (amongst others) against discrimination with respect to race, nationality, religion, conviction and homosexual orientation. With regard to the privacy of workers, the Act on Medical Tests was enacted which prohibits medical tests before hiring personnel, except in extraordinary cases. In those cases, the Act requires doctors and employers to protect the rights of the job applicant who has to undergo a medical examination.

The general reactions to deregulation in the country are reserved. Many people see that the rights of workers are diminishing. For instance the privatisation of sickness payments makes workers more dependent on their employers. On the other hand, flexible forms of work (like dispatching workers agencies and on-call contracts) were accepted after workers found out that they also created job opportunities and that workers got protection when they stayed longer at that job.

One could say that deregulation or flexibilisation is not simply abolishing regulations but replacing outdated regulations by modernised forms of regulations.

Attention to the need for internal flexibility must be greater than before. In this respect it was mentioned above that the introduction of the 'change clause' in the Civil Code and the Taxi Hofman case on good employeeship could promote this.

5. THE ROLE OF LABOUR LAW IN THE 21st CENTURY

The question is raised whether we need a new concept of Labour Law. It seems to me that the role of Labour Law is not changing, but rather the way in which this role is fulfilled. Labour Law has recently taken on an unmistakably more market-oriented approach. But this does not mean that the role to protect workers in their weak position towards the employer has vanished.

The individualisation of Labour Law is very important for many workers and may be necessary to allow Labour Law to survive as a generally accepted set of rules to govern labour relations. The question to be answered in the future is how to respond to new developments and to adapt the concrete rules of Labour Law, all the while preserving the general values of Labour Law and not throwing away its underlying principles. In a world that seems to change rapidly, this question is more current than it has been for some time, but in fact it has always been important. And answering it keeps Labour Law an interesting and important subject.

8. Deregulation and Labour Law: The United States

Daniel H. Foote

In approaching the topic of 'deregulation and labour law' with respect to the United States, it is important to begin by noting the extent to which U.S. labour law is fundamentally premised on the notion of limited government regulation. While one can point to numerous examples of deregulation in the labour field, it would be misleading to speak of a 'trend toward deregulation.' Rather, a flexible, largely unregulated approach to employment issues has prevailed throughout much of U.S. history. Viewed from this perspective, the trend over the past few decades might properly be characterised as a trend toward greater regulation, rather than deregulation; and in numerous respects the trend toward greater regulation continues to this day. Nonetheless, the regulatory approaches taken have been heavily influenced by the flexible, at-will attitude that lies at the heart of U.S. labour law. To give a sense of how deeply rooted that attitude is, this Report begins with a brief examination of the historical background in the United States.

I. HISTORICAL BACKGROUND

One of the most widely quoted statements in the field of U.S. employment law is the following from Horace Gay Wood's 1877 treatise *Master and Servant*:

> With us [in the United States, unlike in England], the rule is inflexible, that a general or indefinite hiring is *prima facie* a hiring at will. ... [U]nless [the parties'] understanding was mutual that the service was to extend for a certain fixed and definite period, it is an indefinite hiring and is determinable at the will of either party.[1]

Regardless of the accuracy of that statement as of the time Wood wrote it,[2] it quickly became a self-fulfilling characterisation. By the end of the 19th century, the view was firmly established throughout the United States, either by state statute or by judicial decision, that at-will employment, subject to termination at any time by

1. Horace Gay Wood, *Master and Servant* 272 (1877).
2. *See, e.g.*, Mayer G. Freed & Daniel D. Polsby, The Doubtful Provenance of 'Wood's Rule' Revisited, 22 *Ariz. St. L.J.* 551 (1990), and articles cited therein.

R. Blanpain (ed.), Deregulation and Labour Law, 147–168

either side (for 'good cause, bad cause, or no cause at all,' according to one popular formulation), represented the norm.

In another key respect, the courts played the central role in ensuring limited government regulation of employment. From the late nineteenth century through nearly the first four decades of the twentieth century, courts at both the federal and state level repeatedly struck down attempts by the states and the federal government to establish laws regulating working hours, wages, workers' compensation, and even workplace health and safety. The most common ground for these decisions was that the laws interfered with freedom of contract, which the courts regarded as one of the fundamental 'liberties' protected by the Fifth and Fourteenth Amendments to the U.S. Constitution. The most famous such case is *Lochner v. New York*.[3] In that 1905 decision, the U.S. Supreme Court struck down a New York statute establishing maximum working hours (10 h per day, 60 h per week) for bakers. Yet some state courts had begun to strike down labour statutes on similar grounds a decade before *Lochner*;[4] and during the so-called *Lochner* era, which extended through 1937, the U.S. Supreme Court alone declared nearly two hundred other state statutes unconstitutional.

Exceptions existed to this pattern of invalidation. For example, in a decision prior to *Lochner*, the Supreme Court upheld limits on working hours for miners.[5] More notably, in a decision just three years after *Lochner*, the Supreme Court upheld the constitutionality of an Oregon statute that limited the working hours *for women*, based on the perceived greater need for protection in that case.[6] By 1919 forty states had established so-called protective legislation mandating maximum working hours for women;[7] and many states prohibited women from certain types of jobs (such as mining or bartending) or prohibited them from late-night work. Nonetheless, to a very great extent, during the *Lochner* era the courts stymied governmental attempts to regulate the workplace.

It is tempting to say that *Lochner* and its progeny reflected an unwavering commitment to freedom of contract, pure and simple. Indeed, Wood himself stated clearly that the at-will rule was simply a presumption to be applied if the parties had not made their intentions clear. Where the understanding of the parties could be fairly inferred from the contract, that understanding would control. Yet, throughout the late 19th century and a substantial portion of the 20th century, judicial interpretations of contract language reflected a strong bias in favour of employers. This resulted in broad employer discretion over virtually all aspects of the employment relationship. As one example, courts interpreted contracts calling for 'permanent employment' or 'lifetime employment' to be no more than contracts of 'indefinite duration.' This in turn meant they were terminable at will by either side.[8] As another example, many courts adopted the so-called gratuity theory of pensions, according to which a promise of a pension was deemed to be merely a gift, which the employer

---

3. 198 U.S. 45 (1905).
4. *See, e.g.*, *Low v. Rees Printing Co.*, 59 N.W. 362 (Neb. 1894) (striking down Nebraska statute setting legal work day at eight hours, with very high premium pay required for overtime).
5. *Holden v. Hardy*, 169 U.S. 366 (1898).
6. *Muller v. Oregon*, 208 U.S. 412 (1908).
7. *See* Claudia Goldin, *Understanding the Gender Gap: An Economic History of American Women* (1990), *reprinted in part in* John J. Donohue III, *Foundations of Employment Discrimination Law* 290 (1997).
8. *See, e.g.*, Sanford M. Jacoby, The Duration of Indefinite Employment Contracts in the United States and England: An Historical Analysis, 5 *Comp. Lab. L.J.* 85, 116–118 (1982).

could withhold at its discretion.[9] Thus, even when employees may have thought they had established clear rights by individual contract, the courts often disagreed.

The judicial system was similarly unsympathetic to worker efforts to engage in collective action. In 1908, the Supreme Court struck down, as an unconstitutional intrusion on the freedom of contract, a federal law prohibiting anti-union discrimination by railroads.[10] Just a week later, the Court held that a union that had organised a boycott could be sued for treble damages under the antitrust laws.[11] Employers quickly availed themselves of this weapon. The most potent weapon for employers, though, was the so-called labour injunction. Up until the enactment of the Norris-LaGuardia Act in 1932, the courts widely granted broad injunctions barring strikes or boycotts, often doing so on an *ex parte* basis.[12]

One might say this is all ancient history. After all, over 60 years have passed since the so-called 'switch in time'[13] occurred in the Supreme Court's 1937 decision in *West Coast Hotel Co. v. Parrish*.[14] That decision upheld Washington State's minimum wage law and ushered in the era of broad judicial deference to economic policy judgements by the legislature. Ever since, the courts have upheld virtually all laws regulating employment relations, unless those laws implicate equal protection or other such constitutional concerns. Nevertheless, the historical background has had a profound impact on the national psyche in the United States. It has helped generate a very strong acceptance, by workers as well as employers, that 'at-will' remains the core concept of the employment relationship; and it has helped foster a resignation to, if not outright acceptance of, very broad employer discretion. In addition, the historical background directly affected the nature of regulation when it finally came.

The centrepiece of federal regulation of collective bargaining is the National Labour Relations Act (NLRA) of 1935 (commonly known as the Wagner Act).[15] It was originally anticipated that collective bargaining would largely eliminate the need for further governmental regulation: the parties themselves would adjust their interests and work out appropriate protections through the collective bargaining process. From the outset, though, union organisation was to be voluntary. The United States has never had a requirement that workers be part of a union or have some other form of designated representative. Even at its peak in 1945, the organisation rate for non-agricultural workers in the United States was only 35.5%.[16] The NLRA prohibits employer domination of unions and employer 'interfere[nce] with, restrain[t] and coerc[ion of] employees in the exercise of the right to self-organisation,'[17] and the

9. *See, e.g.*, *McNevin v. Solvay Process Co.*, 53 N.Y.S. 98 (1898), *aff'd per curiam* 60 N.E. 1115 (N.Y. 1901).
10. *Adair v. United States*, 208 U.S. 161 (1908).
11. *Loewe v. Lawlor*, 208 U.S. 274 (1908) (popularly known as the Danbury Hatters case).
12. *See, e.g.*, Charles O. Gregory and Harold A. Katz, *Labor and the Law*, Chap. IV (3rd ed. 1979).
13. At the time, President Franklin D. Roosevelt had announced plans to expand the Supreme Court from nine to as many as fifteen members, in order to overcome the Court's resistance to New Deal economic reforms. Contemporary observers speculated that Justice Owen Roberts had switched his vote to forestall the court-packing plan, characterising it as the 'switch in time that saved nine.' *See, e.g.*, Jonathan Grossman, Fair Labour Standards Act of 1938: Maximum Struggle for a Minimum Wage, 101 *Monthly Lab. Rev.* 22 (1978).
14. 300 U.S. 379 (1937).
15. The NLRA has been subject to many amendments over the years. As amended, it is currently codified at 29 U.S.C. §§ 151–169.
16. *See, e.g.*, Alvin L. Goldman, *Labour and Employment Law in the United States* 224 (1996).
17. 29 U.S.C. § 158(a).

National Labour Relations Board (NLRB) initially adopted a policy requiring employers to maintain strict neutrality with respect to workers' decision whether to unionise and their choice of bargaining representative. As early as 1941, however, the Supreme Court concluded that this policy probably conflicted with employers' constitutional right of free expression.[18] In the Taft-Hartley Act of 1947, Congress amended the NLRA to permit '[t]he expression of any views, argument, or opinion, or the dissemination thereof,... if such expression contains no threat of reprisal or force or promise of benefit.'[19] Ever since, the basic policy in the United States has been to allow employers to campaign against unionisation, with this right often justified by the rationale that it constitutes an important means of ensuring workers are fully informed regarding the choice to organise.

The centrepiece of federal regulation of the individual employment relationship is the Fair Labour Standards Act (FLSA) of 1938,[20] which regulates wages, hours, and child labour. With respect to wages, the FLSA established a minimum wage, albeit with coverage subject to numerous exemptions, but otherwise left wages subject to collective or individual bargaining.[21] Notably, the FLSA did not attempt to regulate hours directly or to ban late night work. Rather, it adopted only an overtime premium of 50%. Moreover, from the time of its enactment, the FLSA has recognised various broad categories of exemptions from the minimum wage and overtime provisions, including exemptions for executive, administrative, and professional employees.

At the time these two major pieces of legislation were introduced, there was no attempt at the federal level to regulate such other aspects of employment as the hiring or discharge of workers; pensions, health insurance, and other benefits; or workplace safety and health. Nor was there much regulation of such aspects at the state level. Government became involved in job placement through the unemployment system. But there has never been a government monopoly on job placement. The United States had no ban on private placement agencies and did not seek directly to regulate temporary work or part-time work. The fundamental stance of governmental policy in the United States was to establish minimum standards for a limited number of basic aspects of employment, but otherwise to defer to privately shaped accommodations reached through the bargaining process.

Viewed in this manner, the United States historically represented close to the paradigm of a free employment market (albeit one in which courts significantly skewed the terms of the bargaining in favour of employers, as described above). From that perspective, the past forty years have witnessed a continuing trend toward greater regulation of employment in the United States. As of 1940, there were seven key federal statutes dealing with workplace regulation.[22] Twenty years later, in 1960, the number of major federal statutes had increased by only one, to eight.[23] Now there are at least twenty-eight major federal statutes and one executive order dealing with

18. *NLRB v. Virginia Elec. & Power Co.*, 314 U.S. 469 (1941).
19. 29 U.S.C. § 158(c).
20. As amended, 29 U.S.C. §§ 201–219.
21. With the exception of wage and price stabilisation efforts during World War II, the United States has never had an 'incomes policy.'
22. *See* United States General Accounting Office, GAO Report, Workplace Regulation, B-254248, June 30, 1994, GAO/HEHS-94-138 (hereinafter cited as GAO Report), at page 26.
23. Id.

workplace regulation.[24] Between 1960 and 1974, the number of regulatory programs that the Department of Labour administers tripled, from 43 to 134, and that number has risen much further since then.[25] In addition, the past four decades have seen a vast increase in workplace regulation at the state and local level, as well as the advent of a wide range of administrative regulations and judicial decisions governing workplace matters. As the U.S. General Accounting Office concluded in 1994:

- Employers and workers currently face an extensive network of workplace requirements covering a wide variety of workplace activities.... Employers also face a combination of federal and state laws that further increase regulatory requirements.... Because federal, state, and local governments have authority to regulate various workplace activities, employers face a complicated interaction of workplace statutes and regulatory requirements.[26]
- Nevertheless, the trend toward greater regulation has come against the backdrop of a firmly established ethos of flexible, at-will employment. Numerous examples of a flexible approach exist even within the newly adopted regulations, and of movement toward further deregulation. Even more importantly, several major shifts in business and employment practices have highlighted – and in turn heightened – the largely deregulated nature of U.S. employment. The following sections of this Report examine a number of these developments, beginning with developments relating to the individual employment setting.

INDIVIDUAL EMPLOYMENT RELATIONS

A. Anti-Discrimination Statutes

The single largest area of increased regulation is that of employment discrimination law. Beginning with the Equal Pay Act of 1963[27] and Title VII of the Civil Rights Act of 1964,[28] the past thirty-five years have witnessed a steady rise in regulation of status discrimination. The scope of prohibited conduct is large, including discrimination in hiring, promotions, discharge, compensation, and other terms and conditions

24. *See* id. (identifying 26 statutes and one executive order, as of 1994). Over fifty federal laws dealing with some aspect of labour or employment have been enacted between 1994 and the present (search conducted by University of Washington Law Library reference staff). Of those, at least two might be characterised as major pieces of legislation: the Health Insurance Portability and Accountability Act of 1996, 29 U.S.C. §§ 1181–1191, and the Workforce Investment Act of 1998, 112 Stat. 936 (Pub. L. 105–220, 7 August 1998). Incidentally, a selective listing of labour-related bills that have been introduced in Congress since the start of 1997 contains 77 separate bills, see Legislation: Status of Selected Labor Legislation, 105th Congress, *Daily Lab. Rep.*, 17 August 1998. Even allowing for some duplication (where, for example, similar bills have been introduced in both the House and Senate), this number gives a sense of the level of activity relating to regulation of employment matters.
25. *See* Commission on the Future of Worker-Management Relations, *Fact Finding Report* 106 (1994) (hereinafter cited as *Dunlop Commission Fact Finding Report*), and sources cited therein. In a striking indication of the extent of this growth in programs, the Workforce Investment Act referred to in the preceding footnote consolidates 60 programs into three block grants to the states. *See, e.g.*, Pamela M. Prah, Job Training: Clinton Signs Workforce Investment Act; Law Consolidates 60 Training Programs, *Daily Lab.* Rep.,10 August 1998.
26. GAO Report, *supra* note 22, at 27.
27. The Equal Pay Act is currently codified as part of the Fair Labor Standards Act, at 29 U.S.C.. § 206(d).
28. 42 U.S.C. §§ 2000e *et seq.*

of employment. The remedies are substantial. And the range of protected classes is large and has expanded steadily. Title VII prohibits discrimination on the basis of race, colour, religion, sex, or national origin. In 1967, Congress enacted the Age Discrimination in Employment Act (ADEA). That Act originally prohibited discrimination on the basis of age against individuals between the ages of 40 and 65. Its coverage has also expanded. In 1978, Congress extended the upper age limit to 70, and in 1986 it eliminated the upper age limit altogether. Then, in 1990, Congress enacted the Americans with Disabilities Act (ADA),[29] which prohibits discrimination because of disability. In addition, nearly all states and many local communities have their own fair employment practice statutes or ordinances.[30] Many of these laws extend protection to classes other than those covered by federal law, prohibiting, for example, discrimination on the basis of marital status or sexual orientation.

Regulations promulgated by the Equal Employment Opportunity Commission (at the federal level) and by state agencies have amplified the legal requirements. Furthermore, in a number of instances judicial decisions have recognised new causes of action. In some cases, such as the comparable worth doctrine, the cause of action has withered.[31] In others, such as sexual harassment, the new cause of action has flourished.

Some attempts have been made to clarify the applicable standards and thereby streamline the process. In its most recent Term, the Supreme Court contributed to that effort with a series of decisions bringing much greater clarity to the field of sexual harassment.[32] For the most part, though, the developments in this area have all been in the direction of increased regulation, rather than deregulation. In recent years, for example, the ADA has brought a web of complex issues.[33]

In one notable respect, however, the development of employment discrimination law in the United States has resulted in what, at least in Japan, is regarded as a form of deregulation: the elimination of women's protective legislation. Under Title VII, unless a restriction on women's work is based on a bona fide occupational qualification, that restriction is invalid.[34] The courts have held that state protective legislation conflicts with this provision of federal law (which, under the U.S. Constitution, takes supremacy over conflicting state law), and accordingly those state laws no longer are valid.[35]

---

29. 42 U.S.C. §§ 12101–12213.
30. The only states that still do not have fair employment practice statutes are Mississippi and Alabama, *see* Mark A. Rothstein, Charles B. Craver, Elinor P. Schroeder, Elaine W. Shoben, and Lea S. VanderVelde, *Employment Law* 191 (1994) (hereinafter cited as Rothstein, Craver *et al.*).
31. *See, e.g.*, *American Federation of State, County & Municipal Employees v. Washington*, 770 F.2d 1401 (9th Cir. 1985) (rejecting comparable worth argument).
32. *See Burlington Inds. Inc. v. Ellerth*, 66 U.S.L.W. 4634 (26 June 1998) (employer may be held vicariously liable under Title VII for supervisors' sexual harassment of employees, in both quid pro quo and hostile environment contexts); *Faragher v. Boca Raton*, Fla., 66 U.S.L.W. 4643 (26 June 1998) (same result, in case involving only hostile environment issue); and *Oncale v. Sundowner Offshore Servs. Inc.*, 66 U.S.L.W. 4172 (4 March 1998) (Title VII sexual harassment claims may be brought for same sex sexual harassment).
33. That Act calls for 'reasonable accommodation' to the known physical or mental limitations of 'an otherwise qualified individual with a disability,' unless the employer can demonstrate 'undue hardship' to business operations, 42 U.S.C. §12112(b)(5)(A). Needless to say, the definitions of all the quoted terms have been subject to great debate. Moreover, countless issues have arisen concerning the interrelationship between the ADA and health insurance, medical testing, workers' compensation, workplace health and safety, and numerous other areas of regulation.
34. 42 U.S.C. § 2000e–2(e).
35. *See, e.g.*, *Rosenfield v. Southern Pac. Co.*, 444 F.2d 1219 (9th Cir. 1971).

B. Wrongful Discharge

Virtually all of the developments with respect to the regulation of wrongful discharge have come at the state level. Moreover, with the exception of the State of Montana, which adopted the Wrongful Discharge from Employment Act[36] in 1987, nearly all of the regulation has come in the form of judicial decisions, rather than legislation. Nevertheless, outside of employment discrimination, the area of wrongful discharge has seen the greatest increase in regulation over the past few decades.

Over forty states now have recognised judicially both contract and tort (public policy) exceptions to the at-will doctrine.[37] Nearly all the states have recognised one or more of such other employment-related torts as fraud, intentional infliction of emotional distress, intentional interference with contract, or defamation.[38] And courts in approximately ten states have declared the duty of good faith and fair dealing to extend to employment contracts.[39]

The impact of the at-will legacy of course remains strong. Nearly all the states that have adopted contract-based exceptions to at-will, for example, recognise a broad right for employers unilaterally to modify indefinite-term contracts from a 'for cause' to an 'at will' basis. Most do require, however, that any such unilateral modification be clear and unambiguous.[40] In this sense, the doctrine closely parallels one typical pattern of regulation in the United States: it mandates disclosure, but leaves the substantive terms of the relationship to bargaining by the parties.

Still, courts in many states have steadily expanded the protection afforded to workers against wrongful discharge. At least one state, California, has extended these precedents to the wrongful *demotion* context.[41] In turn, that extension may portend still further expansion of the case law to a wide range of other working conditions. In sharp contrast to judicial attitudes of an earlier generation, today many courts strive to find a basis to support employee claims.[42] Indeed, a solid argument can be made that, as a consequence of this ongoing erosion, the attitude of the American public has begun to shift away from the at-will ethos that has prevailed for over a century.

---

36. Mont. Code Ann. §§ 39-2-901 to 39-2-914.
37. *See* Lionel J. Postic, *Wrongful Termination: A State-by-State Survey* xxiv–xxxvi (1994).
38. Id.
39. Id. (only narrowly applied in some of the states, however). To readers from many other nations in the world, it may seem completely unremarkable to learn that a duty of good faith applies to employment contracts. From the standpoint of many adherents to the at-will doctrine, though, this notion is heretical. After all, if the at-will doctrine permits either side to terminate the relationship for no cause, or even for bad cause, how can it possibly be compatible with a duty of good faith? *See, e.g., Murphy v. American Home Prods. Corp.*, 448 N.E.2d 86 (N.Y. Ct. App. 1983).
40. *See, e.g., Swanson v. Liquid Air Corp.*, 116 Wash. 2d 512 (1992).
41. *See Scott v. Pacific Gas and Elec. Co.*, 11 Cal. 4th 454, 904 P.2d 834 (1995).
42. This attitude, of course, is far from universal. Yet the instances in which protection is afforded often generate precedents that are then successfully relied on by subsequent litigants. One example that has attracted considerable attention comes from the State of Washington. An armored truck driver, in direct violation of a firm company rule, left his truck – in order to save a woman who was being attacked by an armed assailant. The company, in strict adherence to established policy but apparently oblivious to public opinion, promptly fired the hero. He sued for wrongful discharge, and the Washington State Supreme Court ultimately upheld his claim, *Gardner v. Loomis Armored Inc.*, 128 Wash. 2d 931, 913 P.2d 377 (1996). The result may seem unsurprising. But in order to reach that result the court had to expand its prior view that 'a clear mandate of public policy' is to be found in 'the letter or purpose of a constitutional, statutory,

In connection with wrongful discharge, one federal statute bears particular note: the Worker Adjustment and Retraining Notification Act (WARN) of 1988.[43] WARN applies to planned plant closings and mass layoffs. It does not seek to control the closings and layoffs directly, however. Rather, as its title implies, it requires employers to provide advance notice of the planned closings and layoffs to employees and to appropriate state and local governments. Thus, WARN fits squarely into the pattern of regulation that treats disclosure as a key prophylactic measure. WARN also is encrusted with exceptions and limitations. In 1993, the General Accounting Office issued an assessment of WARN's effectiveness.[44] The GAO found that many employers evaded the law's requirements by carefully tailoring layoffs to fit within the exceptions. Even where no exception applied, half the employers gave no notice at all and many more gave fewer than 60 days' notice. The GAO called for strengthening WARN's enforcement structure, but to date Congress has not done so.

C. Wages and Hours

In contrast to many other aspects of individual employment relations, the FLSA has remained largely unchanged. The minimum wage has increased modestly in absolute terms (although, in real terms, it has fluctuated considerably over the past 60 years). There have been modest increases in coverage of agricultural workers. The overtime premium has remained stable at 50% of the regular wage rate (the percentage specified in the original 1938 legislation). With very limited exceptions, overtime pay continues to be calculated on a weekly basis, applying to all hours worked in excess of 40 h per week (a figure that has been in effect ever since 1940[45]).

Indeed, as a practical matter, the overtime premium has effectively decreased over time. That premium is calculated on the basis of monetary wages, yet fringe benefits (including health insurance) have approximately doubled as a proportion of total compensation since 1965 alone.[46] Furthermore, the number of American workers covered by the exemptions to the wage and hour provisions of the FLSA has increased over the years.[47] This has resulted in part from a change in industrial

---

contd.
or regulatory provision or scheme [and in p]rior judicial decisions,' *see Thompson v. St. Regis Paper Co.*, 102 Wash. 2d 219, 232 (1984). (This definition of 'public policy' was already at the broadest end of the spectrum among state courts in the United States. Many courts have limited the scope of 'public policy,' for purposes of the exception to at-will employment, to the letter of statutes and the constitution.) Instead, the court extended the scope of 'public policy' to principles found in the 'penumbra' of established law. It remains to be seen whether Washington courts will extend this penumbra any farther. Yet, through decisions such as this, the steady erosion of the at-will doctrine continues.

43. 29 U.S.C. §§ 2101–2109.

44. United States General Accounting Office, Worker Adjustment and Retraining Notification Act Not Meeting Its Goals: Report to Congressional Committees (1993).

45. The 40 h standard was phased in over a three-year period. *See, e.g.*, Willis J. Nordlund, A Brief History of the Fair Labor Standards Act, 39 *Lab. L.J.* 715, 721 (1988).

46. *See, e.g.*, United States Chamber Research Center, *Employee Benefits* 40, Table 17 (1996) (as percentage of wages and salaries, employee benefits increased from 21.5% in 1965 to 41.8% in 1995).

47. Surprisingly, an extensive search conducted by several reference librarians on my behalf could not turn up a clear set of statistics tracking the proportion of the American workforce that has been covered by the FLSA exemptions over the sixty years since the Act was passed.

structure, with more and more American workers falling into the professional and other exempt categories.[48] Another cause has been the piecemeal expansion of the list of exemptions. (As one example, in 1990 Congress directed the Secretary of Labour to adopt regulations exempting most computer programmers from the minimum wage and overtime provisions.[49]) The effective impact of these developments has been further deregulation of wages and hours at the federal level.[50]

A more direct example of deregulation in the wages and hours context is the 1985 amendment to the FLSA permitting public employers to provide compensatory time off (commonly known as 'comp time') in lieu of paying the overtime premium in cash.[51] Some states permit the use of comp time by private employers who lie outside the coverage of federal law;[52] and in recent years there have been proposals to amend the FLSA to permit comp time for private employers covered by that statute, as well.[53] In addition, in recent years there have been proposals to amend the FLSA to allow the averaging of hours over a biweekly period, rather than the one-week period that has been in effect ever since 1938.[54] These proposals have encountered strong opposition from labour, however, and to date none has passed both Houses of Congress (although the House of Representatives did approve a bill for comp time in 1997).[55]

A trend that bears note in this regard is the major recent increase in the proportion of full-time U.S. wage and salary workers with flexible work schedules (*i.e.*, schedules that allow them to vary the time they begin or end work). According to a study conducted by the U.S. Bureau of Labour Statistics, the proportion of such workers increased from 15.1% to 27.6% between 1991 and 1997.[56] Not surprisingly, the highest such rates were reported for executives, administrators and managers, at 42.4%.

---

48. *See, e.g., Dunlop Commission Fact Finding Report, supra* note 25, at 6–8. In this connection, it bears note that the Department of Labour regulations authorise use of a so-called 'short test' for the executive or administrative employee exception, which is used for employees earning at least $250 per week, 29 C.F.R. § 541.1. The $250 figure has not been amended since the mid-1970s, *see* Rothstein, Craver *et al., supra* note 30, at 211.
49. The resulting regulations are found in 29 C.F.R. §§ 541.3, 541.303.
50. The FLSA represents a minimum standard for covered employees. States are free to extend coverage to other workers or to impose higher standards for covered workers. Many states provide broader coverage than the FLSA; and some impose higher standards, such as a higher minimum wage, or a daily overtime requirement (in contrast to the FLSA, which calculates overtime only on a weekly basis, using a 40 h standard).
51. 29 U.S.C. § 207(o).
52. *See, e.g.*, Rev. Code of Washington 49.46.130(2)(b).
53. *See, e.g.*, H.R. 1, 105th Cong. (Working Families Flexibility Act), introduced 7 January 1997, passed by the House of Representatives 3 March 1997.
54. *See, e.g.*, S. 4, 105th Cong. (Family Friendly Workplace Act), introduced 21 January 1997 (also proposing the right for private employers to utilise comp time). Special provisions in the FLSA permit averaging of hours over a two-week period for hospital employees, 29 U.S.C. § 207(j), and over four-week periods for employees engaged in fire protection or law enforcement activities, 29 U.S.C. § 207(k).
55. *See, e.g.*, Court Gifford, FLSA: Senate Votes to Continue Debating Comp-Time Bill; Democrats Offer Alternative, *Daily Lab. Rep.*, 16 May 1997. President Clinton has said that he would support a 'strong' comp time law, but would veto a bill that does not contain sufficient protections for workers, *see* FLSA: Clinton Backs 'Strong' Comp-Time Bill, Expanded Family and Medical Leave Act, *Daily Lab. Rep.*, 25 March 1997.
56. United States Bureau of Labour Statistics, Workers on Flexible and Shift Schedules in 1997, USDL 98-119 (26 March 1998).

D. Benefits

With respect to regulation of benefits, the most important development at the federal level was the enactment, in 1974, of the Employee Retirement Income Security Act (ERISA).[57] On its face, ERISA might appear to be a prime example of *hyper*-regulation. The statute and accompanying regulations are almost mind numbing in their detail and complexity. At another level, though, ERISA represents a quintessentially *laissez faire* approach to regulation.

As the title of the statute implies, one of the main topics covered by ERISA is employee pensions. The statute and regulations go into excruciating detail regarding funding, vesting, forfeiture, and countless other aspects of pension plans. Yet ERISA never requires employers to provide pensions at all, much less attempt to specify how large pensions must be.[58] Furthermore, ERISA has had the effect of sharply limiting regulation of a vast range of benefits other than pensions.

To protect employers from having to deal with a multiplicity of different and potentially conflicting state regulations, ERISA contains an extremely broad pre-emption provision. Section 514 of the Act states that, with certain narrow exceptions, ERISA 'shall supersede any and all State laws insofar as they may now or hereafter related to any employee benefit plan.'[59] 'Employee benefit plan' is defined to include both pension plans and 'employee welfare benefit plans,' or 'welfare plans.'[60] In turn, the definition of 'welfare plan' includes 'any plan, fund, or program' for, *inter alia*, health care; health benefits; accident, disability, death, unemployment or vacation benefits; training programs; day care centres; and prepaid legal services.[61] Thus, ERISA covers a very wide range of benefit plans and pre-empts all state laws 'related' to such plans.

Certain procedural provisions apply to both pension and welfare plans. Notably, these include broad reporting and disclosure requirements, pursuant to which employers must provide all participants and beneficiaries with summary plan descriptions and make more detailed information available to them.[62] In addition, provisions relating to fiduciary duties and a prohibition on adverse treatment for exercising one's rights apply to both types of plans. Yet the treatment of pension and welfare plans is vastly different when it comes to substantive regulation. With respect to pension plans, ERISA supplants state regulation with a pervasive body of federal regulation. In sharp contrast, ERISA contains virtually no substantive regulation of welfare plans.[63] Whether Congress fully appreciated the consequences or not,[64] the upshot of the combination of the broad pre-emption provision with this

57. As amended, 29 U.S.C. §§ 1001–1461.
58. ERISA does contain gender equity provisions; and anti-discrimination rules contained in the Internal Revenue Code seek to compel those employers who provide pensions to extend the plans to lower-ranking employees as well as to highly-compensated employees, *see* I.R.C. §§ 401(a)(4), 401(a)(26), 410(b). Here again, the law does not actually mandate compliance, but it provides a very strong incentive by refusing tax deductions for plans that do not comply.
59. 29 U.S.C. § 1144(a).
60. 29 U.S.C. § 1002(a)(3).
61. 29 U.S.C. § 1002(a)(1).
62. 29 U.S.C. §§ 1023–1025.
63. The one major exception to this statement involves subsequently adopted provisions dealing with the portability of health insurance, discussed below.
64. The original House and Senate bills would only have preempted state law to the extent that the state law related to matters actually regulated by ERISA. The language was changed to its final

lack of substantive regulation is that most types of benefits other than pensions remain free from substantive regulation at either the federal or state level.

The area where this has created the greatest concern is health insurance. (In the United States, as of 1995, about two-thirds of the non-elderly population obtained their health insurance through employer plans, either as employees, retirees, or dependents.[65]) Notwithstanding the ERISA pre-emption provision, states have sought to regulate employer-provided health benefits and other welfare benefits in various ways. With respect to health insurance, one obvious way was to regulate the insurance companies themselves by requiring, for example, that any policies they issue cover specified illnesses or procedures (so-called 'mandated benefit laws').[66] Yet employers who self-insure are able to escape even this indirect regulation; and, not so coincidentally, many U.S. employers have moved to a self-insured basis.[67] This has limited one avenue for state regulation, but states have continued to try to find other means for regulating health insurance and other types of benefits. The Supreme Court has provided some assistance in the process, through narrow interpretations of such terms in the ERISA pre-emption provision as 'plan'[68] and 'relate to.'[69] And when one state law survives a pre-emption challenge, other states are quick to emulate the successful pattern.[70]

One aspect of health insurance that has generated especial concern is the potential loss of coverage, for oneself and one's dependents, if a worker moves from one employer to another or loses a job.[71] This is one major substantive aspect of employer health plans that Congress has dealt with at the federal level. It has now done so twice, first in 1986, in the Consolidated Omnibus Budget Reconciliation Amendment Act (COBRA),[72] and again in 1996, in the Health Insurance Portability and Accountability Act (HIPAA).[73] Both seek to enhance the portability of benefits. COBRA does so by requiring the old employer to continue coverage (mainly at the participant's expense) for 18–36 months from the date on which coverage normally

---

contd.
version in the conference committee. *See, e.g.*, Steven L. Willborn, Stewart J. Schwab, and John F. Burton, Jr., *Employment Law: Cases and Materials* 843 (2nd ed. 1998).

65. John Sheils and Lisa Alecxih, *Recent Trends in Employer Health Insurance Coverage and Benefits* 2 (1996).

66. By its terms, ERISA does not preempt state law 'which regulates insurance, banking, or securities,' 29 U.S.C. § 1144(b)(1). In a 1985 decision the Supreme Court accepted the indirect approach of regulating the types of policies insurance companies could provide to employer plans, *Metropolitan Life Ins. Co. v. Massachusetts*, 471 U.S. 724 (1985); and the states promptly enacted many laws that utilise this approach. In fact, a study published in 1989 found 735 state laws that mandated benefits or coverages, including 38 such statutes in one state alone. John R. Gabel and Gail A. Jensen, The Price of State-Mandated Benefits, 26 *Inquiry* 419 (1989). But virtually impenetrable language in the same section of ERISA has been interpreted as barring any such state regulation of employers who self-insure.

67. Whereas only about 5% of employers self-insured in 1975, by 1987 more than 50% of U.S employers did so. *See* Willborn, Schwab and Burton, *supra* note 64, at 851, and sources cited therein.

68. *See Fort Halifax Packing Co. v. Coyne*, 482 U.S. 1 (1987).

69. *See New York State Conf. of Blue Cross & Blue Shield Plans v. Travelers Ins. Co.*, 514 U.S. 645 (1995).

70. In 1996, in the wake of the Supreme Court's decision the year before in the *Travelers Insurance* case (referred to in the preceding footnote), 33 of the 50 states enacted laws regulating managed care plans, *see* Willborn, Schwab and Burton, *supra* note 64, at 852.

71. This is a serious issue. A recent study found that, in 1994, about 700,000 Americans lost their health insurance each month due to loss of a job, and that the median lapse in coverage was about seven months. *See* Sheils and Alexcih, *supra* note 65, at 9.

72. Codified in part in ERISA, at 29 U.S.C. §§ 1161–1167.

73. Codified in part in ERISA, at 29 U.S.C. §§ 1181–1191c.

would be lost. HIPAA does so by limiting the ability of the new employer to deny health insurance to new applicants. Each of the statutes has given rise to a host of new and complicated questions. Yet both reflect one aspect of the largely unregulated, at-will legacy of the United States: the assumption of extensive employment mobility and the adoption of policies that meet some of the needs created by this mobility.[74]

One other relatively recent piece of legislation relating to benefits deserves mention: the Family and Medical Leave Act (FMLA) of 1993.[75] For the first time at the federal level, this law requires employers to provide leaves for childbirth, for an employee's own illness, and for the purpose of caring for children or other family members with serious health conditions. FMLA contains numerous substantive requirements and has given rise to a host of interpretive issues (including questions relating to the interrelationships among FMLA, ERISA, Title VII, ADA, and various other federal and state laws). In the context of a discussion of deregulation, however, it bears note that FMLA's provisions remain relatively weak. As examples, the Act applies only to employers with fifty or more employees (thus covering only about five per cent of all U.S. businesses, albeit over half of the total employees in the private sector) and the leave is unpaid. Over half the states also have their own laws relating to family and medical leave.[76] Many of those statutes provide more generous leave coverage than FMLA; and, unlike ERISA, FMLA does not pre-empt state laws that establish higher standards.

A final aspect of FMLA that bears note is section 104(b).[77] That section permits an employer to deny restoration to employment for an otherwise eligible employee who is among the highest paid 10 per cent of salaried employees, if 'such denial is necessary to prevent substantial and grievous economic injury to the operations of the employer' and the employer provides the employee with notice of the intent not to restore employment. This provision bears similarities to the executive, administrative and executive exemptions from minimum wage and overtime provisions under FLSA. As in that case, this provision appears to be based in part on the view that high-salaried employees are able to fend for themselves, without the need for statutory protection.

E. Workplace Safety and Health

The key federal statute concerning workplace safety and health is the Occupational Safety and Health Act (OSHA) of 1970.[78] This is a rare example at the federal level of a classic command-and-control statute related to the workplace. In part for that reason,

74. ERISA's pension vesting requirements provide another example of the portability impetus. Traditionally, many pensions in the United States did not vest for twenty or more years. As originally enacted, ERISA required that pensions either vest fully after 10 years or vest gradually, commencing after five years (with full vesting after fifteen years). Out of concern that the vesting process took too long, thereby adversely affecting employees who switched jobs, Congress amended ERISA in 1986 to provide either for full vesting after five years or gradual vesting commencing after just three years (with full vesting after seven), 29 U.S.C. § 1053. In one sense, this represents a tightening of federal regulations; in another, however, it reflects a major U.S. concern with flexibility and mobility.
75. 29 U.S.C. §§ 2601 et seq.
76. *See* Rothstein and Craver *et al.*, *supra* note 30, at 283–284.
77. 29 U.S.C. § 2614(b).
78. 29 U.S.C. §§ 651 *et seq.*

OSHA has been the object of bitter opposition by business and by conservative politicians. That opposition, coupled with numerous other structural factors, has limited the Occupational Safety and Health Administration's[79] ability to adopt new standards. Notably, two of the rare successes in standard setting have involved information disclosure requirements, rather than direct regulation of hazardous substances.[80]

As recently as 1995, several conservative legislators seriously sought to abolish OSHA; and in recent years Congress has passed a number of laws restricting OSHA's activities.[81] Undoubtedly influenced in part by these efforts, the Clinton Administration has made OSHA one of the focal points of its 'reinvention of government.' Among the federal employment-related statutes, OSHA stands as the prime example of formal deregulation efforts. One aspect of the reform efforts is the relatively straightforward, yet very important, policy of making the regulatory process more accessible to employers, employees, and the general public. Steps aimed at that end (many of which also have been adopted by other agencies) include rewriting regulations in plain English, utilising the Internet and other media to make information more accessible, conducting education and outreach activities, improving recordkeeping, and reducing paperwork burdens. In addition, OSHA has sought to achieve a more co-operative regulatory approach, based in part on educating employers and workers and persuading them that co-operation on safety and health is in their mutual self-interest. Steps designed to achieve this objective include so-called Co-operative Compliance Programs, in which workplaces with the worst safety records are identified and given the 'opportunity' to develop special safety plans (with the threat of stricter enforcement if they fail to participate[82]); Voluntary

79. The abbreviation OSHA is frequently used to refer both to the Occupational Safety and Health Act and to the Occupational Safety and Health Administration, which is responsible for its enforcement. Despite the potential confusion, this Report hereafter also uses the abbreviation interchangeably.

80. The first such standard is a 1983 regulation requiring employers to provide employees with access to their own exposure and medical records. For a discussion of this regulation, *see* Benjamin W. Mintz, *OSHA: History, Law, and Policy* 86 (1984). The second is the so-called the Hazard Communication Standard, also adopted in 1983. This standard requires employers who use hazardous chemicals to provide employees with information concerning the hazards and with training on how to use the chemicals safely. *See* 29 C.F.R. 1910.1200.

81. These include laws restricting the OSHA budget and prohibiting OSHA from engaging in certain types of enforcement and rulemaking activities. In the Small Business Regulatory Enforcement Fairness Act of 1996, Pub. L. No. 104–121, 110 Stat. 857, Congress adopted a series of measures requiring OSHA to pay particular attention to the concerns of small businesses (including establishment of an Ombudsman within the Small Business Administration charged with acting as an advocate for small businesses in their dealings with OSHA). Perhaps most significantly, that Act provides for congressional review of all new OSHA standards before they may take effect. This relates to one additional aspect of OSHA that bears note in the context of a discussion of deregulation: the low level of enforcement. In part due to the budgetary limitations imposed by Congress, in 1996 the number of inspections conducted by OSHA dropped to an all time low of 24,024, *see* Willborn, Schwab and Burton, *supra* note 64, at 1196. The level of inspections rebounded somewhat in 1997, to approximately 34,000, *see* Dean Scott, Shantelle Fowler, and Ellen Byerrum, Safety & Health: New Leader of Federal Safety Agency Expects No Major Revisions of Agenda, *Daily Lab. Rep.*, 20 January 1998.

82. In this connection, it bears note that OSHA has continued to utilise its 'megafine' strategy, in which employers with especially egregious safety records are targeted for multi-million dollar fines, *See, e.g.*, Oversight of the Occupational Safety and Health Administration, Hearing Before the Subcomm. on Public Health and Safety of the Senate Comm. on Labour and Human Resources, 105th Cong., 10 July 1997 (Statement of Gregory R. Watchman, Acting Ass't Sec. of Labour for Occup. Safety and Health).

Protection Programs, which recognise worksites for excellence in safety and health reward them with 'Star' ratings; negotiated rulemaking; and a consultation program to provide free (and penalty-free) advice to employers.[83]

Virtually all of these measures are based on approaches that have been implemented previously at the state level.[84] Notably, Joe Dear, who served as Clinton's first OSHA Administrator and was one of the chief architects of the 'reinvention' of OSHA, previously had been director of the Department of Labour and Industries in the State of Washington. That state had achieved great success with similar policies. Whether the 'reinvented' approach will be as successful at the national level remains to be seen. At the federal level, business has fought many of the new initiatives; labour has fought others; and both business and labour have challenged still others.[85] As a result, many of the initiatives remain bogged down in litigation. In short, confrontational attitudes may be so entrenched at the national level that the initiatives will never have a chance to demonstrate their full potential.

F. Other Areas of Regulation

The preceding discussion addresses a number of major areas of regulation. But it represents only a small portion of all the regulatory activity that has taken place in the United States over the past few decades. As the 1994 GAO report on workplace regulation observed, federal statutes enacted prior to 1980 typically involved broad issues, whereas the statutes enacted since the mid-1980s mainly have addressed narrower issues.[86] When one also takes into account the state and local level, the number of statutes and ordinances that concern labour and employment in the United States is staggering. Many of the laws address aspects of privacy.[87] Some (mainly from a few years ago) call for respecting the rights of smokers; others (more recently enacted) call for smoke-free workplaces. Some deal with job references; some with training; some with employee inventions, non-competition agreements, and trade secrets. Most are piecemeal and quite narrow. But the list goes on and on, and it keeps growing.

83. *See* id.; U.S. Dep't of Labor, Occup. Safety and Health Admin., The New OSHA: Reinventing Worker Safety and Health (21 February1995).

84. OSHA permits states to operate their own safety and health plans, provided the state plan ensures substantive standards and enforcement efforts 'at least as effective' as OSHA, 29 U.S.C. § 667. Twenty-two states have approved state plans for public and private sector employees. A number of those states have considerably more extensive regulatory efforts than OSHA. In a broader sense, however, this latitude for state-by-state experimentation represents another relatively deregulated aspect of the U.S. system.

85. *See, e.g., American Trucking Ass'n v. Reich,* 955 F. Supp. 4 (D.D.C. 1997) (successfully challenging regulation requiring employers to report injury and illness data, for failure to comply with standards of Administrative Procedure Act); *Chamber of Commerce of the United States v. U.S. Dep't of Labour*, No. 98–1036, D.C. Cir. (litigation seeking invalidation of the Cooperative Compliance Program; stay prohibiting implementation of the Program granted 17 February 1998; oral argument currently scheduled for 3 December 1998).

86. GAO Report, *supra* note 22, at 26.

87. At the federal level, this includes the Employee Polygraph Protection Act of 1988, 29 U.S.C. §§ 2001–2009, and laws relating to electronic surveillance. At the state level, laws relating to various aspects of worker privacy abound.

DEREGULATORY TRENDS

In contrast to the increasing level of formal regulation discussed in the previous section, one can identify several trends in U.S. business and society that have contributed to an effective deregulation of employment matters. The following section discusses four such trends.

A. Collective Bargaining

The single most important element of deregulation of employment in the United States may well be the steady decline in unionisation rates. In the 1950s, approximately 35% of private sector non-agricultural workers in the United States were union members. By 1997, the proportion had dropped all the way to 9.8%.[88] Moreover, the success of employees in organising unions through NLRB elections has declined sharply. The number of elections held dropped by over 50% between 1975 and 1990, and the success rate of unions in those elections declined from over 70% in the early 1950s to approximately 50% in the period since 1975.[89]

Many labour leaders and other critics contend that these declines are the U.S. Government's fault. Yet one would be hard-pressed to identify specific legislative changes that are responsible. While modest developments have taken place regarding the organisation and election process, the basic structure has remained essentially stable since the enactment of the Taft-Hartley Act in 1947. The level of confrontation has increased sharply, however. Many employers campaign vigorously against unions, utilising a wide range of weapons – some legal (notably including the hiring of permanent replacement for striking workers), some illegal (including firing of workers who engage in union activity and bad faith 'surface' bargaining in the event a union is elected).[90] Some critics attribute at least part of the heightened confrontational stance, including major increases in the use of striker replacements, to President Reagan's 1981 decision to hire permanent replacements for 11,000 striking federal air traffic controllers. Nonetheless, the tools that employers have used to fight unionisation have been in place for many years, thanks in large part to a U.S. Congress that has for much of its history been ambivalent, if not downright hostile, toward unions and collective bargaining.

In its May 1994 Fact-Finding Report, the Commission on the Future of Worker-Management Relations (chaired by former Secretary of Labour John T. Dunlop and widely known as the Dunlop Commission) noted these trends. In its final report, issued later that year, the Dunlop Commission recommended various changes in federal law to facilitate union organisation, including affording employees 'the most equal and democratic dialogue possible,' providing prompt elections, and ensuring prompt relief for discrimination against workers for their union activities.[91] Congress, which has been Republican-controlled since 1994, has not displayed any inclination to pursue those recommendations. To the contrary, members of Congress

88. *See* United States Bureau of Labour Statistics, Union Members in 1997, USDL 98-26 (30 January 1998).
89. *See Dunlop Commission Fact Finding Report*, *supra* note 25, at 67.
90. *See* id. at 68–75.
91. Commission on the Future of Worker-Management Relations, *Report and Recommendations* xviii (1994) (hereinafter cited as *Dunlop Commission Final Report*).

have sought, through oversight hearings and direct letters, to influence the National Labour Relations Board to abandon rulemaking and other efforts that would modestly facilitate union organising.[92] Moreover, when President Clinton utilised an executive order to authorise termination of federal contracts with companies that permanently replaced economic strikers, the U.S. Court of Appeals for the D.C. Circuit struck it down on the ground that it conflicted with the policies of the NLRA.[93]

Whatever the causes, the decline in unionisation levels in the private sector has greatly reduced the influence of collective bargaining as a form of regulation in the United States. There have been substantial increases, however, in 'employee participation' programs and other joint labour-management committees.[94] The legality of these committees has been called into question, in view of the NLRA prohibition on company domination or interference in labour organisations. Indeed, in the 1992 *Electromation* case, the NLRB held that establishment of 'action committees' composed of both labour and management representatives constituted a violation of this prohibition[95] (although the precise parameters of that decision have been subject to considerable debate). In its final report, the Dunlop Commission was generally supportive of employee involvement and recommended that such programs should not be deemed unlawful simply because they involve 'discussion of terms and conditions of work or compensation *where such discussion is incidental* to the broad purposes of these programs.'[96] Congress went much further. The Teamwork for Employees and Managers Act (TEAM), which was approved by both Houses of Congress, would have permitted employers to 'establish, assist, maintain, or participate in any organisation or entity of any kind, in which employees participate, to address matters of mutual interest, *including, but not limited to*, issues of quality, productivity, efficiency, and safety and health.' Labour strongly opposed this bill, and President Clinton vetoed it in 1996. Despite initial statements by Republican leaders that the TEAM Act would again be one of its top priorities in the next session of Congress,[97] they did not renew their efforts to push that bill through.[98] Accordingly, while employee-management committees have continued to spread, the legality of those programs remains in question.

B. Arbitration of Employment Disputes

A second deregulatory trend is the increasing inclusion in employment contracts of clauses requiring the arbitration of all employment disputes. Although grievance arbitration has a long and respected history in the union setting, prior to the 1990s arbitration was not widely utilised in the individual employment setting and was regarded

92. *See* William B. Gould IV, Observations on the Relationship between Law and Politics as Chairman of the National Labour Relations Board, 1994–1998 and an Admonition about the Epigones Who Would Undo Our Initiatives, Speech before the California Labor Federation, AFL-CIO, 22nd Biennial Convention, Oakland, California, 21 July 1998.
93. *Chamber of Commerce of the U.S. v. Reich*, 74 F.3d 1322 (D.C. Cir. 1996).
94. *See, e.g., Dunlop Commission Fact Finding Report*, *supra* note 25, at 29–60.
95. Electromation, Inc., 309 N.L.R.B. 990 (1992), enf'd, 35 F.3d 1148 (7th Cir. 1994).
96. *See Dunlop Commission Final Report*, *supra* note 91, at 8.
97. *See* Pamela M. Prah and Court Gifford, 'Legislation: GOP Workplace Proposals Awaiting Completion when Congress Returns,' *Daily Lab. Rep.*, 27 August 1997.
98. *See* Court Gifford, Legislation: Workplace Bills Put on Hold May Resurface in Next Session, *Daily Lab. Rep.*, 1 December 1997.

as being of questionable legality in that context. That situation changed dramatically in 1991 when the Supreme Court upheld a provision requiring a non-union employee to submit his age discrimination claim to arbitration.[99] Since then, many employers have begun to include, both in employment contracts and in employee manuals, clauses that require arbitration of employment disputes. Although courts have rejected some of these attempts, the trend is very much in the direction of judicial acceptance of compulsory arbitration, subject to certain safeguards (such as the provision of discovery and the opportunity for judicial review).[100] This trend toward compulsory arbitration has been the subject of intense debate.[101] Some observers see mandatory arbitration as a grave threat to employee interests; others see it as a much-needed means of resolving employment disputes efficiently and fairly. Whatever one's views, this development represents a significant step in the direction of deregulation.[102]

C. Contingent Workers

A third trend with significant implications for deregulation is the increase in the contingent workforce. Although the share of part-time workers in the U.S. workforce has remained relatively steady at about 18% of the workforce,[103] the number of workers supplied by temporary help services more than tripled between 1979 and 1992[104] and continued to increase through 1994.[105] Despite widespread perceptions that this trend has continued, official statistics suggest that the level of contingent workers may have levelled off or even declined somewhat since then.[106] Even so, the contingent workforce has broad implications for deregulation in the United States. As of February 1997, contingent workers were estimated to constitute between 1.9% and 4.4% of the total workforce (with that wide range reflecting differences in the methodology used, as well as the difficulty of obtaining precise information about contingent work).[107] Contingent workers are far less likely than regular full-time workers to receive health insurance from their employers or to be eligible for other types of benefits.[108] Moreover, the vast majority of worker protections in the United States are tied to employee status. To the extent workers can successfully be classified as independent contractors, most protections do not apply. Nonetheless, to date the United States has not undertaken any comprehensive steps to regulate contingent employment.

---

99. *Gilmer v. Interstate/Johnson Lane Corp.*, 500 U.S. 20 (1991).
100. *See, e.g.*, *Cole v. Burns Int'l Sec. Servs.*, 105 F.3d 1465 (D.C. Cir. 1997).
101. *See, e.g.*, Richard A. Bales, *Compulsory Arbitration: The Grand Experiment in Employment* (1997), and sources cited therein.
102. The fact that an arbitrator rather than a court decides a claim does not necessarily imply a more lax standard of review. But arbitration awards for individual employment cases have, for the most part, been kept confidential. This has the effect of limiting the impact of such awards on the development of applicable standards.
103. *See, e.g.*, *Dunlop Commission Fact Finding Report*, *supra* note 25, at 21.
104. Id.
105. *See* United States Bureau of Labor Statistics, New Survey Reports on Wages and Benefits for Temporary Help Services Workers, USDL 95–334 (6 September 1995) (hereinafter cited as New Survey).
106. *See* United States Bureau of Labour Statistics, Contingent and Alternative Employment Arrangements, February 1997, USDL 97-422 (2 December 1997).
107. Id.
108. *See* id.; New Survey, *supra* note 104.

In one case that has generated considerable attention, in 1997 the Ninth Circuit Court of Appeals ruled that workers hired by Microsoft Corporation on a special 'contract' basis in fact were 'employees' of Microsoft and thus were entitled to participate in its stock option plan, a major employee benefit.[109] (The decision rested on language contained in the company's documents, rather than an analysis of the work performed by the workers.) Far from leading the way to greater efforts to protect contingent workers, the decision (which involved workers who were already quite highly compensated) appears to have generated a backlash. Microsoft itself rewrote its documents and changed its hiring practices;[110] and Microsoft also promptly sought legislative change that would permit it to treat the categories of workers differentially. As of this writing, the lobbying efforts have not been successful, but Microsoft and other businesses are continuing their efforts to gain legislative protection against claims by contract workers.

D. Layoffs of White-Collar Workers

A final trend that bears mention in connection with deregulation is the widespread layoffs of white-collar employees that have occurred in the 1990s. Despite the strength of the at-will doctrine, as a practical matter, up through the early 1990s both long-term blue-collar workers in major manufacturing industries (such as the automobile industry) and long-term white-collar workers enjoyed high job security. The former category, blue-collar workers in major industries, typically received their protection from union collective bargaining agreements. The white-collar workers generally were protected not by law or formal agreement, but by business custom.

In the early 1990s, the pattern changed for the long-term white-collar employees. Suddenly, many large companies with reputations for lifetime employment began laying off large numbers of white-collar employees. The mass media, including the New York Times in its 1996 series *The Downsizing of America*,[111] provided dramatic anecdotal accounts of this trend. Recently, statistical studies have borne out the media reports (albeit not so dramatically). Overall job security for the U.S. workforce as a whole declined only modestly in the 1990s, but the declines have been more substantial for long-term workers. One study, for example, reported that the annual 'displacement' rate for workers with five or more years of service was higher in 1995 than at any time since the data began in 1979.[112] Moreover, the

109. *Vizcaino v. Microsoft Corp.*, 120 F.3d 1006 (1997), *cert. denied*, 118 S. Ct. 899 (1998).

110. For example, Microsoft compelled many of the workers to go to work for a temporary services agency, which then contracted with Microsoft to supply the workers, *see* id. In addition, Microsoft has announced that it will require all such contract workers to take a break from service after each year of work.

111. The series was originally published in the New York Times during the week of 3 March 1996; it was issued in book form later that year.

112. *See* Daniel Aaronson and Daniel G. Sullivan, The decline of job security in the 1990s: Displacement, anxiety, and their effect on wage growth, in *Economic Perspectives (Federal Reserve Bank of Chicago)*, Vol. 22, No. 1, pp. 17–43 (1998). The estimated displacement rate in 1995 for workers with five or more years of service was 3.4%. 'By comparison,' the authors report, 'the rate for 1982, which was in the middle of a severe recession, was only about 2.5%. We consider this a substantial increase in the risk of displacement for high-seniority workers.' For a discussion of several other empirical studies of workforce participation rates in the United States, *see* Thomas C. Kohler & Matthew W. Finkin, 'Bonding and Flexibility: Employment Ordering in a Relationless Age,' 46 *Amer. J. Comp. L.* 379, 396–401 (1998).

occupational groups with the highest long-term employment levels – professional, managerial, technical, and blue-collar – have experienced the largest declines in job security in the 1990s.[113] Observers have aptly labelled these developments the 'democratisation' of layoffs.[114] Not surprisingly, perceptions regarding job security also have changed. According to a recent study, 'White-collar and college-educated workers were relatively immune to job anxiety during the 1970s and 1980s, but have experienced substantial increases in job insecurity during the 1990s.'[115]

As with the rise in the contingent workforce, this 'democratisation of layoffs' relates to deregulation in two diametrically opposed ways. On the one hand, the layoffs have served as a stark reminder that employment in the United States is fundamentally at-will, even for the managerial class, and thus have reinforced an attitude of resignation to the possibility of dismissal. On the other hand, the layoffs have brought home to the upper middle class just how devastating the loss of employment often is. Given the greater clout of the upper middle class with respect to the policy-making process, this personal appreciation of the implications of job loss may provide added impetus to the movement for greater legislative protection for employment. While the booming economy of recent years has defused much of the pressure for legislative action for the time being, the next recession may well find broader support for legal protection of employment among nearly all classes of U.S. workers.

CONCLUSION

As the preceding account reflects, assessing the degree of deregulation of labour in the United States is far from a simple matter. The underlying ethos traditionally has been that of at-will employment, with minimal government regulation. The decline in unionisation, rise of compulsory arbitration, increase in contingent employment, and other trends in business and society have served to lessen the degree of regulation. Moreover, with the extremely important exception of employment discrimination, in those instances in which the federal government has engaged in workplace regulation, it has usually done so in a relatively non-intrusive manner. The prime example of command-and-control workplace regulation at the federal level is OSHA; and it is no coincidence that that statute has been the focus of the greatest pressure from business for direct deregulation. A far more typical pattern of regulation, as reflected in WARN, ERISA, and the hazardous materials standard under OSHA, is to require employers to disclose relevant information to workers, and then to rely on bargaining by the parties to achieve the proper level of protection. Another common pattern, as reflected in the FLSA and FMLA, is for the legislation to establish a limited number of minimum standards, but otherwise to adopt a hands-off attitude. While one can point to various instances in which federal labour statutes have

---

113. *See* Henry Farber, 'Trends in long term employment in the United States, 1979–1996,' paper prepared for the third public German-American Council Federation Symposium, Labor Markets in the USA and Germany, held at Bonn, Germany, 10–11 June 1997 (findings summarised in Aaronson and Sullivan, *supra* note 112). Aaronson and Sullivan found high increases in displacement rates for highly educated workers, white-collar workers, and workers in the service industries, but not for blue collar workers, *see* Aaronson and Sullivan, *supra* note 112.

114. *See* Aaronson and Sullivan, *supra* note 112.

115. *See* id. (emphasis added).

been strengthened over time, in many other respects (such as the expansion of exemptions from the wage and hour provisions of FLSA) laws have been relaxed. In addition, as reflected by the portability provisions of ERISA, COBRA, and HIPAA, a number of the regulations are premised on a highly mobile job market and in turn have helped to facilitate labour mobility.

Notwithstanding these deregulatory aspects, the overall trend in the United States over the past 40 years has been in the direction of greater regulation of employment. At the federal level alone, the number of major statutes related to labour has more than tripled since 1960, and the number of regulatory programs and narrower statutes has risen even faster. At the state and local level, the rise in regulation has been far more dramatic. The most striking – and most highly publicised – example has been the rapid erosion of the at-will doctrine, almost entirely through the judicial process. Yet that shift has been accompanied by a veritable explosion in state and local legislation and in state and local regulatory programs. Typically, these laws and programs are established on a piecemeal basis. Most specify their own procedures, enforcement structures, and remedies. The procedures and remedies sometimes duplicate each other, sometimes overlap, and occasionally directly conflict. When confusion and tensions arise, as they frequently do, the typical response is not to repeal or simplify one of the existing laws. Rather, the typical response is to enact yet another law, again on a piecemeal basis.[116]

In 1988, Clyde Summers offered the following prediction:

> [T]he proliferation of legal protection of employee rights will greatly increase the complexity of labour law through the turn of the century. ... Courts ... have created complex legal theories in both contract and tort.... Legislation... will make this complex judge-made framework seem simple and coherent, for legislation will almost certainly be a combination of federal, state, and even local regulations. Each statute will have not only its own body

116. As one example, many states have recognised causes of action for so-called negligent hiring and negligent retention. Under these doctrines, an employer may be held liable for death or injuries caused by an employee who should not have been hired initially or should not have been placed in a particular position. (An extreme example of this would be hiring a convicted child molester to serve as janitor at a day care center.) The development of these doctrines has placed greater pressure on employers to undertake careful background checks of new hires; and one traditional tool for doing so has been a reference check with the former employer. At the same time, however, many other decisions have held employers liable for defamation as a result of information provided in response to reference checks. Fear of such liability has led many companies to adopt a policy of providing only extremely limited information about former employees. The resulting inability to obtain reliable information from the prior employer has generated greater pressure on employers to resort to credit reporting services and other sources of information (some of which involve the provision of information that employers are prohibited from asking, under the employment discrimination laws and other laws). This development has led to calls for greater regulation of crediting reporting services and other information providers. As a concurrent development, in a few recent cases, courts have held prior employers liable for failure to notify the new employer, at the time of a reference check, of serious problems relating to the former employee. These cases have created a new fear for employers: they may be liable for defamation if they provide detailed information, but they may be liable on other grounds if they fail to disclose information, as well. One response has been widespread business lobbying for immunity from lawsuits for job references, except in the event of bad faith. Earlier this year, the Republican-controlled Washington State legislature enacted such a law; the Governor, a Democrat, vetoed the bill, out of concern over the impact on workers and on privacy.

> of substantive rules, but also its own administrative procedures and remedies. Present legislation gives no reason to hope that there will be any consistent pattern or systematic co-ordination. Labour law will increasingly change from a troublesome thicket to an impenetrable jungle.[117]

He was right. Labour law in the United States has increasingly become 'an impenetrable jungle.' A graphic illustration of this trend is that, throughout the 1990s, the National Law Journal has consistently rated employment law as one of the top growth areas for legal practice in the United States.

How do the American people feel about the increasing regulation? That was one of the questions the U.S. General Accounting Office sought to answer in a 1994 survey, undertaken at the request of Congress.[118] One may surmise that some of the congressional requesters were hoping to learn of widespread dissatisfaction, which they could then claim as a mandate for aggressive deregulation efforts. If so, the requesters must have been sadly disappointed, for the GAO Report contains the following findings:

> The employer and union representatives we interviewed strongly supported the general goals of the statutes comprising the framework of federal workplace regulation.... The employers and union representatives... generally supported the statutory objectives as well as the actual statutes comprising the framework of federal workplace regulation.... Employers... generally supported most major workplace statutes. For example, many employers, both large and small, stated that OSHA is necessary to protect workers.... Union officials... also supported most workplace statutes, believing that they have led to major improvements in the protections enjoyed by workers and have provided a baseline of benefits upon which workers could improve... through collective bargaining agreements.[119]

The GAO did find concerns, among both employers and union representatives, with various aspects of the way in which the laws are carried out. These included concerns over the adversarial nature of much of the regulatory process, the difficulty in obtaining information from and communicating with the relevant agencies, and unnecessary paperwork requirements. Employers and union leaders both expressed the desire for greater collaboration in the regulatory process. Furthermore, both sides expressed concern over the NLRA: employers seeking greater leeway to utilise labour-management committees, union leaders expressing the need to amend the NLRA to protect workers' rights to organise.

As the GAO Report noted, many of these concerns lay at the heart of two projects that were already underway when the GAO issued its findings in 1994: the 'reinvention of OSHA' and the Dunlop Commission's re-examination of labour-management relations. As discussed above, the goals of the reinvention of OSHA include improved communication and greater collaboration in the regulatory process. Of potentially even greater significance are the Dunlop Commission's

117. Clyde Summers, Labour Law as the Century Turns: A Changing of the Guard, 67 *Neb. L. Rev.* 7 (1988).
118. *See* GAO Report, *supra* note 22.
119. Id. at 48–49.

recommendations. Those recommendations seek to facilitate the organisation of unions and the effectuation of collective bargaining, and at the same time would recognise expanded use of labour-management committees. If successful, these steps would to a considerable extent return U.S. labour relations law to the original ideal of the Wagner Act, in which the parties themselves would adjust their interests and work out appropriate protections through the collective bargaining process. In turn, success in restoring that ideal would likely reduce the pressure for piecemeal regulation by government at the federal, state, and local level.

As discussed above, the reinvention of OSHA remains bogged down in litigation; Congress has not pursued the Dunlop Commission's recommendations for facilitating union organisation; and President Clinton vetoed the TEAM Act, with its very broad authorisation for labour-management committees. Thus, at the moment, none of the major proposed reforms has fared well at the federal level. Until one or more of those reforms is successful, however, Professor Summers' 'jungle' of employment regulation seems destined to become even more impenetrable; and the trend toward ever-increasing levels of regulation seems certain to persist well beyond the turn of the century.